Red Banners, Books and Beer Mugs

Historical Materialism
Book Series

Editorial Board

Loren Balhorn (*Berlin*)
David Broder (*Rome*)
Sebastian Budgen (*Paris*)
Steve Edwards (*London*)
Juan Grigera (*London*)
Marcel van der Linden (*Amsterdam*)
Peter Thomas (*London*)

VOLUME 220

The titles published in this series are listed at *brill.com/hm*

Red Banners, Books and Beer Mugs

The Mental World of German Social Democrats, 1863–1914

By

Andrew G. Bonnell

BRILL

LEIDEN | BOSTON

Library of Congress Cataloging-in-Publication Data

Names: Bonnell, Andrew, 1960-
Title: Red banners, books and beer mugs : the mental world of German Social
   Democrats, 1863-1914 / by Andrew G. Bonnell.
Description: Boston : Brill, 2021. | Series: Historical materialism book series,
   1570-1522 ; Volume 220 | Includes bibliographical references and index. |
Identifiers: LCCN 2020034021 (print) | LCCN 2020034022 (ebook) |
   ISBN 9789004300620 (Hardback : alk. paper) | ISBN 9789004300637 (eBook)
Subjects: LCSH: Sozialdemokratische Partei Deutschlands–History–19th century. |
   Sozialdemokratische Partei Deutschlands–History–20th century. | Socialism–
   Germany–History–19th century. | Socialism–Germany–History–20th century. |
   Marx, Karl, 1818-1883.
Classification: LCC HX273 .B658 2021 (print) | LCC HX273 (ebook) |
   DDC 324.243/07209034–dc23
LC record available at https://lccn.loc.gov/2020034021
LC ebook record available at https://lccn.loc.gov/2020034022

Typeface for the Latin, Greek, and Cyrillic scripts: "Brill". See and download: brill.com/brill-typeface.

ISSN 1570-1522
ISBN 978-90-04-30062-0 (hardback)
ISBN 978-90-04-30063-7 (e-book)

Copyright 2021 by Koninklijke Brill NV, Leiden, The Netherlands.
Koninklijke Brill NV incorporates the imprints Brill, Brill Hes & De Graaf, Brill Nijhoff, Brill Rodopi,
Brill Sense, Hotei Publishing, mentis Verlag, Verlag Ferdinand Schöningh and Wilhelm Fink Verlag.
All rights reserved. No part of this publication may be reproduced, translated, stored in a retrieval system,
or transmitted in any form or by any means, electronic, mechanical, photocopying, recording or otherwise,
without prior written permission from the publisher. Requests for re-use and/or translations must be
addressed to Koninklijke Brill NV via brill.com or copyright.com.

This book is printed on acid-free paper and produced in a sustainable manner.

Printed by Printforce, the Netherlands

Contents

Acknowledgements   VII
Abbreviations   VIII

Introduction   1

1 Ideology, Leadership, and Party Culture: The Lassalle Cult in German Social Democracy   11

2 Between Internationalism, Nationalism and Particularism: From the War of 1870–71 to the July Crisis, 1914   34

3 Attitudes to Labour in the German Social Democratic Party in the *Kaiserreich*   56

4 Social Democracy and the Price of Bread: The Politics of Subsistence in Imperial Germany   76

5 Reds in the Ranks: Social Democrats in the Kaiser's Army   101

6 Reading Marx   128

7 Workers and Cultural Activities: Culture, Sociability, Organisation   151

8 Socialism and Republicanism in Imperial Germany   173

Conclusion   197

Bibliography   201
Index   222

Acknowledgements

Some of the chapters of this book have their own long history, and I am afraid that I may not be able to acknowledge all the debts accrued during their writing.

While the usual disclaimers apply regarding my responsibility for any possible errors or omissions, I have benefitted over the years from discussions of German labour movement history with a number of colleagues, among whom I would like to thank particularly Frank Bongiorno, Matt Fitzpatrick, Dick Geary, and John Moses. I would like to thank Sébastien Budgen for his encouragement and assistance, especially for his encouragement to prepare this book for Brill, and I also thank the other members of Sébastien's informal email group on the history of German Social Democracy for their generosity with their expertise. While teaching German history at the University of Queensland, I have benefitted from working with some very talented postgraduate students, and I thank them here for what I have learned from them.

Colleagues at numerous conferences have provided me with useful feedback. These conferences include: the regular conferences of the Australian Historical Association and the Australasian Association of European Historians, staff-postgraduate seminars at the University of Queensland, the ISOS Conference on Slave, Forced and 'Free' Labour in Comparative Historical Perspective, University of Nottingham, 2010, and conferences of the Australian Society for Labour History.

I am indebted to the archivists and librarians at all the institutions in which I have conducted research for this book – the archives are listed in the bibliography, and it would be tiresome for the reader to list them again here. In particular, however, I would like to thank Dr Anja Kruke of the Friedrich-Ebert-Stiftung (FES), Bonn, for welcoming me as a visiting researcher in the FES in 2012, during one of the research trips on which I gathered material for this project, and for the staff of the FES for all their assistance on this and other visits. I gratefully acknowledge the financial support of the Deutscher Akademischer Austauschdienst for enabling the 2012 visiting fellowship at the FES to take place. I also thank the University of Queensland for supporting periods of research leave in Europe and for funding the research travel that is indispensable for projects such as this one.

It is a pleasure to thank my friends Josef Engel and Mehmet Dökmeci for their hospitality on my research trips to Germany.

I also thank my wife Debbie for putting up with my absences on research trips as well as for all her other support.

Abbreviations

ARS	August Bebel, *Ausgewählte Reden und Schriften*
BA-MA	Bundesarchiv Militärarchiv, Freiburg im Breisgau
Hess. HstAW	Hessisches Hauptstaatsarchiv Wiesbaden
Hess.StAD	Hessisches Staatsarchiv Darmstadt
IISH	International Institute of Social History, Amsterdam
IRSH	*International Review of Social History*
LA NRW	Landesarchiv Nordrhein-Westphalen, Düsseldorf
LAB	Landesarchiv Berlin
MEW	Karl Marx and Friedrich Engels, *Werke* (ed. Institut für Marxismus-Leninismus beim ZK der SED), 39 vols. plus supplementary vols., Berlin, 1956 ff.
NZ	*Die Neue Zeit*
SHStAD	Sächsisches Hauptstaatsarchiv Dresden
SStAC	Sächsisches Staatsarchiv Chemnitz
StAHH	Hamburg Staatsarchiv

Introduction

The German Social Democratic Party was the first million-strong social democratic party, indeed the first truly mass-based political party in the world, and was the main force pushing for the democratisation of Germany before the First World War. The party's inability to bring about such democratisation of Germany in the early twentieth century was to prove fateful for the course of European history. The party has thus been of significant interest to historians over decades. The history of the party in Imperial Germany is widely considered to have been well researched, and justifiably so. Since the pioneering histories of the party by Carl E. Schorske in 1955, Gerhard A. Ritter in 1959, and Guenther Roth in 1963 (to say nothing of Franz Mehring's party history in the 1890s and other older works), there have been a significant number of valuable studies by historians such as Roger Morgan, Helga Grebing, Vernon Lidtke, William Guttsman, Gary Steenson, Stefan Berger and Jürgen Schmidt, among many others.[1] General histories of the party have been supplemented by numerous monographic studies of specific aspects of the party's history, as well as myriad local and regional studies. The history of the German labour movement was also, of course, a major focus of historiography in the former German Democratic Republic.

The question might then arise: why another book on German Social Democracy? There are a number of possible answers. Firstly, while the history of the Social Democratic Party before 1914 has indeed been well-documented, there has been a relative neglect of the topic in recent historiography of Imperial Germany. Since the events of 1989–91 in Europe, from the fall of the wall, to German unification, and the break-up of the Soviet Union, academic fashion has drifted away from labour history. Among historians of Imperial Germany, there has been a greater focus on middle-class culture and bourgeois reform movements, and recently also the history of the aristocracy and the monarchy. History from the viewpoint of the elites has made a comeback, sometimes under cover of the 'cultural turn', sometimes in a return of old-school diplomatic history. Recent textbooks on Imperial Germany are treating the history of German workers and the labour movement as more marginal than might have been the case in the 1980s, and some distinguished historians are even making outright factual errors when it comes to references to the Social Democratic Party (it would

---

1   Schorske 1955; Ritter 1959; Roth 1963; Morgan 1965; Lidtke 1966; Grebing 1966; Guttsman 1981; Steenson 1981; Berger 2000; Schmidt 2018. This list is obviously far from exhaustive.

be invidious to single out individuals here), partly because the extant literature on the topic is simply being read less – partly, in turn, because of the demands of the academic publishing and employment markets for novelty, but there are wider cultural and political trends at work here as well.

Secondly, and related to the previous point, there has been a reaction against those approaches to Imperial Germany, from older Anglo-American liberal historiography to the German Bielefeld School 'critical social history' interpretation, which emphasised a trajectory of 'flawed modernisation', and an insufficiently liberal political culture in Germany as constituting preconditions for the later rise of Nazism. The normative assumptions behind liberal modernisation theory have been held up to sustained criticism since the 1980s, and more comparative approaches to German history have questioned the older emphasis on German 'uniqueness', as if there were one correct and 'normal' path to industrial capitalist society, from which Germany had strayed.

However, the pendulum may have swung too far in the writing of the history of Imperial Germany. Recent work stressing the vitality of middle-class culture and organisational life, reform movements, and mass participation in elections, is tending to replace the older picture of Imperial Germany as a state governed by a reactionary coalition of the Junker class, heavy industrialists, and the monarchy, with an almost Whiggish narrative of reform and progress towards democratisation. Such a narrative occludes the profound structural obstacles towards democratisation if the concept is to be understood as a question of the distribution of political power, as opposed to a set of cultural practices – putting ballots into boxes. James Retallack's recent major study of electoral politics in the kingdom of Saxony from the 1860s to 1918 offers a valuable corrective to the narrative of Imperial Germany as a land of progressive liberal reform and virtual democratisation, demonstrating in impressive detail the determination of the governing elites, both bourgeois National Liberals and Conservative landowners, to resist ceding any real political power to the working class and their political representatives in the Social Democratic Party, and the great lengths to which the elites were prepared to go to prevent any genuine democratisation.[2] Returning the focus to the working class and the organised labour movement, and their confrontation with an authoritarian state structure, can restore the balance in how we look at Imperial Germany, and correct some of the more rose-coloured depictions of recent times.

Thirdly, among historians of socialism, the time may be ripe for a reassessment of the Second International, and more particularly of the pre-1914

---

2 Retallack 2017.

German Social Democratic Party, as a case study in the successful mobilisation of a mass working-class base.³

The Imperial German Social Democrats have been the subject of numerous analyses and critiques, especially in view of their vote for war credits in 1914 and the party's subsequent split.

Critiques of German Social Democracy go back as far as 1910/11, when Robert Michels, for a few years an active party member himself, published his well-known contemporary analysis of the 'iron law of oligarchy' and the capture of the party by its functionaries.⁴ V.I. Lenin famously articulated a critique of the role of the 'labour aristocracy' in the German labour movement, which sought to profit from the fruits of imperial expansion, in seeking to account for the party's support for war credits in 1914.⁵ Carl E. Schorske traced the origins of the split in the labour movement to the different ideological currents in the German Social Democratic Party from 1905 to 1917, seeing the split as inherent within the party's relationship to theory and practice, and thus pre-dating the outbreak of war in 1914 and the response to the Bolshevik Revolution.⁶ Guenther Roth developed the influential concept of 'negative integration' in his study of German Social Democracy, which characterised the party as replicating features of the Imperial German state while isolating itself from practical politics. In Roth's view, sterile oppositionism on the part of Social Democrats was coupled with a kind of perverse mirroring of the Wilhelmine state in the party's own culture and organisation.⁷ The term 'negative integration' was further developed by Dieter Groh, who tied it to the party's ideological tendency to 'revolutionary *attentisme*' – a reliance on a deterministic reading of Marxism as a substitute for a more active kind of engagement with political conditions as they were.⁸

These critiques could all be discussed at much greater length than is available here. Each illuminates an aspect of the truth, but none is fully adequate as an account of the development of German Social Democracy in the half-century before the First World War. Michels' account of the bureaucratisation

---

3   For an important pointer to such a reassessment of Second International socialism, see Lih 2006.
4   Michels 1911.
5   Lenin 1985 [1916], here pp. 283–5.
6   Schorske 1955. As the 'revisionist' controversy has been well covered in Schorske and in subsequent works, I do not propose to go into details about it in this work.
7   Roth 1963.
8   Groh 1973. Groh's usage of 'revolutionary *attentisme*' draws on Erich Matthias' characterisation of German Second International Marxism as '*Kautskyanismus*', stressing the deterministic and *attentiste* side of Kautsky's reading of Marx, Matthias 1957.

of the party and the rise of the functionary stratum captures a dimension of the party's evolution that was observable at the time, but Michels' analysis is embedded in psychological assumptions deriving form Gustave Le Bon and Italian 'social anthropologists', which include the view that the 'masses' had an innate need to revere their leaders. Michels also underestimated the positive benefits of organisation in terms of capacity-building for a workers' movement, as well as the efficacy of the party's internal democratic structures.[9] The Leninist critique of the labour aristocracy bribed with the proceeds of imperialism underplays the importance that skilled workers played in the Social Democratic Party's activist base from the earliest years of the party's existence, and the absence of evidence that skilled workers were less militant than unskilled (often less well organised) workers.[10] Also, Lenin's pamphlet on imperialism overlooks the fact that Germany conspicuously failed to turn a profit on its colonial ventures (with the partial exception of Samoa); indeed, German Social Democrats were very vocal about the costs of colonial expansion, which were passed onto the working class through indirect taxes.[11] (It may have been a different story for the British working class, with the rapid expansion of the textile industry in England being linked to the destruction of Indian textile production and the opening of vast imperial markets for British products.) Schorske's account of the 'Great Schism' captures the widening ideological divide within the Social Democratic Party between revisionists, reformists, and what Hans-Josef Steinberg has characterised as '*Praktiker*' (practically oriented, pragmatic leaders, like Ignaz Auer) within the party,[12] and the revolutionary left wing of the party (with the Marxist Centre, represented by Karl Kautsky, between the two). However, his account arguably understates the enormous and widespread desire within Social Democracy for party unity, partly because of labour movement values putting a premium on solidarity and collective action, and partly because of the importance put on the notion that the party represented the working class as a whole. It took the profound trauma of a world war to split the party, a split sealed by the shocks of the Russian revolution and the acts of violence that accompanied the German revolution of 1918/19. The split of the Second International was not the least consequential effect of what George Kennan called 'the seminal catastrophe' of the twentieth century, leaving Europe's labour movements deeply divided and weakened in the face of violent counter-revolution and fascism in the interwar period and beyond. The

---

9   For a critique of Michels with particular reference to the trade unions, see Eisenberg 1989.
10 See Geary 1981, pp. 53–4.
11 On this, see Bonnell 2018.
12 Steinberg 1979.

term 'negative integration' has stimulated much useful analysis and discussion, but it also calls for a more differentiated analysis. In the sphere of Social Democratic cultural policy and activities, for example, it is possible to discern contrasting trends towards efforts at positive integration into bourgeois culture supported by the party's right wing, on the one hand, and an approach of more critical and selective appropriation of bourgeois culture, viewed through the prism of Marxian 'historical materialism' on the left of the party.[13]

Based on recent research into the movement culture of the party, this study will pose a contrary question: why the Social Democrats were as successful as they were in creating a mass working-class party under the conditions of an authoritarian imperial state. Instead of reading the history of German Social Democracy backwards from 1914 to ask why the party failed, it might be useful to consider how the party was successful in becoming as large as it did, both in terms of membership and in terms of electoral support, prior to the outbreak of the First World War.

A large part of the answer to this last question is the salience of class in Imperial Germany, and the success of Social Democracy in becoming the main political representative of the working class, with the exception of sections of Catholic workers in some parts of Germany. Again, the analysis of Imperial Germany as a class society has become less fashionable in the last couple of decades, and other cleavages within German society have perhaps received more attention. Over thirty years since Geoff Eley called for a joining of two histories – those of the German working class and of the Social Democratic labour movement – we seem to have moved further from that goal, rather than closer to it.[14] However, it is difficult to argue that Imperial Germany was not profoundly divided along class lines, and that class location was a very strong and fundamental determinant of the life chances and experience of Germans. At the most basic level of health and life expectancy, Imperial Germany was clearly highly unequal. Official statisticians did not tabulate life expectancy by class as such, but certain proxies such as the prevalence of tuberculosis and infant mortality rates, for which evidence from specific regions exists, show that there was a significant gulf in life expectancy rates between workers and upper-class Germans, as one would expect from the large differences in access to medical care, differences in housing and living conditions, nutrition, and working conditions.[15] In 1912, the sociologist Alfred Weber diagnosed a com-

---

13   See Bonnell 2005.
14   Eley 1986 [1984]. Eley acknowledges the contributions of Mary Nolan and Dick Geary, in particular, in this endeavour.
15   Spree 1988. On housing, see von Saldern 1995.

mon life pattern among industrial workers of declining physical strength and health from the age of around 40 on, which would result in loss of better-paid employment, and increasing insecurity and poverty (in contrast to the middle and upper classes, who typically experienced greater material security and prosperity in the latter part of their working lives).[16] In terms of education, most Germans' schooling finished with the end of elementary school, and at the opposite end of the educational spectrum, only a very few Germans of working-class background made it into the country's universities. Along with gender, class was the most important structural determinant of Germans' life chances.[17]

The salience of class divisions in Imperial Germany was reinforced by the political system and by workers' experiences of their interactions with the state. Even though Bismarck introduced universal manhood suffrage for the Reich in 1871 (from the age of 25, which meant that many workers had been in the paid workforce for a decade before they could vote), state- and municipal-level franchise laws often entrenched class privilege through voting systems weighted by property qualifications – most notoriously in Prussia, which contained most of Germany's territory and population, but other states followed suit (such as Saxony in 1896), especially in response to rising levels of support for Social Democracy. The veto power of parliaments' upper houses, often dominated by the landed interest, remained a check on democratisation, as did the monarchical system at the apex of the Imperial German state. The extent to which the law favoured the state against the political representatives of the working class, not only during the outright ban on socialist activity between 1878 and 1890, persuaded many workers that 'class justice' was a reality.[18] The fiscal system of the Empire, with its heavy reliance on regressive indirect taxes and tariffs on the national level, rather than progressive income or wealth taxation, was also perceived as exacerbating inequalities in ways that had a direct impact on workers' everyday lives.

As Hans-Ulrich Wehler pointed out in his magnum opus, *Deutsche Gesellschaftsgeschichte*, Marxism, in the form in which it was disseminated from the 1870s on, was successful in gaining a following among German workers because it made sense to them as an analysis of the social, economic, and political condition of Imperial Germany, as 'a realistic analysis of their own lived reality'. It also offered a perspective beyond the current society, pointing to the pos-

---

16   Quoted in Tennstedt 1981, p. 157.
17   On the condition of the German working class generally, see Ritter and Tenfelde 1992; Wehler 1995, pp. 772–804.
18   Hall 1977, Part 2.

sibility of a better state of affairs for workers, and providing a guide to the fight for greater political emancipation in practice.[19] While some recent writers have tended to play down the fact,[20] German Social Democracy was self-consciously a class-based movement, seeking to give a political voice to organised workers, especially in urban areas and industrial districts, and especially (though not exclusively) to secularised workers or those from a Protestant background. This is not to suggest that the German workers constituted an ideal-typical homogeneous factory proletariat – the high level of involvement of skilled craft workers in the party is well-documented, and the party also enjoyed the support of some 'deserters' or 'fellow-travellers' from other classes as well ('*Überläufer*' or '*Mitläufer*' were two terms used at the time). But its bulwarks of support were the places where the urbanised or industrial workforce was most strongly present and most well-organised (as contemporaries well understood).

The present work sets out to show in greater detail how the German Social Democratic Party was successful in mobilising its mainly working-class base precisely through the combination of addressing the real concerns of workers in the present, in a society that was experienced as highly stratified by class, and offering a radical, transformative perspective, that promised a qualitatively different kind of social order. This combination of addressing real problems in the present along with a promise of radical change in the future led to the well-known theoretical tensions between the revisionist and reformist right wing of the party and the more revolutionary left wing. But the party's ability to address workers on both of these levels, a capacity which was perhaps most clearly demonstrated by the long-term party leader August Bebel, contributed powerfully to its success in mobilising its mass following.

Rather than offering another chronological survey of the evolution of Social Democracy in Imperial Germany, the present study seeks to investigate how the party successfully mobilised its working-class base through exploring specific themes. Firstly, the rise and decline of the personality cult around the party founder Ferdinand Lassalle sheds light on the culture of the party in its early decades, but also on its ideological evolution as it moved away from such a personality cult. The figure of Lassalle also served as a rallying point during the years of persecution of Social Democrats during the anti-Socialist law and beyond, quite apart from any influence of Lassalle's own doctrines.

---

19 Wehler 1995, pp. 798–9, quotation p. 798.
20 Gabriel 2014, for example, while interesting and informative, suffers from a tendency to neglect the party's working-class base, remaining on the level of discourse analysis, while at the same time overlooking the importance of working-class identity in socialist discourse in Germany.

The relationship between nationalism and allegiance to particular German states became a pressing issue in the years of German unification 1864–71, which coincided with both the formation of a German labour movement independent from liberal tutelage and the formation of the International Workingmen's Association (First Association), with which German socialists sought affiliation. The tensions between socialist internationalism and the new mass ideology of nationalism will form the subject of the second chapter.

Constitutive of working-class experience was the experience of wage labour under capitalism, and German Social Democrats' attitudes to work will be considered in another chapter. Discussions in the German Social Democratic press in the 1870s reflected the continuing influence within the party of elements of a craft-worker ethos, reflecting the party's early social base among skilled craft-workers. Also fundamental to working-class experience was the matter of daily subsistence: workers' everyday food and drink. The Social Democratic Party was able to convey to its members a seamless political narrative that connected their daily experience of rising food prices with a tax system biased in favour of the wealthy, with the unequal power relations entrenched in the political system, and the need to organise and become politically active on the part of workers in order to remedy the situation.

In an age of mass compulsory military service, workers were exposed to the very direct exercise of state power on their persons when they were called up to serve in the army. At the same time, the Imperial German army, as the Kaiser occasionally reminded his subjects, was intended to support the status quo in the German state as well as protecting Germany from potential external adversaries. This element of the individual German male's experience of the authoritarian state in a very concentrated manner for the two to three years of military service left traces on many people's lives, as considered here in Chapter 5.

The next chapter considers the circulation of socialist, specifically Marxian, ideas among the organised labour movement. It is generally agreed that few workers sat down to read Marx's *Capital* at any length (although a few clearly did!). However, the availability of cheap newsprint and pamphlets, as well as the labour movement's culture of meetings and oral communication, clearly helped to diffuse versions of Marxian thought.

Following on from the diffusion of Marxian ideas among rank-and-file Social Democracy, there is the question of the republican sympathies of party members *vis-à-vis* notions of residual popular monarchism (in an age in which the invention of traditions, including monarchical tradition, was being ramped up in an effort to stabilise the existing political order). Socialist republicanism had to contend with potentially repressive legislation that shielded the monarchy from criticism, but there is plenty of evidence that, with some degree of regional variation, organised Social Democratic workers did not revere the monarchy or the individuals sitting on Germany's array of thrones.

Clearly, a thematic study could look at other themes as well. Instead of a separate chapter on gender, I have sought to consider the dimension of gender in each chapter here. Potentially, more could be said here about transnational aspects of the German Social Democratic Party. I have touched on these elsewhere.[21]

The evidence for this study comes from research over many years into the politics and culture of Germany's Social Democratic Party. In order to get closer to the ways in which the party was able to mobilise its base, wherever possible I have tried to recover the voices, words, and thoughts of rank-and-file members of the party themselves. Sometimes these come through in the reports of party meetings which appear in the Social Democratic Party's extensive output of newspapers, sometimes, like insects preserved in amber, the words of working-class members of the party are preserved in the often otherwise formulaic prose of political police reports (especially where utterances have been seen to be potentially evidence for prosecution). I have perused many hundreds, indeed thousands, of meeting reports, archival or in newspapers. A particularly valuable source of working-class opinion is the collection of police surveillance reports of workers' pubs in the Hamburg state archives.[22]

Clearly, as with any primary sources, such sources need to be read critically: political police were always keen to find any signs of dissent within Social Democratic ranks, as well as evidence of any prosecutable activities or statements, while party accounts preferred to project a picture of unity. Despite these expected differences, the large mass of accounts of party meetings and activities presents a remarkably consistent picture of a self-consciously oppositional, professedly class-based movement, which pitted itself against the phenomena of economic inequality, undemocratic and authoritarian government, and militarism, and which saw itself as working towards a more democratic, egalitarian, and peaceful future. It was a vision of the future that appealed to workers in their millions before the outbreak of the Great War.

Note: Earlier versions of some of the chapters in this book (Chapters 1, 2, 6, and 8) were previously published in the *Australian Journal of Politics and History*. They have been substantially revised and expanded for this publication,

---

21 E.g. Bonnell 2013 and 2018.
22 Evans 1989.

incorporating substantial additional research. Part of Chapter 3 draws on work previously published in the *International Review of Social History*, as well as on an unpublished paper presented at the ISOS Conference on Slave, Forced and 'Free' Labour in Comparative Historical Perspective, University of Nottingham, 2010.

CHAPTER 1

Ideology, Leadership, and Party Culture: The Lassalle Cult in German Social Democracy

In Germany, the 'separation of proletarian democracy from bourgeois democracy' (Gustav Mayer), the founding of an independent social democratic party based on a working-class membership, occurred in 1863 after a group of Leipzig workers dissatisfied with the tutelage of middle-class liberals over workers' associations invited the former 1848 revolutionary, advocate, and writer, Ferdinand Lassalle to take on the leadership of such a party.[1] Lassalle's 1862 pamphlet, *Workers' Programme. On the Particular Connection of the Current Historical Period with the Idea of the Workers' Estate*, had articulated the concept of a higher historical mission for the working class (or 'estate', *Stand*, in Lassalle's formulation), and attracted the attention of radical democrats and workers disillusioned with middle-class progressive liberal politics. The General German Workers' Association (Allgemeiner Deutscher Arbeiterverein, or ADAV) was subsequently founded in Leipzig on 23 May 1863, with Ferdinand Lassalle elected the inaugural President of the ADAV, with an initial five-year term.[2] Lassalle's agitation among workers lasted 15 months before his death in August 1864. He left behind a party which claimed 4,610 members, of whom over half were in the Rhineland (especially in and around the manufacturing towns of the Wuppertal area and Solingen), with other centres of membership including Hamburg, Berlin, and Leipzig and its surrounding industrial regions.[3]

Lassalle was a charismatic, flamboyant figure, who ran the ADAV in an autocratic, centralised way, and who sought to energise supporters directly through his public speaking tours. After his death, a kind of posthumous personality cult grew up around Lassalle, which has been commented on by a number of historians. Contemporary observers of the Social Democratic Party at the end of the nineteenth century, such as the political sociologist and former Social Democratic Party member Robert Michels, noted its existence – Michels came to see

---

[1] Letter from Otto Dammer, Wilhelm Fritzsche, and Julius Vahlteich, on behalf of the 'central committee for the convening of a general German workers' congress', to Lassalle, 4 December 1862, in Na'aman with Harstick, 1974, pp. 352–3.
[2] Statutes of the ADAV in Dowe and Klotzbach 1973, pp. 138–9.
[3] Mehring 1980, pp. 137–42. There is some uncertainty around the early membership figures of the ADAV, however.

it as proof of an innate need among 'the masses' for veneration of leaders.[4] Many later historians of the pre-1914 German Social Democratic Party, from Wolfgang Abendroth to Helga Grebing and Vernon L. Lidtke, have also pointed to the persistence of a 'Lassalle cult'.[5] The existence of a 'Lassalle cult' throws up some interesting questions, particularly in view of its persistence in the Social Democratic Party even after the party had already adopted an 'orthodox' Marxist programme in 1891. Despite the supremacy of Marxism as the party ideology, and the fact that the leadership of the party was dominated by old 'Eisenachers' (representatives of the second German Social Democratic Party, founded in Eisenach in 1869), such as August Bebel and Wilhelm Liebknecht, who had been strongly opposed to the 'Lassallean' strain of Social Democracy, the personality of Lassalle remained prominent in the party's folklore well into the early years of the twentieth century, in many ways more prominent than the figure of Karl Marx. The Lassalle cult was perhaps at its most intense in the period between Lassalle's death in 1864 and the unification of the 'Lassallean' with the 'Eisenacher' social democratic groups at the Gotha Congress of 1875. However, as will be seen, it persisted (albeit in a more subdued form) beyond Gotha, and also survived the banning of the party from 1878 to 1890 and the adoption of the Marxist Erfurt Programme in 1891. The Lassalle cult throws up interesting questions around the ideological development of socialism in Germany, the notion of leadership in the early phases of the labour movement, and ideas relating to party organisation, as well as questions around political symbolism and secularisation.

In 1873, Bebel wrote to Friedrich Engels:

> The Lassalle cult must be stamped out, there I agree with you entirely, and Lassalle's errors must also be opposed, but with caution [...]
>
> You must not forget that Lassalle's writings have, in fact created through their popular language – that cannot be argued away – the basis of the socialist views of the masses. They are ten, twenty times as widely distributed as any other socialist writings in Germany, such is the considerable popularity of Lassalle. This popularity has been elevated to a

---

4 Michels 1911, pp. 62–8.
5 Abendroth 1974, pp. 17 f.; Grebing 1966, p. 68; Lidtke 1985, pp. 112–14. While Lassalle festivals were far more numerous than Marx festivals, Lidtke erred in stating that the latter did not take place (p. 195). See, for example, the Marx memorial celebration held by the 'Karl Marx' Reading Club in Berlin in March 1891 (*Vorwärts*, no. 57, 8 March 1891), and in subsequent years. Scholarly treatments of the Lassalle cult include: Herzig 1988, pp. 321–3; Welskopp 2000, pp. 365–9; Walter 2013; and, most recently, Hake 2017, Chapter 6.

cult by the means (well-known enough to you) employed by the Countess [Sophie von] Hatzfeldt, [Johann Baptiste von] Schweitzer and others, and if this cult, thanks to the healthy sentiments of the masses and to our own activity, has already declined and continues to decline, it would still be unwise to injure these feelings by inconsiderate actions.

In our own party the Lassalle cult has just about disappeared, but all the same, there are still areas, such as the Rhineland and Silesia, in which it finds adherents ...[6]

Another socialist leader, Julius Vahlteich, a Leipzig shoemaker who had been one of the workers who invited Lassalle in 1862 to head a workers' congress, wrote looking back on this period: 'It took us ten long years of hard and thoroughly unedifying struggle, to get the fanatical Lassalle cult out of the heads of the workers'.[7]

The Lassalle cult had begun, at the latest, with Lassalle's death (the result of a duel over an aristocratic young lady, Helene von Dönniges – an incongruous end for a people's tribune, but one that did not forestall the growth of the posthumous personality cult). After the sensational news was despatched throughout Germany, and after the first funeral demonstration by 4,000 socialists and republicans in Geneva, where Lassalle had died, Lassalle's friends and political associates began to compete for shares in his political legacy.[8] Countess Sophie von Hatzfeldt, intimate friend and patron of Lassalle (whom he had represented in her sensational divorce case against her abusive husband), planned to send Lassalle's embalmed body, which she had transported from Geneva, in state around Germany. After thousands of workers attended memorial demonstrations in Frankfurt and Mainz, Hatzfeldt's project was foiled by the police and Lassalle's family, with the Prussian police confiscating Lassalle's body after its arrival in Düsseldorf following a request for intervention by Lassalle's mother. A protest gathering of 1,500 followers of Lassalle, led by the countess, at Cologne-Minden station failed to dissuade the police from removing the body from her custody. Lassalle was then quietly laid to rest in the new Jewish cemetery of Breslau (now Wrocław), the city of his birth.[9]

More significant than the contest over Lassalle's body – symptomatic though it was – was the contest over his party, the ADAV, which Lassalle had treated

---

6 Bebel 1980a, pp. 401–2.
7 Vahlteich 1978 [1904], p. 36.
8 Na'aman 1971, pp. 782 ff.; von Uexküll 1974, p. 130. On the Countess von Hatzfeldt's unsuccessful attempts to enlist Marx in the service of the Lassalle cult, see Hirsch and Pelger 1982.
9 Kling-Mathey 1989, pp. 146–7.

almost as his personal property, leaving authoritative instructions to his successors in his testament.[10] The struggle for control over the ADAV – and of the splinter groups which broke away from it – took on an increasingly sectarian character, as different leaders and parties claimed to represent the 'true Lassalle', in attempts to benefit from the Lassalle cult, which at the same time they helped to perpetuate.[11] Johann Philipp Becker, the veteran socialist (a member of the League of Communists in the 1840s, and a representative of the International Workingmen's Association in Switzerland) wrote in September 1865:

> since the Messrs. [Moses] Hess, von Schweitzer and B[ernhard] Becker claim for themselves alone the right of 'individual opinion and superior knowledge' and claim to be solely capable of interpreting Lassalle's writings, they attempt to declare the contents of the same – according to their own privately convenient views – to be holy, incontrovertible dogma. Conscious of their own lack of authority, they try to lean on Lassalle, who is thus made out to be the infallible Son of God and Messiah (whereby Lassalle's mother cuts a very odd figure as the Mother of God), in order, like other priests, to invoke the threat of danger to the religion and in order to be able to chase all the blind believers into the only sheep-pen that confers on them the promise of salvation.[12]

Lassalle himself had helped to pave the way for the quasi-religious nature of this personality cult. In his last speech, at Ronsdorf (22 May 1864), Lassalle's hubris was perhaps at its peak, vanity and dictatorial pretensions marked the speech, while Lassalle himself was carried away by the enthusiastic reception he received from thousands of Rhenish workers: 'this must be what it was like at the founding of new religions!' he wrote to the Countess Hatzfeldt.[13] The Ronsdorf speech closed with an exhortation to the effect that, if he were done away with, he expected some successor to arise and take vengeance.[14] When Lassalle died after being wounded in the duel three months later, these words were seen by some as a presentiment of martyrdom. For many members of the

---

10   Na'aman 1971, pp. 785f. See also Na'aman 1974, pp. 396–400.
11   See Morgan 1965, pp. 36–43; Mehring 1980, p. 171ff.
12   Johann Philipp Becker, 'Warnung für Warnung', article in the *Nordstern*, Hamburg (September 1865), cited in Dlubek et al. 1964, p. 68. Schweitzer and Bernhard Becker were at this time competing for leadership of the ADAV.
13   Cited in Na'aman 1971, p. 739.
14   Text of the Ronsdorf speech in Lassalle 1891–93, Vol. II, pp. 840–72. For comments on the speech, see Mehring 1980, pp. 147–9; Na'aman 1971, pp. 732ff.

ADAV, as Eduard Bernstein later wrote, 'it was impossible to grasp the idea that Lassalle had really been the victim of a common love affair. They believed in a premeditated blow, the work of opponents who wished to remove the dangerous agitator from the scene, and they feted the fallen leader as the victim of a dastardly political intrigue'. Thus developed, Bernstein continued, 'a true Lassalle cult', partly the work of the Countess Hatzfeldt, but partly due to 'the manner in which Lassalle had personally presented himself to workers'.[15]

An examination of the manifestations of the Lassalle cult reveals a quasi-religious character, or, at the least, an extreme form of hero-worship, in its early phases. Helga Grebing has written that the cult supplied a substitute for the residual religiosity of the working class, as a cult 'in which the wavering between Christian religion and secularised reality became more than clearly evident'.[16] The disillusioned co-founder of the ADAV, Julius Vahlteich, who subsequently went over to the 'Eisenacher' Social Democratic Workers' Party (Sozialdemokratische Arbeiterpartei, or SDAP), put it succinctly: 'Lassalle became a god and his supporters became his faithful'.[17] The Lassallean newspaper, the *Neuer Social-Demokrat*, published a leading article in 1871, in the lead-up to the seventh anniversary of Lassalle's death, with the title 'Crucify him, crucify him', placing Lassalle in the ranks of the crucified victims of the ruling class throughout history.[18]

One focus for the Lassalle cult was the celebration of the anniversaries of Lassalle's birth and death. In Augsburg, the minutes book of the local chapter of the ADAV records that preparations for the first anniversary of Lassalle's death (1865) preoccupied the group for four weeks' meetings prior to the commemoration, with the meeting after the ceremony given over to discussion of the success of the event and its resonance in the local press. The first *Lassalle-Feier* in Augsburg had a sombre, funereal character, beginning with music and closing with the performance of a tragic play, with two local ADAV members giving speeches to a reportedly quiet and attentive audience.[19] In 1872, Lassalle's death continued to be commemorated in Augsburg, this time with the aid of singing clubs and a brass band.[20] In 1868, Lassalle's birthday was celebrated in Oederan (in Saxony) with *tableaux vivants* showing 'Lassalle as a boy', 'Lassalle as

---

15 Eduard Bernstein, 'Lassalle und seine Bedeutung für die Sozialdemokratie', Introduction to Lassalle 1891–93, Vol. I, pp. 180 f.
16 Grebing 2007, p. 27.
17 Vahlteich 1978 [1904], p. 36.
18 'Kreuzige ihn, Kreuzige ihn', *Neuer Social-Demokrat*, 21, 18 August 1871.
19 Murr and Resch 2012, pp. 84–6, description of *Lassalle-Feier*, p. 86.
20 *Der Volksstaat*, 69, 28 August 1872.

a youth', 'Lassalle as public speaker' and 'Lassalle on his death bed'.[21] Lassalle's death was also the subject of a *tableau vivant* at a festival of the Hildesheim ADAV in 1870, where 'Lassalle at the duel' was depicted.[22] Lassalle festivals were also held in Breslau, Lassalle's birth and burial place (in 1870 and subsequent years),[23] in Dresden (Lassalle's birthday, 1871),[24] and Leipzig (where the ADAV had been founded).[25] The Breslau commemoration of the tenth anniversary of Lassalle's death in 1874 was particularly elaborate, presided over by Wilhelm Hasenclever and other leaders of the ADAV, with a deputation from the Allgemeiner Deutscher Frauenverein (General German Women's Association) led by Bertha Hahn, taking part, which laid a red-embroidered cushion on Lassalle's grave. The motto on the cushion read:

> Your name will turn red the peoples' dawn
> May your spirit make fertile our field of harvest.

The cushion was followed by a laurel wreath and 100 other wreaths from 52 towns and cities (all under the eyes of a large contingent of police).[26] These represent just a sample of the early Lassalle festivals.[27]

As well as *tableaux vivants*, male-voice choirs and speeches – all features which became normal components of workers' festivals, Lassalle festivals were also the occasion for the recitation of poems dedicated to the fallen leader (such poems often also being part of a *tableau vivant* or sung by the choirs). Poems celebrated Lassalle as being like 'God's lightning bolt', which unleashed

---

21   Rüden 1973, p. 31. (In Rüden, cited as 'Oderau'. There was a small ADAV-*Gemeinde* in Oederan in the Kreishauptmannschaft of Zwickau, and subsequently a *Gemeinde* of the LADAV there. Offermann 2002, attached CD-ROM, pp. 521–2.)
22   Ibid.
23   *Der Volksstaat*, 71, 3 September 1870; Müller 1975 [1925], pp. 133, 143–4.
24   *Der Volksstaat*, 28, 5 April 1871.
25   *Der Volksstaat*, 71, 2 September 1871.
26   Müller, *Die Geschichte der Breslauer Sozialdemokratie, Erster Teil*, pp. 143–4.
27   A perusal of the Lassallean newspaper *Neuer Social-Demokrat* from 1871 to 1874 shows Lassalle festivals increasing in number. In 1871: Berlin, Hamburg and Ottensen, and Chemnitz; in 1872: Berlin, Hamburg, Altona, Ottensen, Bremen, Lübeck, Kiel, Duisburg, Barmen, Elberfeld, Hannover, Barmbeck, Düsseldorf, and Delitzsch; in 1873: Berlin, Ottensen, Harburg, Altona, Mannheim, Breslau, Barmen, Duisburg, Frankfurt, Brandenburg, Bremen and environs; in 1874: Berlin, Essen, Hamburg and the nearby localities of Pinneberg, Altona, Harburg and Uetersen, Barmen, Duisburg, Breslau, Lübeck, Dorfgaarden, Hannover, Zittau, Delitzsch, Glauchau, Rückingen, Essen, Neumünster, Schönwalde, Gelsenkirchen, Bautzen, and Karlsruhe. A planned *Lassalle-Feier* in Bremen in 1874 was banned by the city authorities.

the wrath of the disinherited.²⁸ Another poem (like the one just mentioned, from 1865) can be cited as typical:

> Heil sei Dir, Mann von grosser Ehre,
> Der uns erteilt so gute Lehre,
> Der Du gekämpft mit Ernst und Freud!
> Du lebst fur uns in Ewigkeit!²⁹

> Hail to thee, man of great honour,
> Who taught us such fine lessons,
> You who fought in earnest and with joy!
> For us you live eternally!

For the seventh anniversary of Lassalle's death, in 1871, the ADAV's paper, the *Neuer Social-Demokrat* published a poem with the lines:

> Lassalle schallt's, als ob es Engel riefen,
> Lassalle tönt es hoffend hier wie dort.
> Lassalle klingt es aus der Seele Tiefen,
> Lassalle hallt's in fernsten Landen fort.³⁰

> Lassalle! rings out, as if in angels' voices,
> Lassalle! the hopeful cry here and yonder,
> Lassalle! sounds from the depths of our souls,
> Lassalle! resounds around the globe.

For the same occasion, the *Neuer Social-Demokrat* published an article which explicitly compared Lassalle, the 'saviour of mankind' with Christ. Lassalle's mental (or spiritual) bearing could only be compared with 'the spiritual bearing [*geistige Haltung*] of that great Nazarene after his death on the cross [!]'.³¹

In a somewhat similar vein were songs like 'Eine feste Burg ist unser Bund, wie ihn Lassalle geschaffen' ('A sure fortress is our league, as Lassalle created it'),

---

28 Rüden 1973, p. 31.
29 Ibid.
30 Cited in Steinberg 1979, p. 20.
31 *Neuer Social-Demokrat*, 27, 1 September 1871, cited in ibid. The *Neuer Social-Demokrat* drew the same direct comparison, of Lassalle with Christ, in an editorial for Good Friday in 1873. See *Der Volksstaat*, 32, 19 April 1873, which criticised the editorial.

and the 'Lassallean Confession of Faith', printed in the *Freie Zeitung*, the organ of the Lassallean splinter party sponsored by the Countess Hatzfeldt, which began:

> I believe in Ferdinand Lassalle,
> The Messiah of the nineteenth century ...[32]

The most successful and enduring song produced by the Lassalle cult, however, appealed not to religious sentiments but to secular revolutionary tradition, by using the melody of Rouget de Lisle's *Marseillaise*. Jakob Audorf's *Arbeiter-Marseillaise* was written shortly after Lassalle's death and was first performed at the memorial demonstration in Hamburg in 1864. It was to become the German labour movement's single most popular song, sung at countless meetings, demonstrations, and festivals. The first verse ended

> Nicht zählen wir den Feind,
> Nicht die Gefahren all',
> Der Bahn, der kühnen, folgen wir,
> Die uns geführt Lassall'.

> We do not count the foes,
> Nor the dangers all,
> We follow the path of boldness,
> Shown us by Lassalle.

The last verse contains the idea of Lassalle's personal legacy living on after him

> Ist auch der Säemann gefallen,
> In guten Boden fiel die Saat.
> Uns aber bleibt die kühne Tat,
> Heil'ges Vermächtnis sei sie allen![33]

> Though the sower may have fallen.
> The seed has found good ground.
> His bold deed is left to us.
> A sacred legacy to us all!

---

32 Quoted in Fricke 1964, p. 88.
33 Lidtke 1979, pp. 63 ff., 74 f.

Audorf's *Arbeiter-Marseillaise* was included in five out of six commonly used songbooks of the German labour movement used by Lidtke for his study of songs of the movement.[34] It was regularly sung at occasions such as party congresses: the congresses of 1875, 1880, 1883 and nearly every congress from 1890 to 1914 closed with the song, setting a pattern followed by many other types of party meetings.[35]

However, Lassalle's name was not invoked only on ceremonial occasions. Striking workers at Mönchen-Gladbach in October 1871 (who described themselves as 'strict Lassalleans') closed a proclamation with cheers to Ferdinand Lassalle, the sacred rights of labour, and the united league of the workers.[36]

The Lassalle cult also found expression in graphic media at this time. Copies of photographs of Lassalle (and of other leaders) were reproduced and advertised for sale in the party press.[37] In April 1872, *Der Volksstaat* contained an advertisement for an allegorical print showing Lassalle, 'that courageous fighter against the power of capital' in full figure, in the act of casting down the golden calf (representing Mammon) from its pedestal and trampling it underfoot.[38] In October of the same year, the printer (J.H. Born, Elberfeld) announced that 6,000 copies had already been sold and that a new edition was in print.[39] This particular print was widely distributed – Karl Kautsky recalled in his memoirs that he often saw this picture in workers' dwellings in Austria.[40] Its wide and lasting popularity is also testified to by a remark from the socialist literary critic Edgar Steiger, who wrote (in the context of the debate on socialism and naturalist literature in 1896) that if the workers were still lacking in appreciation of the arts, this was not their fault, but the failure of the party, with whose permission 'those frightful Lassalle-pictures (with *Frack*, flag, rocks and calf) are hawked from door to door'.[41]

---

34 Lidtke 1979, p. 61; see also Lidtke 1985, pp. 112–14; Mehring 1980, pp. 172 f.; Lammel 1984, p. 20.
35 Lidtke 1979, p. 65; Brauer 2012, pp. 54–8.
36 *Der Volksstaat*, 88, 1 November 1871. As 'strict Lassalleans', the strikers felt it necessary to point out that they did not believe that trade union organisation or strike activity could ultimately solve the 'social question', in keeping with Lassalle's sceptical teachings on trade unions, but they were striking for specific and justified industrial claims.
37 See e.g. the advertisement of H. Knieling, Dresden, in *Der Volksstaat*, 14, 15 February 1871.
38 *Der Volksstaat*, 33, 24 April 1872. While the existence of such material in the Lassallean papers, such as *Neuer Social-Demokrat*, is unremarkable, it is significant that this also appears in the rival 'Eisenacher' paper, *Der Volksstaat*.
39 *Der Volksstaat*, 87, 26 October 1872.
40 Kautsky 1960, p. 306.
41 Steiger, *Das arbeitende Volk und die Kunst*, Leipzig, 1896, cited in Fülberth 1972, p. 96.

During the years of Bismarck's anti-Socialist law from 1878 to 1890, in which the party, its organisations and publications were banned, such pictures became contraband, smuggled into Germany from Switzerland and England, along with the party newspaper *Der Sozialdemokrat*, and other social democratic propaganda. The Prussian political police kept an eye out for the importation of pictures of Lassalle and of Karl Marx (pictures of whom also circulated as contraband in significant quantities).[42] People could be convicted for selling pictures of Lassalle, as happened to the Berlin carpenter Fritz Bolger in June 1884.[43] In April 1885, the Berlin police became aware of a consignment of busts of Lassalle, but they observed that these failed to find any buyers because of their complete lack of resemblance to their subject.[44] When the anti-Socialist law lapsed in 1890, a number of booksellers, cigar-makers and other supporters of the Social Democratic Party in Berlin and Brandenburg tried to mark their new political freedom by exhibiting the picture of Lassalle conquering the power of Capital in the shape of the golden calf in their shop windows. Despite the expiry of the anti-Socialist law, the Prussian political police found grounds to harass such open adherents of Social Democracy (such as possession of still-banned Social Democratic songbooks or formal offences against the laws governing the press).[45]

It should be noted that manifestations of the 'Lassalle cult' were not confined to the ADAV or its avowedly 'Lassallean' offshoots. The distinction sometimes drawn (by historiographical orthodoxy in the former German Democratic Republic, for example)[46] between the 'Eisenachers' who were well on the way to becoming consistent Marxists, and the ideologically backward 'Lassalleans', does not stand up to close examination. (This error partly has its origins in Marx's 'Critique of the Gotha Programme'.) The party's leading theoretical authority after Friedrich Engels' death, Karl Kautsky, wrote: 'Theoretically both branches of German social democracy were Lassalleans. Marx's teachings were hardly known to anyone in Germany [in the 1860s and early 1870s] except in the form which Lassalle gave them – without naming their originator. What separated the two sides were questions of party organisation [... and] dif-

---

42 Landesarchiv Berlin (= LAB), A Pr. Br. Rep 030 Berlin C, Nr. 9061: Acta des Königlichen Polizei-Präsidii zu Berlin, betreffend bildlichen Darstellungen, 1883–1910.
43 LAB, A Pr. Br. Rep 030, Nr. 9061, Bl. 29.
44 LAB, A Pr. Br. Rep 030, Nr. 9061, Bl. 46.
45 LAB, A Pr. Br. Rep 030, Nr. 9061, Bl. 87–130.
46 Conversely, West German Social Democrats often tended to depict the party as descended from Lassalle in opposition to Marx and Marxism, whereas the party's ideological genealogy was always more complex.

ferences over tactics'.⁴⁷ To this might be added differences over the national question – the ADAV tending to accept Prussian dominance over a 'Lesser Germany', while the 'Eisenachers', based mainly in Saxony and Southern Germany, opposed Prussian hegemony over these territories.⁴⁸ Bernstein wrote: 'We were more or less all socialist eclectics' in this period, adding: 'and anyone who brings to mind the state of social development in Germany at the beginning of the 1870s, and the level of development of the socialist press and propaganda, will not be surprised at that'.⁴⁹ Even Bebel, one of the key figures of the 'Eisenacher' SDAP, recalled that he:

> like almost everyone who became socialists at that time, came to Marx via Lassalle. Lassalle's writings were in our hands before we even knew one work of Marx or Engels. The extent to which I was influenced by Lassalle is clearly shown by my first brochure *Unsere Ziele* ['Our Goals'], which appeared at the end of 1869. Towards the end of 1869, however, I first found ample time and leisure to read the first volume of Marx's *Das Kapital*, which had appeared in late summer of 1867, and that was in prison.⁵⁰

The other leading figure among the 'Eisenachers' was Wilhelm Liebknecht, sometimes regarded as Marx's principal emissary in Germany. However, the opinion of contemporaries and of later historians is virtually unanimous that theoretical questions were not the strong suit of the 'soldier of the revolution', Liebknecht.⁵¹ The existence of theoretical weaknesses in the Gotha Programme was due as much to such factors as to any tactical need to make theoretical concessions to the Lassalleans. An examination of *Der Volksstaat*, the organ of the 'Eisenachers', suggests that no strict doctrinal distinction was drawn between 'Lassalleanism' and 'Marxism'. Lassalle's writings were advertised by the paper's publisher (in greater number than those of any other social-

---

47   Kautsky 1960, p. 306, cf. also p. 367.
48   See Morgan 1965, pp. 2f., and on the national question Chapter 2 below.
49   Bernstein 1894/95, p. 103. Bernstein gives a candid account of the state of reception of socialist theory at this time, noting his own susceptibility to the teachings of Eugen Dühring, along with the influence of Dühring on many other leading Social Democrats. See also Steinberg 1979, p. 13.
50   Bebel 1980a, pp. 107f. Cf. *Unsere Ziele*, in Bebel 1995–97, Vol. 1, pp. 61–110, in which Lassalle is cited more frequently than Marx: in particular, pp. 80ff. in which Bebel defends Lassalle's views on state assistance for producers' cooperatives.
51   See, for example, Kautsky 1960, pp. 374f.; Bernstein 1978 [1928], pp. 45f.; Steinberg 1979, p. 14.

ist),[52] and the columns of the paper were occasionally made open to the 'Lassalle'scher ADAV', one of the ADAV's successor factions which had split from the main ADAV under Schweitzer's leadership.[53] Not Lassalle, but his successors, especially J.B. von Schweitzer, were the target of *Der Volksstaat's* polemics. Of some interest is a notice published in *Der Volksstaat* asking contributors to the paper 'to avoid the expression *Lassalleans* as a description for members of Schweitzer's association. Many of our party comrades proudly call themselves Lassalleans and – like us – regard these pseudo-socialists as *defilers* of the man to whom the German workers owe so much gratitude'.[54] Against this background, it is not surprising that commemorative prints celebrating the unification of the two socialist parties at Gotha in 1875 could show Marx and Lassalle side by side, expressing the belief that the two men's views could be easily harmonised,[55] nor is it surprising that the Lassalle cult persisted after Gotha and through the period of the Anti-Socialist Law, even if its excessively messianic overtones tended to fade away.

Many of the workers' associations banned during the period of the Anti-Socialist Law bore the name of Lassalle – there were 'Lassalle Dramatic Clubs', 'Singing Club Lassallias', etc.[56] Police reports recorded that on Lassalle's birthday and anniversary of his death (as well as on certain other significant socialist anniversaries), red flags were displayed in some towns, flown from towers, factory chimneys and trees.[57] Lassalle festivals continued to be held despite restrictions – one in Köpenick, on the South-Eastern outskirts of Berlin, in 1885 (attended by some 5,000 people), ended with stones being thrown at police who tried 'to prevent inflammatory speeches' and to remove a red flag from the area of the assembly.[58] Similar scenes took place in 1887 in Grünau near Berlin, and elsewhere, on the occasion of a banned *Lassalle-Feier*.[59] In Altona near Hamburg, a *Lassalle-Feier* was held in 1887 with 700 people in

---

52 E.g. *Der Volksstaat*, 82, 12 October 1872, Beilage.
53 E.g. *Der Volksstaat*, 21, 11 December 1869.
54 *Der Volksstaat*, 18, 1 December 1869.
55 Cf. Grebing 1985, pp. 79–80.
56 See Fricke 1964, pp. 135 ff. For example, Hessisches Hauptstaatsarchiv Wiesbaden (= Hess. HStAW), Abt. 407. Polizeipräsidium Frankfurt am Main, Nr. 701: Gesangverein Lassalleania 1869–1878 and Nr. 702: Akten betreffend [Dramatischen] Club Lassalle in Bockenheim 1878.
57 Fricke and Knaack 1984, p. 194 (citing six-monthly summary report of Berlin political police, 30 July 1883), 244 (report of 1 November 1884), and 268 (report of 6 July 1884).
58 Fricke and Knaack 1984, pp. 294–5 (report of 24 July 1886).
59 Fricke and Knaack 1984, pp. 324–5 (report of 15 November 1887).

attendance after police banned the posters publicising the event.[60] In Breslau, police guarded Lassalle's grave every birthday and death anniversary to prevent demonstrations at the graveside, and they also removed any red-ribboned wreaths, or wreaths consisting of red flowers, that were placed by mourners who managed to dodge the police guard.[61] At the end of August 1890, just a month before the formal expiry of the Anti-Socialist law, a brigade of troops was reportedly moved closer to Berlin in anticipation of unrest on the occasion of the *Lassalle-Feier*. The commemorations went off without incident, however.[62]

That the repression of these years may have done more to ensure the persistence of a Lassalle cult than to stamp it out is suggested by the short play 'Lassalle in Police Custody' (1897), performed by the socialist agitational theatrical troupe, *Gesellschaft Vorwärts*, under Boleslaw Strzelewicz, in which a Social Democratic agitator is arrested in a South German town by a policeman who, when told that a socialists' gathering is to celebrate Lassalle's birthday, believes that the visiting agitator is the notorious Lassalle himself.[63] The play's butt is the stupidity of the authorities, but it also touches on the theme that although Lassalle is dead (and therefore beyond the reach of the police), his ideas and spirit live on.

The period of the Anti-Socialist Law saw the establishment of Marxism as the official party ideology, a process beginning roughly with the appearance of Engels' *Anti-Dühring* and culminating in the adoption of the Erfurt Programme. In the process, the eclectic nature of the party's ideology was superseded, and with it all specifically Lassallean views. Steinberg writes that Lassalleanism 'ceased to play any role from the end of the Anti-Socialist Law'.[64] However, as Engels complained in letters to Bebel, this did not mean that the Lassalle personality cult had ceased to exist: 'To complete the victory of the [Lassalleans] you have made that moralistic piece of rhymed prose, in which Herr Audorf celebrates Lassalle, into your party song. And during the thirteen years of the Anti-Socialist Law there was of course no chance of the party taking action against the Lassalle cult'.[65]

---

60   LAB A Pr. Br. Rep. 30, Nr. 14086, Bl. 206.
61   E.g. LAB, A Pr. Br. Rep. 30 Berlin C, Nr. 8987, Bl. 153 (1880); Nr. 8988, Bl. 155 (1884).
62   Sächsisches Hauptstaatsarchiv Dresden, 11250, Nr. 115, Bl. 129: Report of the Saxon Military Plenipotentiary in Berlin, Colonel von Schlieben, 31 August 1890.
63   Knilli and Münchow 1970, pp. 326–34.
64   Steinberg 1979, p. 118n54. Cf. Jorke 1973.
65   Engels and Luise Kautsky to Bebel, 1–2 May 1891, in Blumenberg 1965, p. 416; cf. also Engels to Bebel, 6 October 1891, p. 445.

Even if 'Lassalleanism' was dead in doctrinal terms (Lassalle's notion of state-funded producers' co-operatives must have seemed increasingly antiquated in a period marked by the rise of huge industrial cartels and finance capital, and the open hostility of the Imperial German and Prussian states to Social Democracy made any strategy aiming at collaboration between the state and the labour movement moot), Lassalle remained an important symbol-figure in the party's folklore, ceremonial and cultural activities into the early years of the twentieth century.

Lassalle festivals continued to be a major event in the Social Democratic calendar. For example, in 1891 several Lassalle festivals were held in Berlin and its environs alone. Some celebrations took place as open-air excursions, following the pattern of the clandestine gatherings of the anti-Socialist law years, and also taking advantage of perhaps the last fine Sunday of summer, while others took to those beer halls and entertainment venues that were willing to host Social Democratic functions. The Third Berlin *Wahlkreis* (Electoral District) hired a special train to take over 1,000 people to its celebration at Schmöckwitz, while the Second Wahlkreis took to lake-side Friedrichshagen on Berlin's South-Eastern outskirts, where about 5,000 people took part in festivities during the day. In both Schmöckwitz and Friedrichshagen, police observed participants carrying red banners and wearing Lassalle medallions or pins, red carnations, and red ribbons or sashes. The indoor celebrations typically featured a bust of Lassalle, decorated with red sashes or wreaths, and red flags hung in the hall. Seven to eight thousand people attended the highly successful celebration of the fourth *Wahlkreis*, with singing clubs and *tableaux vivants*, and police estimated about 5,000 in the Sixth Wahlkreis, in the Eiskeller in the Chausseestrasse, where Lassalle's one-time adversary Wilhelm Liebknecht gave the speech. The Polish socialists in Berlin had their own Lassalle festival, as did the carpentry workers, the shoemakers, the singing club *Vorwärts*, the comrades from Rixdorf and Britz, as well as those from Adlershof, Grünau and Johannisthal.[66] The *Lassalle-Feier* became a regular fixture in the Berlin party organisation during the 1890s, with each *Wahlkreis* hosting its own events, despite occasional difficulties. Bad weather affected participation in 1893; the 1894 celebrations were scaled back out of consideration for the Berlin 'beer boycott', which the party was conducting against Berlin's major breweries over an industrial dispute (see Chapter 4); and in 1895 the celebrations planned by the Fourth *Wahlkreis* in Berlin's East End were banned by the police while those in other districts were able to con-

---

66   See reports in *Vorwärts*, 203, 1 September 1891, Beilage; the police file in LAB, A Pr. Rep. 30, Nr. 15432, Bl. 6–81.

tinue. The *Lassalle-Feier* still attracted thousands of Berlin workers at the end of the 1890s, however.[67]

Throughout the 1890s, and to some extent thereafter, Lassalle festivals were held annually in numerous places in Germany, being particularly popular in the Rhineland and Westphalia.[68] Lassalle's grave in Breslau continued to be a site for Social Democratic commemorative activities, which could now take place legally, albeit still under police oversight. On 30 August 1891, following a memorial celebration in a meeting-hall the previous evening, some 700 people, divided into smaller groups, paid their respects at Lassalle's grave, with wreaths laid from the local workers' association, the reading and discussion club 'Lassalle', the Breslau paperhanger-apprentices, the united Breslau hatmakers, Social Democratic groups from outlying places like Karoitsch and Oplau and from as far afield as Offenbach and the German Reading Club in Stockholm.[69] Also paying their respects were a group of women laying a wreath on behalf of the women and girls of Breslau. Under the Prussian law of association, women would still be banned from political organisation and activity until 1908. Police noted the particularly conspicuous involvement of women in the Lassalle commemorations.[70]

Images of Lassalle also continued to feature in other demonstrations, at which his bust or picture was displayed, or at which he was the subject of *tableaux vivants*.[71] At party congresses, too, pictures or busts of Lassalle were displayed along with those of Marx and Engels, and *tableaux vivants* representing Lassalle were shown.[72]

---

67 LAB, A Pr. Rep. 30, Nr. 15432, Bl. 145 (1893), 162 (1894), 181–182 (1895). This file provides exhaustive coverage of Lassalle festivals in Berlin down to 1899 inclusive.

68 See Lidtke 1985, pp. 78, 195, 205f. On Lassalle festivals in Leipzig and environs, 1894–95, see Sächsisches Staatsarchiv Leipzig 20028, Amtshauptmannschaft Leipzig Nr. 2719.

69 LAB Pr. Br. Rep. 30 Berlin C, Nr. 8990, Bl. 32. On the commemorations of Lassalle's death in 1892, see the same file, Bl. 78; for 1895, Bl. 193; for 1897, Bl. 235.

70 LAB Pr. Br. Rep. 30 Berlin C, Nr. 8990, Bl. 32–33; for other instances of women participating in significant numbers, see ibid, Bl. 78, 193. It is tempting to speculate on whether aspects of Lassalle's personality and biography (defender of a wronged Countess, the dashing orator, and his death for love) exercised a particular appeal to women, given the conventions of women's popular literature in this period, but sources do not really allow us to explore the gender dimension of the Lassalle cult in any depth.

71 Examples of busts of Lassalle at Social Democratic Party festivities and events are too numerous to list, but for indicative examples, see Lidtke 1985, pp. 89, 154, 195; Guttsman 1981, p. 176. At a *Lassalle-Feier* of the Berlin First Wahlkreis held in Köpenick in 1895, Lassalle busts (presumably small ones) were raffled off among the participants. LAB, A Pr. Rep. 30, Nr. 15432, Bl. 181.

72 For examples, see *Protokoll des Parteitages der Sozialdemokratischen Partei Deutschlands. Abgehalten zu Halle a.S., 1890*, Berlin, 1890, p. 11; *Protokoll des Parteitages ... Gotha, 1896*,

There was also a continuing market for Lassalle paraphernalia: Lassalle pictures remained popular room decorations among workers (occasionally with embroidered mottoes, which replaced the Bible verse or proverb often found in German homes), and Lassalle watches, Lassalle pipes (with a portrait painted on the bowl of the pipe), Lassalle lapel-pins and medals, and Lassalle beer mugs and playing cards were all available.[73] In addition, although Lassalle's ideas no longer played a part in the debates of party theoreticians, his popularly-written books and pamphlets continued to be read among workers. Library records suggest that – as far as socialist theoretical literature was concerned – only Bebel's *Die Frau und der Sozialismus* exceeded them in popularity.[74]

As Peter Brandt and Detlef Lehnert recently observed, the Lassalle cult waned in the early 1900s, the fortieth anniversary of Lassalle's death (1904) being the last occasion on which Lassalle festivals took place widely and on a large scale.[75] Lassalle commemorations did not disappear entirely, however. To return to Breslau, for example: in 1907 a group of 24 Social Democratic bicyclists who rode in formation to lay a wreath on Lassalle's grave were charged by the police with taking part in an illegal procession.[76] In December 1913, Karl Haberland, representing the old Lassallean stronghold of Elberfeld, suggested to the *Parteiausschuss* (the federally constituted consultative body that accompanied the work of the executive, the *Parteivorstand*, from 1912 on) that the

---

Berlin, 1896, p. 62; Knllli and Münchow 1970, p. 498. The police file on Berlin's Lassalle festivals also contains photographs of three characteristic *tableaux vivants*: 'Three cheers for Ferdinand Lassalle', showing a bust of Lassalle, wearing a red sash, beside a red flag, and with a 'worker' standing on each side of it; the 'Marseillaise', featuring a revolutionary crowd; and 'Labour paying tribute to liberty'. LAB, A Pr. Rep. 30, Nr. 15432, Bl. 91–93. The photographs were sold by the Verein für Volksthümliche Kunst (association for popular art), Berlin.

73 See the fine example of a beer mug with portraits of both Marx and Lassalle on the cover of Groschopp 1985. There are also examples of Lassalle beer mugs in the German Historical Museum, Berlin: http://www.dhm.de/datenbank/dhm.php?seite=5&fld_0=KG101022 (last retrieved 29 January 2018) and in Mannheim's Technoseum: http://technoseum.faust-iserver.de/rech.FAU?sid=C6AC935D2&dm=1&auft=0, both dated ca. 1890, with the latter showing Lassalle in the pose of victor over the golden calf. On the 'commercialisation' of the Lassalle cult, see also Welskopp 2000, p. 369.

74 Steinberg 1979, pp. 131, 139, 141. However, on the diffusion of works by Marx and Engels, see Chapter 6 below.

75 Brandt and Lehnert 2014, p. 10.

76 International Institute for Social History, Amsterdam, Wolfgang Heine Nachlass, no. 79. Paul Löbe and Breslau (questionnaire of party executive, dated Berlin, July 1907. Löbe's response to the questionnaire received by Heine on 11 August 1907). For the (more conventional) commemoration of the anniversary of Lassalle's death in Breslau in 1906, see *Volkswacht* (Breslau), 203, 1 September 1906.

party should mark the fiftieth anniversary of Lassalle's death with one final grand *Lassalle-Feier*. The proposal met with no interest from the rest of the Parteiausschuss, and was not pursued.[77]

Robert Michels, writing in 1910, had observed the Lassalle cult as a member of the Social Democratic Party (in which he was active from 1902 to 1907), and attributed it to the 'childish character of proletarian psychology'. 'The masses', Michels wrote, 'experience a profound need to prostrate themselves, not simply before great ideals, but also before the individuals who in their eyes incorporate such ideals'.[78] He continued: 'It is a point of honour with the masses to put the conduct of their affairs in the hands of a celebrity. The crowd always submits willingly to the control of distinguished individuals. The man who appears before them crowned with laurels is considered *a priori* a demigod'. Lassalle, who was celebrated as 'poet, philosopher, and barrister', is cited as an example.[79] However, while Michels' sociological reflections on the German labour movement continue to stimulate debate among its historians, few will be satisfied by his generalisations on mass psychology. In particular, they do not explain the changes in, and gradual fading away of, the Lassalle cult.

To some extent, the Lassalle cult conforms to Max Weber's typology of 'charismatic leadership'.[80] The charismatic leader, a man (invariably a man in Weber's description of the phenomenon) of unusual gifts, emerges during a time of crisis, claiming to represent a particular mission, a mission which involves a radical break with the past – in particular, with traditional authority. Much of this applies to Lassalle and his role in the early 1860s; also pertinent are Weber's observations on the problems of successors to the charismatic leader, who may attempt to derive their authority from having been designated by the original leader,[81] and the 'routinisation' which follows charismatic leadership, with its replacement by the 'powers of tradition or of rational socialisation'.[82] Thus in the case of Social Democracy, for example, the

---

77   Protokoll der Partei-Ausschuss-Sitzung vom 19. und 20. Dezember 1913, in *Protokolle der Sitzungen des Parteiausschusses der SPD 1912 bis 1921*. Nachdrucke (ed. Dieter Dowe), Berlin and Bonn, 1980, Bd. 1, p. 64.
78   Michels 1962, p. 96; cf. German original: Michels 1911, p. 67, where Michels refers to the particular '*Seelenzustand des Proletariats*'. Michels did not use the word 'childish' in the German original edition, but his translators inferred it from the context and general sense of this section.
79   Michels 1962, pp. 100 f.; cf. Michels 1911, p. 72.
80   See Weber 1967 [1948], pp. 245–53; Weber 1968, pp. 18–27, 48–65; cf. also Bendix 1962, pp. 298–328.
81   Weber 1968, p. 55.
82   Weber 1968, pp. 54 ff.; Weber 1967, p. 253.

growth of a party bureaucracy, replaced the charismatic leader – the process described in detail by Michels.

While aspects of Weber's typology can help to illuminate aspects of the Lassalle cult, a causal explanation can only be arrived at by reference to the historical stages of development of the German labour movement under the specific social conditions of the time. The main precondition for the Lassalle cult was the relative lack of maturity of the German working-class movement in the 1860s, industrialisation in Germany having 'taken off' only in the preceding decade.[83] Despite the later onset of industrialisation in Germany, a separate socialist party appealing to a working-class base came into being in Germany earlier than in Britain, for example. The Marxist scholars Wolfgang Abendroth and Hans Jürgen Friederici both stressed the absence of a fully-formed, self-conscious industrial proletariat in this period as a major factor permitting the emergence of a personality cult.[84] In the absence in this period of a stratum of working-class 'organic intellectuals' and of a proletarian organisational tradition, bourgeois intellectuals like Lassalle necessarily played a significant role in the early social democratic party organisation, although skilled craft workers who had acquired some education in workingmen's associations, like August Bebel, were not far behind them.[85] It is also important to bear in mind the education available to German workers in this period from a school system which stressed monarchical and religious values at the expense of independent thought.

In addition to this school background, many workers had their first experience of workingmen's associations in Catholic or Protestant-run Workers' Educational Associations.[86] It is therefore not surprising that, during the early stages of Social Democratic organisation, workers sought to express the value they placed on their political activity in forms borrowed from religious tradition, which enjoyed popular currency and which offered a vocabulary and a ceremonial which traditionally connoted high ideals.[87] It is perhaps worth noting that much of Lassalle's agitation took place in strongly Catholic areas, for example, the Rhineland (where, according to Franz Mehring, 'so many [workers] still lived under the mental thrall of ultramontanism').[88]

---

83 On the formation of the German working class, see Kocka 1983 and Zwahr 1978.
84 Abendroth 1974, pp. 17 f.; Friederici 1985, p. 212.
85 See Geary 1981, pp. 48 f.
86 E.g. August Bebel, who, although not a believer, valued his experience in a Catholic Workers' Educational Association in 1859–60. Bebel 1980a, p. 43.
87 On the appropriation and repurposing of traditional ceremonial and formal elements to express new symbolic content, see Tenfelde 1982, pp. 45–84.
88 Mehring 1980, p. 148.

The religious language in which the Lassalle cult was framed, and its borrowings from religious imagery, have attracted interest from scholars of the relationship between Social Democracy and religion, such as the theologian Heiner Grote and the historian Sebastian Prüfer. Grote dedicated the first substantive chapter of his study of Social Democracy and religion from the founding of the ADAV to the Gotha unification congress of 1875 to an examination of the Lassalle cult, emphasising the aspects of the cult of the dead, its ritual elements, and the recourse of socialists to religious language when commemorating Lassalle.[89] Grote considered that the cult 'always had a backward, provincial and ultra-petit bourgeois character, and [it] flourished in areas that included some that had previously been known for their susceptibility to conventicle movements' (as was the case in the Wuppertal area, which was also a centre of early textile production). For Grote, the cult was also a sign that the Social Democratic movement had not been ready to grapple with the world that confronted it, turning inwards to practice a personality cult, until it learned the lesson that such a cult was not the path to effective social and political action.[90] Grote (writing a few decades before the current inflationary use of the term 'political religion', for example in studies of fascist ideology and culture) suggests that socialists were reaching for some kind of substitute religion, and they only found a fully secular alternative belief system to replace religion when Social Democrats became fully familiar with Marxism.[91] Sebastian Prüfer also considers the prevalence of religious vocabulary and concepts among socialists in the pre-1848 period, along with points of contact between early proponents of communism and notions of primitive Christianity that seemed in the early nineteenth century to offer precedents for communist social ideas (although Prüfer also acknowledges a reaction against such religious-tinged

---

89 Grote 1968, pp. 8–25.
90 Grote 1968, p. 25. Dieter Dowe's analysis of the breakaway Lassallescher ADAV, which, under the influence of Countess von Hatzfeldt, claimed to be the true heir to Lassalle's doctrine, argued that it drew its members from small towns and relatively less developed regions (such as Erzgebirge villages, the Harz mountains, etc.), as opposed to the larger ADAV, with its groups in cities like Hamburg, Berlin, Munich, and the industrialising Rhineland. Dowe 1989, pp. 135–47. The more comprehensive analysis of available membership data by Toni Offermann significantly qualifies this distinction, finding broad similarities in the appeal to skilled craft workers and emerging factory workers as well as activity in mining regions, with only some local peculiarities in the LADAV's membership (e.g. the Erzgebirge and the more rural region around Bremen and Oldenburg). Offermann 2002, pp. 230–2. There is a great wealth of information on the CD-ROM enclosed in Offermann's book.
91 Grote 1968, pp. 232–5.

conceptions of socialism among Social Democrats by 1875).[92] Against this background, Prüfer stresses the religious and ritual elements in the Lassalle cult in the 1860s, while diagnosing a reaction against the synthesis of socialist and religious elements by the mid-1870s.[93]

Suggestions that the Lassalle cult indicates an innate need for religious belief systems or a continuity with earlier forms of religious enthusiasm (as in Grote's waves of conventicles) need to be set against the background of processes of secularisation among the working class in this period. It may be true, as Jürgen Schmidt has recently pointed out, that recent research has argued that secularisation is a more complex and less uni-directional process than sometimes assumed.[94] It nonetheless remains the case that the Social Democratic Party increasingly drew support from workers who had left their parish church towers behind – the enormous population movements that kept the German industrial revolution supplied with labour power took workers away from their ties to local churches, just as it freed from the daily supervision of local landowners. The German elites in the late nineteenth century were concerned about the shortage of church buildings in the large cities and industrial regions where workers lived, as shown by the frantic efforts to build new churches in Berlin under Kaiser Wilhelm II. In turn, the rise of Social Democracy, and its promotion of secular, scientific, and materialist ways of seeing the world helped to reinforce the trend towards the secularisation of its supporters' mentalities.[95] There were, of course, regional differences: hostility to the state church as a prop of autocratic government, and agitation in favour of leaving the church, were more pronounced in Berlin, and other parts of Prussia, and Saxony than in Bavaria or the South-West. And there were Catholic regions, where, as Franz Mehring complained, workers remained under 'the mental thrall of ultramontanism', and were more likely to join the Christian trade unions and Catholic workers' associations than their Social Democratic counterparts.[96]

If the early Lassalle cult was an expression of the theoretical and practical immaturity of German Social Democracy, the period of repression in the 1870s

---

92 Prüfer 2002, pp. 273–87.
93 Prüfer 2002, pp. 287–94.
94 Schmidt 2015, p. 22. See also Kocka with Schmidt 2015, pp. 291–305.
95 See Lidtke 1980, pp. 21–40; Schmidt 2011, pp. 39–59. On the church building wave in Berlin in the 1890s, see Lange 1967, pp. 70–1.
96 On the Christian (predominantly Catholic) labour movement, see Brose 1985; for a rich local study of the problems encountered by the Social Democratic Party in a largely Catholic area, but also showing the challenges that working-class radicalism posed to the conservative leadership of the Catholic Centre Party, see Nolan 1981.

and 1880s saw the Lassalle cult shed many of its quasi-religious trappings and take on a new function. The celebration of Lassalle festivals became one means (among others) of asserting the continued survival of socialist ideals despite persecution during and after the anti-Socialist law.

Finally, the use of Lassalle as a symbol-figure in the 1890s and, to some extent, thereafter, suggests a strategy on the part of the party leadership to construct a party tradition which could counter the dominant official traditions and rituals of the German Empire, providing the German labour movement – as a rapidly growing mass party which was now sufficiently large and organisationally developed to sustain it – with its own subculture. The period 1890–1914 saw strenuous attempts on the part of the authorities (partly as a result of the challenge of Social Democracy) to invent nationalistic traditions which would establish the legitimacy of the Reich: the Social Democrats in their turn constructed an alternative set of traditions.[97] This can be seen perhaps most clearly in the socialist calendar, which replaced the official religious, national and militaristic festivals with secular or specifically socialist days of celebration.[98] In place of Easter, Social Democrats celebrated 18 March, the anniversary of the outbreak of the 1848 Revolution in Germany and of the Paris Commune;[99] May Day was of international importance from 1890 on, following the resolution of the Second International in Paris in 1889 that established it as a festival of labour; and Lassalle festivals, commemorating the anniversary of Lassalle's death (31 August) had the advantage that they almost exactly coincided with Sedan Day (the anniversary of the decisive battle in the Franco-Prussian War and a major patriotic festival).[100] The Lassalle festival thus had the significance of a counter-demonstration to one of the main nationalistic and militaristic festivals – the festival, indeed, which commemorated the very manner in which the Empire had been founded, from above, by 'iron and blood'.[101] In Altona in 1872, near Hamburg but within the borders of Schleswig, members of the ADAV responded to a police ban on the attendance of women at the local Lassalle commemoration by staging a massive

---

97 See Hobsbawm 1984; see also Mosse 1975.
98 See Lidtke 1985, pp. 77f.
99 It is possible that the anniversary of Marx's death (14 March) was overshadowed to some degree by the older socialist March celebration. On the memory of 1848 in the German labour movement, see Bouvier 1998, specifically on Social Democratic commemorations of March 1848: pp. 1182–8 and Bouvier 1988.
100 On Sedan Day and other patriotic and monarchist commemorations, see Schellack 1988.
101 Steenson 1981, p. 145. See *Der Volksstaat*, 106, 15 September 1875, for an account of a mass meeting at Leipzig, at which Sedan Day was criticised, with the Lassalle anniversary consciously opposed to it.

counter-demonstration to the Altona Sedan festival, swamping the patriotic torchlight procession with protesting workers and drowning out the military band music with the *Arbeiter-Marseillaise*.[102] The following year, in September 1873, the Lassallean Wilhelm Hasenclever led a mass meeting of the ADAV in Berlin as an internationalist counter-demonstration against Sedan Day. At that meeting, Wilhelm Hasselmann referred to the fact they had just previously celebrated the *Lassalle-Feier*, 'a fine contrast to the Sedan-Festival!'[103] The theme of the Lassalle festival as a socialist antipode to the chauvinist and increasingly militarist Sedan Day persisted in the Social Democratic press into the 1890s.[104] In Frankfurt am Main in 1895, the police responded to this challenge to patriotic sentiment by banning a combined Social Democratic function in honour of both Lassalle and the recently deceased Friedrich Engels that would have clashed with celebrations of the 25th anniversary of the Battle of Sedan (although, incongruously, the combined Lassalle-Engels festival went ahead in Wiesbaden, the seat of the relevant *Regierungsbezirk*, or government administrative region).[105]

As far as the enduring popularity of the *Arbeiter-Marseillaise* is concerned: given that the song's popularity outlasted the Lassalle cult, remaining a party anthem down to 1914, it probably owed its success less to its references to the party founder than to the stirring revolutionary associations of the melody. There was a strong and lasting interest among German Social Democrats in the heritage of the French Revolution, and a tendency to see their own movement as forming part of a continuous radical heritage of popular emancipation from 1789 to the 1848 revolutions and onward.[106] The song was banned during the period of the anti-Socialist law, so that singing it also became a manifestation of defiance of the authoritarian state.[107]

After the unification of the ADAV and SDAP, for the sake of party unity, particularly in the face of repression and powerful opposition, Social Democratic leaders felt it necessary to project a harmonious image of the party's history: hence differences between Lassalle and Marx were played down, and

---

102   Laufenberg 1911, pp. 475–6.
103   *Neuer Social-Demokrat*, 102, 5 September 1873. Report of the speeches in *Neuer Social-Demokrat*, 103, 7 September 1873.
104   E.g. 'Zum 31. August', *Vorwärts*, 203, 31 August 1895 and 'Sedanrummel und Arbeiterbewegung', *Vorwärts*, 206, 4 September 1894.
105   Documented in Hess. HStAW, Abt. 407, Nr. 515, Bl. 69–93 (reference to Wiesbaden festival, featuring Max Quarck and Wilhelm Liebknecht, Bl. 93).
106   See Bouvier 1982; Bouvier 2012; Ducange 2012; on the revolutionary associations of the *Arbeiter-Marseillaise* itself, see Lammel 2002, pp. 217–26.
107   Atzrott 1971 [1886], p. 4, citing the *Reichs-Anzeiger*, 250, 1878.

both were celebrated as founders of the movement – Marx as the theoretician, Lassalle as the pioneering political leader.[108] 'Eisenacher' leaders such as August Bebel swallowed their differences with Lassalle – and in due course the living Bebel eclipsed the dead Lassalle in the esteem of rank-and-file Social Democrats. Lassalle, rather than the exiled Marx, was also used as a counter-figure to the symbol-figures of Prussian-German nationalism: the Kaisers and Bismarck, the 'Iron Chancellor' being the subject of a widespread nationalistic personality cult.[109] Lassalle's prominence in the 'heroic years' of the 1860s made him seem a worthy antagonist and counterpart to Bismarck, and as the party became more established after the anti-Socialist law, Lassalle continued to serve as a reminder of its early years of struggle.[110] The posthumous personality cult around the – in some respects improbable – figure of Ferdinand Lassalle can thus be traced back to the particular circumstances prevailing in the 1860s as the working-class movement detached itself from bourgeois liberalism; and its persistence, transformation and eventual decline are closely bound up with definite stages of the Social Democratic Party's development. As the party gained in numbers, organisational depth and theoretical consistency, with a new generation of working-class leaders and functionaries, the Lassalle cult gradually became superfluous.

---

108   See Bebel to Engels, 30 March 1891, in Blumenberg 1965, pp. 408–9. Bebel objected to the publication of Marx's strong criticisms of Lassalle in the commentaries on the Gotha Programme on the grounds of their potential impact on both the new and inexperienced party members who had joined during the anti-Socialist law period and on those thousands of comrades who had already demonstrated their willingness to make sacrifices for the party, and who would be outraged at harsh criticism of Lassalle.

109   On the Bismarck cult, see Mosse 1975, pp. 36, 64, 67, 95; Nipperdey 1968, esp. 577–82; Stürmer 1971, pp. 312–14. Gerwarth 2005 focusses mainly on the Weimar period.

110   For example, a Lassalle festival at Solingen in 1897 took as its theme the party's 'heroic years', with the performance of 'Twelve Years of Banishment' by C.M. Scävola. Lidtke 1985, p. 153. It was known in this period that Lassalle had held secret negotiations with Bismarck but the relevant correspondence was only made public in the 1920s by Mayer 1928.

CHAPTER 2

Between Internationalism, Nationalism and Particularism: From the War of 1870–71 to the July Crisis, 1914

In the history of German Social Democracy, there have been a number of critical junctures at which Social Democrats have been confronted with the 'national question', sometimes with the additional complications brought by war.[1] The 'national question' has been problematical for Social Democrats, given the historical traditions adhering to the notion of a German nation-state since Bismarck's anti-liberal and anti-democratic solution to the 'national question' in 1870–71 on the one hand, and ideas of socialist internationalism on the other. The issue of the vote for war credits by the Social Democratic Reichstag deputies in August 1914 is perhaps the most-studied example of German Social Democracy's response to war and to the 'national question', and a variety of explanations have been offered for the behaviour of the Social Democratic Party majority in that crisis, ranging from theories of bureaucratisation or the formation of 'oligarchic' party structures, to the emergence of a labour aristocracy and 'embourgeoisement' of the party's membership, to notions of the 'nationalisation of the masses' through the ideological offensives of pro-imperialist groups in German society or the 'negative integration' of the Social Democratic Party into Imperial German society through processes of self-exclusion, sterile dogmatism and an attitude of so-called 'revolutionary *attentisme*'.[2] In this chapter, the response of German Social Democrats to the challenge of war and the problem of national unification in 1870–71 will be examined, a response shaped as much by the competing demands of internationalism, nationalism, and particularism as by the normal demands

---

1 See Conze and Groh 1966; Wehler 1971 [1962]; Groh and Brandt 1992.
2 Out of the considerable body of writing on this area, only a few representative works can be cited here. On bureaucratisation and tendencies towards 'oligarchic' power structures, see Michels 1911; for the notion of a 'labour aristocracy' bought off with the profits of imperialism, Lenin 1985 [1916]; on the impact of nationalism, Mosse 1975; on 'negative integration', Roth 1963 and Groh 1973. For a useful concise survey of these and related issues, see Geary 1984, esp. pp. 107–26. For a nuanced analysis of the Social Democrats' reactions to the outbreak of the First World War, which stresses the existence of widespread anti-war sentiment among the party's rank and file while suggesting that the party leadership partly acted out of rational political calculation in voting for war credits, see Kruse 1993.

of working-class politics. The situation in 1870–71 is of particular interest as it saw both the genesis of the Bismarckian Reich and crucial formative years for the German labour movement, and the response of party leaders to the crisis provided a potential template for future conflicts.[3] Following the analysis of the Social Democrats' response to the events of 1870–71, there is room for further reflection on the party's relation to nationalism and internationalism in Imperial Germany.

As noted in the previous chapter, there were two competing social democratic parties in Germany in the 1860s: the ADAV (*Allgemeiner deutscher Arbeiterverein*, or General German Workers' Association), founded by Ferdinand Lassalle in 1863, and led in 1870 by Johann Baptiste von Schweitzer, who had emerged as the most able of Lassalle's successors. The ADAV had, from its inception, broken with middle-class progressive liberalism, but in doing so had become identified with aspects of Bismarckian policy, in particular the efforts for a Prussian-dominated *kleindeutsch* (lesser German) solution to the 'national question', whereas the rival Social Democratic Workers' Party (*Sozialdemokratische Arbeiterpartei*, or SDAP), founded at Eisenach in 1869, was strongly anti-Prussian under the influence of August Bebel and Wilhelm Liebknecht, and had links with particularist groups in Saxony and other states. There were organisational and ideological differences between the two groups – the 'Eisenachers' considered the ADAV to be run in a dictatorial fashion by Schweitzer, given the centralised constitution bequeathed by Lassalle – but the distinctions between the theoretical positions of the respective parties were still somewhat blurred, with Lassallean notions common among SDAP leaders. The most fundamental antagonisms between the two socialist parties were perhaps to be found over the 'national question'. At the same time, both groups maintained links with the International Workingmen's Association (subsequently known as the First International), and proclaimed adherence to its principles.

In 1864, the ADAV claimed 4,610 members, of whom over half were from the Rhineland, especially from the area around Elberfeld-Barmen, where workers from the textile industry were suffering the effects of intensified competition and technological change.[4] Solingen ('the German Sheffield') and Hamburg were also important centres for the ADAV.[5] The ADAV also recruited members

---

3   Again, the literature on German nationalism and the unification of 1870–71 is vast. For introductory surveys, see Schulze 1985 and Stürmer 1984, especially the bibliographical essays in each work. Also of interest is Hughes 1988. See also Seyferth 2007.
4   Mehring 1980, p. 137.
5   Mehring 1980, pp. 137 ff. On early Social Democratic organisation in Solingen, see Renzsch 1980; for Hamburg, see Trautmann 1983.

from Saxony, but was to face competition there from the largely Saxon-based SDAP by 1869 (and its forerunner organisations prior to 1869). The membership consisted mainly of workers, but as yet industrial factory workers played a minor role compared with skilled craftsmen with a pre-existing tradition of organisation. In Hamburg, for example, the 909 members of the ADAV in 1868 included 245 tailors, 198 joiners and carpenters, 169 cigar-makers and 111 shoe-makers.[6]

After the death of Ferdinand Lassalle in 1864, the ADAV suffered a series of splits, and conflicts between rival leaders. Some of these conflicts were related to the personal ambitions of Schweitzer and other figures. However, there were also divisions relating to Schweitzer's attitude towards the Prussian government and the national question, with some ADAV members professing loyalty to a Lassallean conception of social democracy, but expressing opposition to Schweitzer's pro-Prussian views. In particular, Hamburg and Braunschweig (both of which were in the position of being self-governing enclaves surrounded by Prussian territory) were centres of opposition to Schweitzer within the ADAV. When Schweitzer attempted in 1869 to shore up his position with a sudden merger with the 'Lassallean ADAV' associated with Lassalle's erstwhile patron the Countess von Hatzfeldt, some of the Braunschweig leaders (notably Wilhelm Bracke) and some of the Hamburg leaders left the party in protest, some making contact with August Bebel and the group that became known as the 'Eisenacher'. Wilhelm Bracke thus became one of the founding figures of the SDAP along with Bebel and Liebknecht, leading a substantial Braunschweig delegation at the party's founding congress.[7] Despite the loss of members at this time, the ADAV's ninth congress in Berlin in January 1870 was attended by delegates representing 8,062 members.[8] It should also be noted that, despite Lassalle's negative attitude towards trade unions (on the basis that trade-union work was powerless to override the 'iron law of wages' which Lassalle had postulated), his successors found it necessary to found and work with trade union organisations. The ADAV's January 1870 congress was followed by a congress of the ADAV's trade union federation, which had been founded in 1868 and consisted of 20,674 members in early 1870. However, the strongly centralised organisation and Schweitzer's dictatorial leadership contributed to a significant decline in membership from 1869 onward.[9]

---

6 Trautmann 1983, p. 169.
7 Morgan 1965, p. 28; Offermann 2002, pp. 200–11. On the labour movement in Braunschweig, see Eckert 1965, with reference to Bracke's break with Schweitzer and shift towards the 'Eisenacher', pp. 87–102; Schildt 1986, pp. 407–36.
8 Mehring 1980, p. 360.
9 Ibid; Fricke 1987, Bd. 2, pp. 873–7.

At the SDAP's Stuttgart congress in June 1870, delegates claimed mandates from some 15,000 workers, although the actual number of active SDAP members at the time may have been closer to 10,000.[10] The SDAP newspaper *Der Volksstaat* had somewhat more than 3,000 subscribers in June 1870, but lagged behind Schweitzer's *Social-Demokrat* with approximately 5,000.[11] Judging from the list of mandates for the Stuttgart congress, well over a third of the SDAP's membership came from Saxony, with significant groups also in Baden and Württemberg, Bavaria and Hesse, as well as recruiting from the industrial centres of the Rhineland, Hamburg and Berlin (along with a significant Braunschweig contingent).[12] That the SDAP's main strength was in Saxony is also demonstrated by election results. The SDAP was represented in the North German Reichstag by August Bebel and Wilhelm Liebknecht, both originally elected to Saxon constituencies in 1867 as members of the Saxon People's Party. The Lassalleans had five seats in the Reichstag in 1870, Elberfeld-Barmen, Lennep-Mettmann and Duisburg (in Rhineland-Westphalia), Chemnitz and Freiberg (in Saxony).[13] The social composition of the SDAP was not unlike that of the ADAV, despite the SDAP leadership's previous close involvement with Southern German middle-class democrats.[14] The SDAP emerged as an independent Social Democratic Party in 1869 only after four years of joint agitation involving workers' educational associations, especially in Leipzig, and the German People's Party and subsequently the Saxon People's Party. Bebel and Liebknecht became involved with the middle-class German and Saxon People's Parties partly because they felt (in contrast to Schweitzer) that the Prussian government was the major enemy of the workers' movement, rather than the progressive-liberal sections of the middle classes, and partly because of their opposition to Prussian domination of Saxony and Southern Germany. They saw in Prussia the most repressive and reactionary state in Germany, in particular as far as restrictions on the press and freedom of association were concerned.[15]

10 *Protokoll über den ersten Congreß der social-demokratischen Arbeiterpartei zu Stuttgart, 1870* (Leipzig, 1870; Reprint Glashütten/T., 1971), p. 9; Mehring 1980, p. 363.
11 Fricke 1987, p. 502; Mehring 1980, p. 352.
12 *Protokoll [...] Stuttgart, 1870*, pp. 59–61. Note that the total of 15,000 (p. 9) also included some members of the Zurich German Workers' Educational Association.
13 Fricke 1987, Bd. 2, pp. 722–36. For details on the electoral organisation and regional bases of electoral support of the social democratic parties in the North German Confederation, see Pollmann 1989, pp. 164–95.
14 Welskopp 2000, pp. 99–137, summarising the key point on p. 118; Offermann 2002, pp. 222–32.
15 A point emphasised by Bebel in his speech to the North German Reichstag attacking the proposed Reich constitution on 6 December 1870, in Bebel 1995–97, Vol. 1, pp. 131f.

(Liebknecht had in fact moved to Leipzig after being arrested and deported from Prussia in 1865 as a direct result of his anti-Bismarckian political agitation in Berlin).[16] The SDAP's views on the national question, especially as far as Bebel and Liebknecht were concerned, were strongly coloured by the particularism represented by the Saxon People's Party. The Saxon bias of the SDAP was somewhat modified by the location of the party's Central Committee in Braunschweig as a concession to the former Lassalleans who acceded to the SDAP in 1869, with a Control Commission based first in Vienna (symbolising the *grossdeutsch* sympathies of the party), then in Hamburg. The party organ, *Der Volksstaat*, however, remained in Leipzig and reflected the views of the Leipzig leaders.

Both the ADAV and the SDAP identified themselves with the programme of the International Workingmen's Association, although the practical consequences of such identification were limited by the nature of the International itself (as a bureau of propaganda and debating platform, with slender financial resources at its disposal) and by the Prussian laws of association, which prohibited associations from 'organisational contact' with bodies in other countries.[17] After the foundation of the International in London, Johann Philipp Becker, a veteran of the 1848 revolution, started a Section in Geneva, which was divided into a French and German Section in early 1865. The latter became the base for a tireless campaign of propaganda and recruitment in the German states, which reached a peak in 1868–69.[18] Through Becker's monthly journal *Der Vorbote*, and the work of adherents of the International in Germany, the programme of the International, drawn up by Karl Marx, became disseminated, and its prestige among workers gradually increased. This was sometimes expressed in acts of practical international solidarity, for example, during the 1868 strike of building workers in Geneva, financial support was sent from all over Germany.[19] In 1869, Nuremberg workers collected money for locked-out ribbon weavers and silk-dyers in Basel, despite police attempts to prevent the collection.[20] Poignantly, in light of subsequent events, in June 1870, *Der Volksstaat* printed a message to the SDAP's Stuttgart party congress from striking metal-

---

16 Dominick 1982, pp. 113–14; Schröder 2013, pp. 144–5.
17 Morgan 1965, p. 91n. The funds in the treasury of the General Council of the International during the period 1868–70 seem to have fluctuated between about £5 and £15, although the International could raise larger sums for specific purposes through appeals to its affiliates. Institute of Marxism-Leninism of the CC, CPSU n.d., pp. 104, 148, 151, 233.
18 Morgan 1965, pp. 74 ff.
19 Morgan 1965, p. 93.
20 Institute of Marxism-Leninism of the CC, CPSU n.d., p. 73.

workers in Paris, calling for all possible assistance that German comrades could render them, a call endorsed by *Der Volksstaat*.[21]

Liebknecht and Bebel also kept in direct contact with Marx and Engels in London, and saw themselves as furthering the aims of the International in Germany. Even Schweitzer sought to gain the backing of Marx and Engels, and worked to disseminate the ideas of the first volume of *Das Kapital* when it appeared in 1867. In 1868, the ADAV issued a public declaration of solidarity with the principles of the International, and Schweitzer, mindful of the strong support for the International within the ADAV, and despite his differences with Liebknecht and Becker, continued to emphasise his support for the programme and activities of the International, adding that only the laws of association, whose abolition he demanded, prevented the ADAV from joining it as a party.[22] Also in 1868, the Federation of German Workers Associations' Congress at Nuremberg declared itself in agreement with the programme of the International, at the instigation of Liebknecht and Bebel. Bebel and Liebknecht, together with Julius Motteler, were also active in founding a federation of 'International Trade Unions' in Germany, the title signifying their allegiance to the principles of the International. Characteristically, in contrast to the rigidly centralised ADAV-aligned unions under Schweitzer, the International Trade Unions had a more democratic and more federal structure.[23]

The outbreak of the Franco-Prussian war in July 1870 thus found the labour movement divided between Schweitzer's close identification with Bismarckian Prussia at one end of the spectrum and the federalist 'Greater Germany' conception of Liebknecht, who refused to reconcile himself with the settlement of 1866 and the establishment of the North German Confederation, at the other. Furthermore, tensions existed within both parties over the national question. At the same time, however, both professed adherence to a common conception of international working-class solidarity. Schweitzer explained the labour movement's internationalism in the following terms:

> The reactionary or anti-popular elements – in particular, open or concealed absolutism, the rule of the military, nobility and priests, and the capital power of the 'liberal' bourgeoisie – all weigh more or less upon the working people in the whole of the modem civilised world. Since those elements hostile to the people support each other reciprocally within

---

21 'Politische Übersicht', *Der Volksstaat*, 48, 15 June 1870.
22 Morgan 1965, p. 94; Mayer 1970 [1909], p. 282.
23 Fricke 1987, pp. 865–8; cf. Moses 1982, Vol. I, pp. 48 ff.

the various states and beyond *state* borders, the struggle against those anti-popular elements and their rule can only be conducted with success through international cooperation of the working people.[24]

This internationalism was placed under a severe strain when a war broke out in which German workers would be ordered to fire upon French workers.

As war approached, the Leipzig *Volksstaat* expressed scepticism about Bismarck's version of the French-Prussian negotiations and concluded that it was the task of the workers' party 'to work with all [its] energy for the abolition of conditions which make it possible for any Bonaparte or Bismarck to disturb world peace and at a whim send hundreds of thousands to death and cast millions into misery'.[25] The view of the *Volksstaat* reflected the conviction of Liebknecht and Bebel that there was little to choose between the Caesarism of one side or the other.[26] With the withdrawal of the Hohenzollern candidature for the Spanish throne, *Der Volksstaat* saw an end to the crisis, noting with satisfaction that judgement had been passed on the policy of Prussian expansionism, concluding that the North German Confederation was politically bankrupt and that only a reversal of 'the work of 1866' could prevent Germany from being a plaything of foreign powers.[27] With the Ems telegram incident and the ensuing French declaration of war, however, a dramatically new situation had developed. *Der Volksstaat* declared that: 'Our interests demand the destruction of Bonaparte'. It added that: 'Our interests are in harmony with those of the French people', given that the democratic forces in France were strongly opposed to Bonaparte, the pillar of reaction in Europe, and that Bonaparte was resorting to war in order to prop up his throne and destroy the social republican movement in France. At the same time, *Der Volksstaat* continued to insist that: 'Our position regarding the creation of 1866 remains the same as it always was. We do not lose sight of the fact that Bismarck and Bonaparte were allies in 1866, and that Bonaparte would not have been able to attack Prussia today, if Germany had not at that time been torn asunder by Prussia. We categorically refuse to call this war a German war. Thanks to the year 1866 only a *part* of Germany can enter the struggle, and it is not even certain that as before in 1866, Germans will not fight against Germans. But now the removal of Bonaparte is the order of the day'.[28]

---

24 Mayer 1970 [1909], p. 282.
25 *Der Volksstaat*, 13 July 1870.
26 Bebel 1995–97, Vol. 1, pp. 48 f.; Dominick 1982, p. 190.
27 *Der Volksstaat*, 17 July 1870.
28 *Der Volksstaat*, 20 July 1870.

This was to be the position of Liebknecht and Bebel during the first phase of the war – opposition to Napoleon III but at the same time refusal to accept that the North German Confederation as created and led by Bismarck could be a legitimate bearer of national interests. On 17 July, a regional congress of the SDAP convened by Liebknecht and Bebel in Chemnitz and attended by about 150 delegates, passed a resolution condemning a war fought for dynastic interests and proclaiming solidarity with the antiwar efforts of French democrats and workers.[29] The regional congress followed a meeting attended by 2–3,000 workers in Chemnitz the previous day which had expressed similar sentiments.[30] On 21 July the North German Reichstag was called upon to pass a war credit bill for 120 million *Taler*, which was passed unanimously except for the abstention of Bebel and Liebknecht. Their abstention was based on the view that the present war was a dynastic war, undertaken in the interests of the Bonaparte dynasty, in the same way as the war of 1866 had been a dynastic war. Bebel and Liebknecht declared themselves unable to grant the war credits, as this might be interpreted as a vote of confidence in the Prussian government, whose actions in 1866 had prepared the ground for the present war. At the same time, a refusal of the credits might have been seen as sanctioning the 'criminal policies' of Napoleon III. They affirmed that 'as opponents on principle of every dynastic war, as social republicans and members of the International Workingmen's Association which opposes all oppressors without regard to nationality', they could neither vote for nor against the war credits, and expressed the hope that the peoples of Europe would learn from this experience and overthrow militarism and the rule of one class over another.[31]

Bebel and Liebknecht's stand was principled and – at a time when the press (skilfully manipulated, or simply bribed, by Bismarck) and the government were whipping up patriotic outrage at French aggression – courageous, affirming their democratic opposition to Prussian militarism and authoritarian rule and reaffirming socialist internationalism. However, while this stand had some support among Saxon and Bavarian workers (as shown by meetings in Leipzig, Chemnitz and Munich), there were strongly opposing views even within the SDAP, notably within the Braunschweig central committee, nominally the governing body of the party. On 16 July an assembly in Braunschweig, attended by about 2,500 people, convened by Bonhorst, Bracke and other Braunschweig Social Democrats, echoed Bebel and Liebknecht in their condemnation of dynastic wars and in their declarations of sympathy for the French workers

---

29   *Der Volksstaat*, 20 July 1870, also 23 July 1870. See also Dominick 1982, p. 192.
30   *Der Volksstaat*, 20 July 1870.
31   Bebel 1995–97, Vol. 1, p. 117; *Der Volksstaat*, 23 July 1870.

who were labouring under Bonapartist oppression. However, the Braunschweig gathering differed from the Leipzigers in declaring Germany to be the injured party. 'Napoleon and the majority of the so-called representatives of the French people are the frivolous disturbers of the peace ... of Europe'. It was the duty of the German people to oppose them, accepting a defensive war as an 'unavoidable evil', while keeping in mind the need to work against the social and political conditions that made such a misfortune possible, and that this should not be a war against the French people.[32] Wilhelm Bracke, treasurer and key figure in the Braunschweig committee, argued that it was necessary to support the national movement in the face of Napoleon's attack, with a view to the ultimate creation of a unified and democratic state.[33] Bracke later explained that his position was governed by two considerations:

> 1) that the French democracy would necessarily gain breathing space if the war, conducted energetically by Germany, led to the collapse of the French imperial throne.
> 2) that, with the huge upswing that the national idea in Germany must take, a unification of Germany, perhaps with the involvement of the people and under the influence of Social Democratic workers, must take place, and that subsequently the 'national question' would no longer have a disruptive and inhibiting influence on the great democratic and social democratic movement.
>
> With these thoughts in mind, we considered the declaration of our party friends in the Reichstag to be an error, especially as the national movement was showing an extraordinary depth, and we had reason to fear that the Social Democratic movement, if it resisted the national movement, might temporarily be entirely swallowed up by it.[34]

Writing to August Geib, chairman of the party control commission in Hamburg (which co-existed with the Braunschweig central committee), Bracke questioned not only the tactical wisdom of Liebknecht's position (calling it a 'colossal tactical error'), but also the idea that

> someone shall, for the sake of his justified international standpoint, *deny the national*. If the excess of national feeling is to be criticised, as is the

---

32 *Der Volksstaat*, 23 July 1870; Eckert 1985, pp. 126–7, with text of the resolution of the meeting in the Braunschweig Turnhalle, pp. 129–30.
33 Seidel 1986, p. 73.
34 Seidel 1986, p. 75f.

excess of *narrower* patriotism (particularism), then it is likewise with the excess of cosmopolitanism. All three are justified and it is necessary to establish the necessary harmony between them. The international idea can after all only be realised *between* individual *nations*.

Bracke feared that Bebel and Liebknecht had departed too much from popular national feeing, and risked appealing only to a hard core of 'social republicans' and Saxon particularists, concluding: '*In matters of such importance, pure negation is fatal*'.[35]

Bracke's views coincided to some extent with those of Friedrich Engels, who criticised Liebknecht's policy of abstention as impractical. Engels regarded the war as a legitimate defensive war against Napoleon III and French chauvinism, and hoped that the French workers would benefit from a defeat of Napoleon, and that the German labour movement would gain from national unification. Engels also hoped that a German victory might also enhance the position of the German sections within the International, which supported Marx against the Bakuninists in France.[36] On 7 August *Der Volksstaat* published the first address of the General Council of the International on the war, which declared the war to be a defensive war on the German side. However, Marx's condemnation of Prussia's part in preparing the ground for war from 1866 on had to be omitted from the *Volksstaat* for legal reasons. *Der Volksstaat* did print, in italics, Marx's statement that 'if the German workers allow the present war to lose its strictly defensive character and to degenerate into a war against the French people, victory or defeat will prove to be equally disastrous'.[37]

As it had long supported Prussia's external policies, the ADAV under Schweitzer initially found itself in a less difficult position than the SDAP when war broke out. Before the declaration of war, Schweitzer's *Social-Demokrat* placed the entire blame for the coming conflict on Napoleon III for his extreme and humiliating demands against Prussia, which left the King of Prussia no alternative but to act as he did.[38] On 17 July a leading article in the *Social-Demokrat* by Wilhelm Hasselmann declared Bonaparte to be the mortal enemy of socialism, so that the duty to defend the fatherland coincided with the defence of socialism. At the same time, however, the *Social-Demokrat* conceded that, by

---

35   Wilhelm Bracke to August Geib, 29 July 1870, in Eckert 1965, pp. 133–4; Seidel 1986, p. 77. Emphasis in original.
36   Engels to Marx, 15 August 1870, in Marx and Engels 1966 (hereafter MEW), Vol. 33, pp. 39–41. Cf. Wehler 1971 [1962], p. 55.
37   *Der Volksstaat*, 7 August 1870; cf. MEW, Vol. 17, pp. 3–8.
38   Mayer 1970 [1909], p. 388.

strengthening national hatred and militarism, the war would damage the cause of socialism.[39] In an assembly attended by thousands in Berlin, Schweitzer set out the position of the ADAV in three resolutions: firstly, that only in a society based on exploitation, and in the correspondingly reactionary state structures, could a state of war arise so suddenly. Secondly, Napoleon was declared to be the offender against peace and Germany was fighting in defence of its independence and honour. Thirdly, it was declared that the meeting believed the overwhelming majority of the enlightened French people to be against the machinations of their government, and it was hoped that French democrats would succeed in putting a stop to them. These resolutions were accepted without opposition.[40] The Lassallean deputies in the North German Reichstag, Schweitzer and Wilhelm Hasenclever, approved the war credits, as did the cigar-maker Friedrich Wilhelm Fritzsche, a former Lassallean but now a member of the SDAP. Hasenclever saw his vote not as a vote for war as such, but rather wished that, since war had now broken out, the 'good-for-nothing of Europe', Napoleon III, would be defeated and overthrown.[41]

Hasenclever argued for the position of the ADAV in a meeting at Leipzig on 26 July, debating with Bebel and Liebknecht in person. Hasenclever reiterated that the war was defensive in nature, reproaching Bebel and Liebknecht for creating an impression of German disunity abroad, which lent encouragement to Napoleon. Bebel and Liebknecht responded, the latter describing the war as the inevitable product of Bismarck's policies. The majority at the meeting backed Bebel and Liebknecht – according to the report in the SDAP's *Volksstaat*, their party members constituted a majority of those attending. *Der Volksstaat* hat to concede, however, that Hasenclever won over many who had endorsed the position of Bebel and Liebknecht the previous week.[42] In the North German Confederation as a whole, however, the position of the Leipzigers seems to have represented very much a minority view.[43]

---

39 Ibid.
40 Mayer 1970 [1909], p. 389.
41 Heid 1989, p. 28. See Hasenclever's account of the debate in his memoir, Hasenclever, n.d. [1877/1987], pp. 89–90. In terms that alarmingly anticipate the racialised discourse of German nationalists referring to the French occupation of the Rhineland in the 1920s, Hasenclever cited the need to prevent occupation of Germany by French African colonial troops, pp. 90, 91.
42 *Der Volksstaat*, 30 July 1870.
43 For evidence on public opinion in July 1870, see Seyferth 2007, pp. 30–44, who points to the particular pressures exerted on those dissenting from Bismarck's war policy (but who inexplicably refers repeatedly to Liebknecht as 'Karl', rather than Wilhelm, confusing father and son!).

The situation was transformed when the war entered a second stage, after the German victory at Sedan (1–2 September), the surrender of Napoleon III and the proclamation of a French Republic. As soon as the news of the Republic reached Germany, the Braunschweig committee of the SDAP issued a manifesto addressed to all German workers, dated 5 September 1870, which declared that an 'honourable peace with the French people' was in Germany's interest, since a dishonourable peace would only constitute a truce until France was able to rise up against such a settlement, and that it was 'the duty of the German *workers*, for whom the unity of interests between the German and French people has become a sacred conviction, and who see in French workers only their brothers, with whom they are united by a single fate and a single striving, to demand such a peace for the French Republic'. The Manifesto (of which 10,000 copies were distributed, in addition to its being printed in *Volksstaat*) also condemned plans for an annexation of Alsace-Lorraine.[44] Bracke wrote that after Sedan 'there could no longer be any question of a difference between us [the Braunschweig Committee] and our Leipzig friends ... Our task was to oppose the greed for annexations and the continuation of the war, and to work for a fair peace with the French Republic'.[45] Four days after the appearance of the Manifesto, Bracke and three other members of the Braunschweig Committee (Leonhard von Bonhorst, August Kuhn and Samuel Spier), as well as the printer Sievers, were arrested and transported in chains and under heavy guard to the fortress-prison Lötzen.[46] The Braunschweig Manifesto had, however, laid down the guideline for Social Democrats regarding the war – from late September onwards every issue of *Der Volksstaat* bore the headline: 'A fair peace with the French Republic! No annexations! Punishment of Bonaparte and his accomplices!' On the French side, the French workers' associations and sections of the International called for a German withdrawal back across the Rhine. However, as Hans-Ulrich Wehler points out, there was no common Franco-German action initiated or co-ordinated by the General Council of the International.[47]

By this time, with the realisation of those war aims recognised as legitimate by most German Social Democrats – the defence of German territory and the overthrow of Napoleon III – and the transformation of the war into a war of conquest and annexation, not only was the SDAP now united in opposition to the continuation of the war, but the Lassalleans were coming to join

---

44 *Der Volksstaat*, 11 September 1870; facsimile of the manifesto as a handbill in Eckert 1965, pp. 138–9; Seidel 1986, p. 82.
45 Seidel 1986, p. 82 (ellipsis in original).
46 Seidel 1986, p. 83; Eckert 1965, pp. 129, 144–6.
47 Wehler 1971 [1962], p. 54.

them in their stance. This was demonstrated in November, when the North German Reichstag was called upon to vote additional war credits. In his speech to the Reichstag on 26 November, Bebel stated that, while he considered himself a good patriot and a good German, and while he condemned the provocative actions of Napoleon III, he stood by his earlier view that the war was a dynastic conflict, and a consequence of the events of 1866. With regard to the existing situation, he argued that the French Republic was the legitimate expression of the present mood of the French people, and that there was no good reason why peace could not be concluded with it, were it not for German demands for the annexation of Alsace-Lorraine, which he condemned, on the grounds that the overwhelming majority of the population of Alsace-Lorraine had 'not the slightest desire to join this German state under the Hohenzollerns'. In Bebel's view, the principle of nationality had to take second place behind the principle of self-determination. Taken to its logical conclusion, given the non-German minorities within Germany, and the German-speaking groups outside Germany, the principle of nationality would lead to war without end. Bebel closed with a resolution on behalf of Liebknecht and himself declaring that the defensive war had become a war of conquest, demanding a renunciation of annexations and a prompt conclusion of hostilities, and rejecting further war credits.[48] In the vote held on 28 November, Bebel was joined by Liebknecht, Fritzsche, the Lassalleans Schweitzer, Hasenclever and Fritz Mende, the democratic liberal Reinhold Schraps and the liberal Hannoverian Heinrich Ewald in voting against the credits. Hasenclever subsequently defended the ADAV's rejection of credits with the argument that the ADAV opposed war in general as a 'barbarity' and was particularly opposed to a war of conquest, now that it had assumed such a character.[49] Hasenclever also asked: 'Who fights the battles, who provides the hundreds of thousands of soldiers? The working class ... Are not the workers the ones on whom the misery of war always weighs the most?' At the same time Hasenclever maintained that in a case of the fatherland being wrongfully attacked, the workers would do all in their power to defend it, and later commented acidly on the patriotism of the bourgeoisie, which was revealed in its true light by the fact that capitalists only subscribed

---

48   Bebel 1995–97, Vol. 1, pp. 118–29.
49   In his memoirs, Hasenclever wrote: 'Of course I voted against them [the second round of war credits], because we no longer had to fear that Zouaves and Turcos [French colonial troops] would disport themselves on German soil, because there had been quite enough bloodshed, because the defensive war had turned into a war of conquest, and because the planned annexation of Alsace-Lorraine struck me as not only unjust but also as ruinous for Germany'. Hasenclever n.d. [1877/1987], p. 91.

to war loans when victory and profit seemed certain.⁵⁰ Some years later, Hasenclever framed his thoughts on the turning point of the war in verse:

> The fatherland is in danger!
> And again the loud cry is raised:
> Yet after just a few weeks' time
> The great danger had passed.
>
> But the German Michel
> Beat the neighbour boy black and blue,
> And still it wasn't enough –
> The horror of war raged on [...].⁵¹

On 6 December, attacking the proposed constitution for the nascent German Reich, Bebel went so far as to claim that 'the whole war is more or less being conducted [against our party ...] It was believed that by winning the war, we [i.e. the Social Democrats] would be defeated, and with us, of course, the people [...]', and created an uproar in the Reichstag by proclaiming a republic as the ultimate goal of the German people.⁵²

The Social Democrats' stand against annexations and a continuation of the war was not without repercussions, as already seen in the example of the arrest and imprisonment of the members of the Braunschweig committee. Hasenclever became the target of patriotic agitation in his Duisburg electorate, with a petition condemning his 'treasonous' voting behaviour gaining 11,223 signatures, some of which were from workers.⁵³ In December, Hasenclever was called up for military service and sent to the front in France, the only Reichstag deputy to serve in the war as a private soldier.⁵⁴ (Hasenclever, a tanner's son from the Sauerland, had served as a one-year volunteer in a Westphalian infantry regiment in 1857, and was subsequently called up again during the crisis of 1859, during the war against Denmark in 1864, during the war of 1866, and finally once more in December 1870. His experiences in the army

---

50   Heid, Vinschen and Heid 1989, pp. 30f., 34 (ellipsis in original). See the article 'Die beiden Reichstagsabgeordneten', in Schweitzer's newspaper, *Agitator*, 2, no. 1, 7 January 1871 for these quotations in the context of an article that reiterates the distinction between support for a defensive war before Sedan and opposition to a war of conquest thereafter.
51   Heid, Vinschen and Heid 1989, p. 29.
52   Bebel 1995–97, Vol. 1, pp. 134f.
53   Heid, Vinschen and Heid 1989, pp. 30, 34.
54   Heid, Vinschen and Heid 1989, pp. 29f.; Hasenclever n.d. [1877/1987], pp. 92–132.

made him into a resolute critic of Prussian militarism.)[55] Meanwhile, Bebel and Liebknecht were arrested on 17 December, along with Adolf Hepner, their colleague on the editorial staff of *Der Volksstaat*. They were in gaol awaiting trial for high treason when the new German Reich was proclaimed.[56] In the first election for the new Reichstag on 31 March 1871, Bebel was the only Social Democratic candidate elected (in Glauchau-Meerane in Saxony). Following this electoral debacle, Schweitzer withdrew from politics, to be succeeded by Hasenclever as president of the ADAV, and the *Social-Demokrat* ceased publication.

In an interesting postscript to the war of 1870–71, in August 1871 the successor paper to the *Social-Demokrat*, now called the *Neuer Social-Demokrat*, carried a report that German occupation troops outside Paris had been fraternising with French socialists, adding that: 'there are still many Lassalleans standing in front of Paris. During the war the socialist principle has to no small extent been spread in the German army'.[57]

The following conclusions can be drawn from this brief examination of the response of German Social Democrats to the war of 1870–71. Firstly, the Social Democrats of both parties expressed opposition to the war in principle, believing it to be a consequence of exploitative and oppressive social and political structures, and that it was conducted at the expense of workers on both sides. Social Democrats made a distinction between the régime and the people of France, arguing that war might advance the cause of French democracy. Secondly, that this argumentation was not merely casuistic is shown by the principled opposition of both socialist parties to a continuation of the war and to an annexationist policy once Napoleon had been deposed and any military threat to Germany had been averted after Sedan. A sincere commitment to socialist internationalism was also demonstrated by Liebknecht's and Bebel's courageous and controversial declarations in support of the Paris Commune (an episode deserving of separate treatment, which would go beyond the framework of this chapter). Thirdly, most Social Democrats acknowledged the right – and indeed the duty – of national self-defence. As a result of Bismarck's diplomatic manoeuvres and the patriotic outrage generated by the manipulated press and the government, most Germans were prepared to accept the war as a war of self-defence, and when the Social Democrats did oppose the war's continuation, it was in the face of a forceful patriotic

---

55 Heid, Vinschen and Heid 1989, pp. 16–33, 311 f.; Hasenclever n.d. [1877/1987]. See Chapter 5 below.
56 See Leidigkeit 1960.
57 *Neuer Social-Demokrat*, 1, no. 21, 18 August 1871.

backlash.⁵⁸ Fourthly, to Social Democrats in Saxony and Bavaria, represented by Bebel and Liebknecht, especially those who had until very recently been aligned with South German bourgeois democratic and particularist groups, the concept of a 'war of national defence' begged the question of how the nation itself was to be defined, and the principle of 'self-determination' was declared to take precedence over the principle of 'nationality'. To these people, the settlement of 1866, the formation of the North German Confederation, and the subsequent founding of the Reich in 1871 represented not the unification, but the division of Germany, with the exclusion of Austria and the subordination of Southern and Central Germany to the rule of the Hohenzollerns and Prussian reaction. This argument threatened to split the SDAP until the foundation of the French Republic united Social Democrats against what had become overtly a war of conquest. The division between the SDAP leaders in Leipzig and the Prussian-based ADAV presented itself as a struggle between Saxon and South German particularism on the one hand, and collaboration with Prussian aggrandisement on the other (with the Braunschweig Committee of the SDAP attempting to take a middle position). However, despite the different views on a Bismarckian *kleindeutsch* solution to the 'national question', once it was a fait accompli the major stumbling block to the unification of the German socialist labour movement was removed, and a process was set in motion which culminated in the national unification of German socialists at Gotha in 1875. For the next generation of Social Democrat leaders, however, the lessons of 1870 were ambiguous; in 1914, the 'social patriots' in the majority of the Social Democratic Party would invoke the principle of national self-defence also proclaimed in 1870, while the anti-war minority could draw inspiration from the stand of Bebel and Liebknecht.

In his recent concise survey of 'workers in modernity', Jürgen Schmidt has pointed to the limitations on international solidarity of workers, writing that 'there is nothing to heroicise when it comes to international and transnational solidarity', pointing to resentment of cheap competition from foreign workers, for example, in certain historical contexts.⁵⁹ However, rather than measuring the extent of international solidarity in practice against an abstract ideal standard, it may be worth taking a step back and reflecting on why there was as much emphasis on international solidarity as there was among workers organised in Social Democratic parties and their affiliated unions from the birth of the Ger-

---

58 On Bismarck's manipulation of the press and public opinion during the war, see Lipgens 1964; Seyferth 2007.
59 Schmidt 2015, p. 178. Sabine Hake also tends to discount the existence of working-class internationalism, Hake 2017.

man labour movement. Why did textile workers from Saxony, shoemakers in Hamburg, Ruhr miners and Berlin machine-workers feel they had a common cause with building workers in Geneva, weavers in Basel, and metalworkers in Paris, and why did the rival Social Democratic parties (prior to unification in 1875) feel the need to compete for the endorsement of a small committee in London purporting to represent workers internationally? Especially at a time in Europe when the principle of allegiance to a nation-state was being strongly promoted as overriding older confessional and dynastic identities, the emphasis placed on internationalism by the nascent workers' movement is striking in itself.

A few reasons for the appeal of internationalism to rank-and-file Social Democrats can be suggested. Firstly, the early labour movement recruited members largely from the ranks of skilled artisans, who had a tradition of spending part of their formative training years travelling, including across state borders, and many of the early socialist leagues joined by German artisans were outside German states, in France, Belgium, or Switzerland, where they benefitted from less repressive political and legal conditions than was typically the case in Germany.[60] The German labour movement was thus transnational from its earliest phase of development. Secondly, German radical democrats and socialists drew inspiration from the revolutionary tradition of 1789, and the attitudes of many of the generation of Lassalle and Wilhelm Liebknecht had been shaped by the events of 1848, which could be seen as a continuation of that revolutionary experience. These revolutions had been international in their scope and ramifications, with the universalist principles of 'liberty, fraternity and equality' meeting the resistance of Europe's anti-democratic dynastic states. Thirdly, the bourgeois liberal leadership of the German national movement had tended to accord workers second-class status in its organisational life, and the divergence of economic interests between the liberal bourgeoisie who led the national movement and the workers was becoming more and more salient during the strikes and beginnings of trade unionism in the German states in the 1860s. The growth of class identity among German workers reinforced both this separation from bourgeois nationalism and the belief in a common class identity with workers outside Germany.[61] Against this background, socialist internationalism clearly had a significant appeal to workers (which is not to deny that internationalism could sometimes meet with conflicting interests or ideas).

---

60 See Schraepler 1972.
61 See Morgan 1965, pp. 230–1. The prestige of the International among German workers and socialist activists is a major theme of this work.

The internationalist strain in Social Democratic thought was strengthened by the events of the anti-Socialist law in Germany from 1878 to 1890: the party's organisation, newspaper, and congresses, operated in exile, in Switzerland, Britain, and Denmark. The repressive conduct of the German state towards Social Democracy reinforced the primacy of socialist principle over the allegiance to the nation-state. When the Second International was founded in Paris in 1889, the German party was still illegal in its own country, but after the expiry of the anti-Socialist law in 1890, the German party's size and organisational capacities resulted in the German party becoming the *de facto* leader of the International.

Even if internationalism might be supposed to be relatively remote from the everyday experiences of German workers, it is possible to find frequent expressions of internationalist sentiment, especially at times of major international crises. One very rich source, discovered by Richard Evans in the Hamburg State Archives in the 1980s, is the collection of *Vigilanzberichte*, surveillance reports, by members of the Hamburg political police, whose daily rounds included sitting incognito in workers' pubs, eavesdropping on workers' conversations and reporting back on anything that might be of interest to their superiors, While careful source criticism is warranted with this source as with any other – the political police filtered and selected the material, and it is not always possible to distinguish when 'organised' workers (members of the unions or the Social Democratic Party) are speaking (although sometimes this is apparent from context or content of the conversations), these glimpses of 'pub conversations' from Imperial Germany provide many insights, and are as close to the *vox populi* of pre-1914 workers as we are likely to get.[62] On the basis of his having combed through many hundreds (perhaps thousands) of these reports, Evans found: 'If the political police hoped to find in Hamburg's evidence that the ordinary worker was patriotic enough to reject the internationalism of the Social Democratic leadership, they were [...] gravely mistaken'.[63] Specifically, Evans discovered a profoundly sceptical attitude towards the Reich's colonial and imperial policies.[64] To take one example from the files: in 1902, workers in Krichelsdorf's pub refused to express patriotic outrage over the reports of the murder of a German envoy in China, with one worker stating that the fault

---

62   Evans 1989 includes a substantial edited selection of these reports, organised thematically. See also Evans 1990, pp. 124–91. In the present work, I have supplemented Evans' material with my own samples from these files from the Hamburg Staatsarchiv (hereafter StAHH), as indicated for specific citations.
63   Evans 1990, pp. 176–7.
64   Evans 1990, pp. 176–8; with many examples, Evans 1989, pp. 341–60.

was at least partly on the European side: how would we respond, he asked, if we were occupied by foreigners who took our land without any payment and treated us the way Chinese have been treated by foreigners? One of his companions added that he blamed the missionaries for trying to force Christianity onto the Chinese: it was only natural that the Chinese responded violently to this intrusion.[65]

Richard Evans did note a degree of prejudice against Poles among Hamburg workers, especially when Polish workers were employed to undercut German workers' wages, although there was also opposition to government policies of Germanisation in Polish-speaking territories. In principle, Social Democratic workers believed that Poles should enjoy equal rights, but they also stressed that Poles needed to assert their right to equality by joining unions and the Social Democratic Party, and not go a separate way.[66] In one exchange noted by the police, in February 1905, against the background of revolution in Russia, a Polish worker apparently long resident in Hamburg lamented that the Polish nobility showed too little solidarity with the oppressed Polish people. He was angrily reproved by a German comrade for nourishing the nationalistic illusion that the nobility could be anything but an exploiter of the people, whether in Germany or Poland. The German Social Democrat concluded emphatically: 'I shit on all nationality and stand with Social Democracy, which is international'.[67]

From 1905 to 1907, workers followed the revolutionary events in Tsarist Russia with great interest and sympathy. In late January 1905, the news of the unrest in St Petersburg was greeted as a factor that might prompt the German government to make concessions to the striking miners in the Ruhr (at this time, lists for collecting money to support the striking Ruhr workers were on display in many Hamburg pubs).[68] There was also sympathy for the Russian revolutionary movement in its own right: Hamburg workers considered the Russian labour movement to still be in its infancy, but they predicted that the repression by, and untrustworthiness of, the Tsar would spur it on to greater things, as 'the workers had learned to know themselves and had realised that only in compact masses and not as petitioners, but demanding with force, they could achieve

---

65   StAHH, 331–3, 5286, *Vigilanzbericht* of Schutzmann Hinz, 15 March 1902 (unfoliated).
66   Evans 1990, pp. 179–80; Evans 1989, p. 366. For a complaint about Polish and Italian workers being used to undercut wage rates for unskilled workers (such as earth-workers), see StAHH, 331–3, 5298, *Vigilanzbericht* of Schutzmann Noroschat, 9 July 1906 (unfoliated). For criticism of Prussia's repressive policies towards Poles, see StAHH, 331–3, 5286, *Vigilanzbericht* Hinz, 6 September 1902.
67   StAHH, 331–3, 5288, *Vigilanzbericht* of Schutzmann Hinz, 25 February 1905 (unfoliated).
68   StAHH, 331–3, 5288, *Vigilanzbericht* Hinz, 28 January 1905.

something'.[69] Workers expressed contempt for Tsar Nicholas II, branding his departure from St Petersburg as cowardice.[70] By 20 February, workers received the news of the killing of Grand Duke Sergei Aleksandrovich, uncle of the Tsar and Governor-General of Moscow, by a Socialist Revolutionary, with the opinion that as wrong as assassination was in itself, the act was an understandable reaction of a people driven to extremes: the Grand Duke had deserved his punishment.[71] Sympathy for the Russian revolution was not confined to sentiments: the Social Democratic Party called on its members to donate money to aid the family members of the victims of Tsarist counter-revolutionary repression. By the time of the Essen Party Congress in September 1907, nearly 340,000 Marks had been raised, plus another 25,000 Marks pledged to assist the Russian Social Democratic Party in its campaign for the Duma elections.[72] Cultural activities were held to demonstrate and deepen the sense of solidarity with the Russian workers, as well as to help raise money for the victims of Tsarist repression, like a performance of Maxim Gorky's play *The Lower Depths* shown for the party members of Berlin's Fourth Reichstag electoral district in August 1905.[73] The 1906 May Day commemorative newspaper displayed a cover illustration of German workers shaking hands with Russian revolutionaries.[74] During the winter of 1908–09, at a time of frequent complaints about the increases in the prices of essential commodities and rising employment, one Hamburg worker was heard to state: 'We Social Democrats are united in this respect, that things will not start getting better for us until we take the workers of Russia as an example to follow and make a good clean sweep of the lordships up above us'.[75]

Practical expressions of international solidarity were not confined to climactic world events like the 1905 Russian Revolution. For example, in November 1908, the Hamburg waterside workers' union called on its members to sup-

---

69 Ibid, 14 February 1905; cf. also 8 March 1905; StAHH, 331–3, 5302, *Vigilanzbericht* of Schutzmann Kramer, 25 January 1905 (unfoliated), 28 October 1905.
70 StAHH, 331–3, 5302, *Vigilanzbericht* Kramer, 25 January 1905.
71 StAHH, 331–3, 5288, *Vigilanzbericht* Hinz, 20 February 1905. Another worker was more direct: 'It's a good thing that they've got rid of the worst of these scoundrels [*Schufte*]'. StAHH, 331–3, 5302, *Vigilanzbericht* of Schutzmann Kramer, 18 February 1905.
72 *Protokoll über die Verhandlungen des Parteitages der Sozialdemokratischen Partei Deutschlands. Abgehalten zu Essen* […], Berlin, 1907, p. 61. For demonstrations on the Russian Revolution and collections of money for the families of Tsarist repression in Bremen, see Staatsarchiv Bremen, Bestand 4, 14, 1 Politische Polizei, XII. A.3.b.2.
73 Political police report, Exekutive, IV. Kommissariat, Berlin, 19 August 1905, Landesarchiv Berlin (hereafter LAB), A.Pr.Br. Rep. 30, Nr. 14146, Bl. 84.
74 Achten 1979, p. 128; Nordrhein-Westfälisches Landesarchiv Düsseldorf, Reg. Düsseldorf 42814, Bl. 30 ff. (distribution in Düsseldorf region).
75 StaHH 331–3, 5320, *Vigilanzbericht* of Schutzmann Mebus, 15 January 1909 (unfoliated).

port a strike by their counterparts in Christiania (Oslo), Norway. Hamburg's maritime workers were warned that the Norwegian employers would be seeking strike-breakers from Hamburg, and the union called on workers not to act as strike-breaking crew on Norwegian ships. Police constable (*Schutzmann*) Mebus, whose regular rounds at this time included waterfront pubs, overheard workers expressing sympathy for the striking Norwegian workers and a strong aversion to strike-breakers:

> It would never occur to an honest and genuine sailor to stab the dockworkers in Christiania in the back, for that would be too much for his sense of honour.

> But one should really refuse to go out to sea on the same ships as such people [strike-breakers], and if one has to after all, then there are other ways and means to get rid of these people; you can just simply let a lump of coal fall onto such a fellow's head, or he falls overboard ...[76]

The political police were always on the lookout for evidence of illegal or seditious behaviour on the part of workers, and these remarks may also reflect a rough culture among Hamburg waterside workers that was often at odds with the respectable image customarily promoted by Social Democratic Party functionaries.[77] The relevant point in the context of this chapter is the evidence that the enforcement of solidarity with fellow workers of another nationality was seen as something self-evident when it came to supporting workers striking for their rights. Similarly, the German Social Democrats and the Free Trade Unions declared their solidarity with the Swedish general strike of 1909, with the Social Democratic press warning against attempts at recruiting strike-breakers in Germany, and calling on German party and union members to donate funds to support the Swedish strikers.[78]

---

76   StaHH 331–3, 5320, *Vigilanzbericht* of Schutzmann Mebus, 23 November 1908; in same file, union flyer calling for boycott of Norwegian ships in solidarity with striking workers in Christiania (Oslo) attached to report dated 20 November 1908.
77   See Grüttner 1984; Grüttner 1982.
78   *Vorwärts* carried regular tallies of donations in August–September 1909. See also *Vorwärts*, 190, 17 August 1909, 'Der allgemeine Aufstand in Schweden' (leading article); *Vorwärts*, 197, 25 August 1909, 'Der Riesenkampf in Schweden' (leading article); *Vorwärts*, 208, 7 September 1909, 'Vom Riesenstreik in Schweden' (leading article); C. Legien, 'Aufruf zur weiteren Unterstützung der Ausgesperrten und Streikenden in Schweden', *Vorwärts*, 209, 8 September 1909. By the end of September, the Berlin trade union commission had collected close to 200,000 marks. *Vorwärts*, 229, 1 October 1909, 1. Beilage.

In late 1912, Social Democratic Party members took place in large-scale protests against the threat of war in the Balkans, calling for peace and demanding that the Great Powers refrain from interfering in the region.[79] In July 1914, another, more deadly Balkan crisis loomed and in the last week of the month over half a million members and supporters of Social Democracy all over Germany staged protest meetings which in large cities spilled over into massive street demonstrations.[80] The reasons for the swift collapse of the anti-war movement and the Social Democratic Party leadership's support for war credits in the Reichstag a few days later would require a separate treatment to do them justice, but simple accusations of 'betrayal' will not suffice. A complex of factors were at work: the pace of events and the realisation that the protests had failed in their object once mobilisation began; the German government's monopoly of information and the skill with which it presented the war as a defensive fight against the Tsarist empire, an even greater *bête noire* of European socialists than the Kaiser's regime; and the threat of immediate military repression, with Germany being placed under potential martial law once mobilisation and an official state of preparation for war were declared.

The legacy of 1870–71 was a mixed one: different conclusions could be drawn in a given situation from the approval for a defensive war (especially against a repressive foreign regime) versus the opposition to a war that became a war of conquest. The fact that the party split relatively quickly and profoundly once it became apparent that Germans were not in immediate danger of being overrun by the Tsar's Cossacks demonstrated that the legacy of socialist internationalism was not extinguished by the 'experience of August 1914'.

---

79 *Hamburger Echo*, 244, 22 October 1912, 'Der Balkankrieg und die Sozialdemokratie. Eine Massendemonstration der Hamburger Arbeiterschaft'; StaHH 331–3 V330 Bd. 14 (unfoliated), police reports on meetings dated November 1912; *Leipziger Volkszeitung*, 245, 21 October 1912, 'Die Massen sprechen!' and 251, 28 October 1912, 'Der Aufmarsch der 90,000'; *Vorwärts*, 270a, 18 November 1912, Extra-Ausgabe: 'Friedensarbeit! Die internationale Demonstration gegen den Krieg'.

80 Boll 1980, p. 89; Kruse 1993, pp. 30–42; Kruse 1989. For police records of the protests in Berlin, see LAB, A Pr. Br. Rep. 30, Nr. 15805; for the protests in Hamburg, StAHH, 331–3, S23511 Versammlungen und Demonstrationen anlässlich der österreichisch-serbischen Auseinandersetzungen 1914.

CHAPTER 3

Attitudes to Labour in the German Social Democratic Party in the *Kaiserreich*

> Through the extension of machinery and the division of labour, the proletarians' work has lost all independent character and thereby all charm for the workers.
>
> MARX and ENGELS, *Manifest der Kommunistischen Partei*, 1848

∴

> To be able to transform money into capital, the owner of money must find the free worker available on the commodity market, free in the double sense, that he disposes of his labour power as his commodity as a free person, and that on the other hand he has no other commodities to sell. He is free, untied and unencumbered, of all things necessary for the realisation of his labour power.
>
> MARX, *Das Kapital*, Bd. 1, II, 4

∴

If one sets out to investigate the history of *mentalité* of the Social Democratic Party members of the *Kaiserreich*, it is clear that work, and attitudes to work, must be a significant element in such an investigation. The German Social Democratic Party in the *Kaiserreich* defined itself as predominantly a workers' party, and recruited its members mainly from the industrial, urban working class, broadly defined, including many skilled craft workers. The creation of a party of workers reflected the emerging conviction that the experience of wage labour united men (and eventually also women) into a class with common political interests. The experience of a working life under industrial capitalism that divided the worker's days into hours in which an employer determined the use of his or her labour power and the limited self-determined time that a worker could enjoy was fundamental to the worker's life experience, and it is not surprising that the campaign for a shorter working day was one of the most vital demands of the organised labour movement. The experience of working in an industrialised workforce may have given workers a new communicative horizon that enabled the emergence of a working-class consciousness, but this communicative horizon was also hedged around by labour discipline and attempts to restrict the scope of worker organisation.

How, then, to approach the history of attitudes to labour among the Social Democratic rank and file? A number of themes and avenues for investigation suggest themselves.

Firstly, the question arises of what sources can offer access to the experience and thoughts of rank-and-file Social Democratic workers, and what these sources can be expected to do. One fairly familiar and well-studied source is the body of working-class autobiographies written by workers – and former workers (sometimes turned party functionaries) from late nineteenth- and early twentieth-century Germany. These sources are open to the obvious criticism that workers who published memoirs were *ipso facto* atypical,[1] but all source material in this field is more or less mediated and source criticism is a constant duty of the historian in any case. Mediated by literary convention, the expectations of publishers and editors, and filtered by memory after later life experience outside the workshop or factory, working-class autobiographies still offer us some first-hand evidence of the experience of labour in this period.[2]

Of 33 Social Democrats' autobiographies analysed by Jochen Loreck, the large majority of the workers (not all of these memoirists were working-class) were skilled workers who had learned a trade, and some expressed a strong aversion to factory labour. The opportunity to gain advancement as a master, greater mobility, including the traditional craftsman-journeyman's *Wanderschaft* that many of these writers found a formative experience (fourteen of Loreck's sample had been journeymen), the fellowship of craft-based organisations and the conversation and personal relations with other apprentices or workers in a workshop, were all factors that made skilled work more attractive than factory labour to these writers, in addition to the intrinsic value of learning the skills for a trade that could provide a degree of security for life.[3] Exceptions to these skilled workers in Loreck's sample were the factory worker Moritz Bromme and the rural labourer Franz Rehbein. Bromme described the rigours of poorly paid piecework in dusty and unhealthy factories. Bromme fre-

---

1 See Kelly 1987, pp. 2–3.
2 For reflections on working-class autobiography, see Sinjen 2015, Ch. 5. Sinjen argues that working-class autobiographies achieved a degree of emancipation from bourgeois literary models, reflecting the different trajectories of working-class lives and less of a focus on the development of the author as autonomous individual subject.
3 Loreck 1977, pp. 141–4.

quently changed his workplace, and experienced periods without income due to ill-health. He worked in button factories, as a maker of slippers, and a stint as a waiter, before getting a job with a tool and machine factory in Gera, where he made drill bits, again paid by the piece, and he experienced constant work intensification through reduction in the rates and the need to work ever longer hours to feed his family. Fifteen years of such factory work ended with his incapacitation from lung disease.[4] Describing his work making drill bits, Bromme wrote:

> when one is working on a lathe with an automatic release, like my new one was, one can only speak of repetitive gripping with the hand, aside from setting up, and grinding and measuring the steel; one becomes a machine oneself and has only a purely mechanical action to perform.[5]

In a similar vein, the factory worker Carl Fischer described how his 'work became a torment': 'Too often one had to do the work of two men, now the spine became stiff and bending over became difficult'. He summed up: 'the spirit for work [*Arbeitsgeist*] sank to zero'. Fischer also vividly described the toll that hard and repetitive labour took on his body, with arms that felt weak and useless after carrying and working on stone.[6]

For skilled craft workers, on the other hand, work could be a source of identity and pride, at the same time as they experienced economic pressure from low wages, or increasing pressures from the capitalist market in the case of masters who had made themselves independent. Wilhelm Keil, a wood-turner (like August Bebel, who specialised in ornate door handles) recalled with pride a black-varnished 'smoking set' he had made out of peach-tree wood at the end of his second year of apprenticeship, which had been successfully exhibited at a show of craft products by apprentices, and which he kept for the rest of his life. At the same time, however, he recalled the Spartan standard of living allowed by his pay at that time.[7] Keil also travelled as a journeyman, going as far afield as London as well as several German cities. Philip Scheidemann, who also had fond memories of his journeyman days, as a compositor, derived 'great pleasure' from his work, especially when he was working in the university

---

4   Bromme 1971 [1905].
5   Bromme 1971 [1905], p. 252.
6   Carl Fischer (from his memoirs 1903–04), cited by Schmidt 2015, pp. 74, 113. Fischer's autobiography was not amongst those analysed by Loreck, who focussed on people who joined the Social Democratic Party.
7   Keil 1947, Vol. 1, p. 37.

town of Marburg and got to read works of scholarly or literary interest.[8] After learning the printing trade, he entered the service of the Party as a newspaper editor. As Thomas Welskopp has pointed out, August Bebel himself described in his memoirs the other side of the skilled artisan's existence: 'the misery of the small master', with which Bebel had become thoroughly acquainted, subject to market pressures requiring him either to deliver goods on long-term credit, despite the immediate need to meet his own expenses, or face dependency on a merchant who shaved his profit margin to the minimum, while his political activities then aroused the hostility of local business-owners, who drove him to the edge of ruin through their boycott of his products.[9]

As for the unskilled worker: Franz Rehbein described the drudgery of the life of the rural labourer, including the long days during the harvest season when he rose at 3.00am to return home for supper at nine or ten in the evening, and then the threshing work that could also involve 100-hour weeks. Like Bromme, Rehbein was also incapacitated from work-related injury (in Rehbein's case, losing his right arm in a threshing machine).[10]

Other contemporary sources on workers' attitudes include the compilations and investigations of middle-class social reformers and researchers such as Paul Göhre, a Protestant theology graduate and adherent of Friedrich Naumann's National Social party, who worked incognito in a factory for three months to study the workers and their views on life, and Adolf Levenstein, who conducted surveys of workers in 1908.[11] Klaus Tenfelde succinctly summarised the findings of Levenstein's subsequent work on 'the worker question', drawing on his surveys: no workers surveyed reported taking pleasure in their work, with miners, for example, describing difficult and unpleasant, even hellish, working conditions. Some workers attributed their lack of pleasure at work to the demands of capitalism, adding hypothetically that voluntary work, or work under different social conditions, might be a source of pleasure.[12]

It is also possible to mine the Social Democratic press for expressions of Social Democratic attitudes to labour. Again, the press does not give unmediated access to the experiences and thoughts of rank-and-file Social Democratic workers. But it is clear that organised socialist workers were often also news-

---

8   Scheidemann 1929, Vol. 1, p. 45.
9   Welskopp 2010, p. 60; Bebel 1980a, pp. 147–8.
10   Rehbein 1985: on life and work as a rural labourer, see especially pp. 241–85; on Rehbein's injury, pp. 284–5.
11   Göhre 1891. Göhre subsequently joined the Social Democratic Party, standing on the revisionist right wing of the party; Levenstein 1909.
12   Tenfelde 2010, pp. 130–1, citing Levenstein, *Die Arbeiterfrage*, Munich, 1912.

paper readers, and the high circulation figures of party papers, including their many regional and local organs, suggest that this was the era of Brecht's famous 'worker that reads'. In addition to the party dailies, or their weekly or twice-weekly local equivalents, the humorous paper *Der Wahre Jacob* gained a genuine mass readership. If one allows for a multiplier factor of two to three readers per copy, it would not be unrealistic to assume that most Social Democratic Party members got to see copies of *Der Wahre Jacob* regularly, plus a good number of family members of Social Democrats. *Der Wahre Jacob* depicted workers as characterised by strength and honesty, often by implicitly contrasting workers with their political and ideological opponents or with unflattering depictions of bourgeois or aristocrats. One can also note the gendered iconography of stylised depictions of workers in publications such as *Der Wahre Jacob*: the strong, manly worker, his masculinity emphasised by a squarely trimmed full beard, sometimes swinging a heavy hammer, a symbol of his strength. At the same time, proletarian servant girls were contrasted positively with their bourgeois mistresses: domestic servant girls were modest and unaffected, naturally poised, and possessed of innate good sense, while their mistresses were depicted as idle, vain, and foolish. Both the male and female working-class stereotypes portrayed in *Der Wahre Jacob* testified to a belief in the innate dignity of labour.[13]

As well as contributing to the formation of attitudes among the Social Democratic rank and file, the party and trade-union press occasionally contains direct (if not unfiltered) expressions of the views of the rank and file, for example in reports of discussions at party meetings and other gatherings of organised workers in the lively and very extensive organisational culture of the labour movement.

Such expressions of opinion can also sometimes be found in political police reports of meetings (again, an unavoidably somewhat selective source). Such reports vary greatly in how informative they are. Unusually informative on the opinions of Social Democratic workers are the reports on working-class opinion collected by the Hamburg political police, discovered and partially published by Richard Evans (as noted in Chapter 2). In addition to record-

---

13   *Der Wahre Jakob*, 1884–1933 is now conveniently accessible in full colour electronic format on the website of Heidelberg University library, at http://digi.ub.uni-heidelberg.de/diglit/wj. For analysis of some aspects of the symbolic iconography of the labour movement's culture and self-presentation, see Petzina 1986, although a number of contributions to the volume focus more on the Weimar Republic than on Imperial Germany. Hake 2017 stresses the gendered dimension of Social Democratic cultural production, and the emphasis on masculinity in the socialist iconography of the idealised proletarian.

ing workers' political views, the police also noted their complaints over occasional scarcity of work on the docks, low wages, arbitrary treatment of workers in the workplace, working hours (and endorsement of the labour movement demand for the eight-hour day), unsafe working conditions and workplace accidents.[14]

It is possible to find evidence of the change from the mental world of the skilled artisan to that of the 'class-conscious wage worker', a transition that was still very much in progress in the early decades of the German Social Democratic labour movement. It can be argued that the pride of the skilled artisan in his work was still in evidence in labour movement discourses in the 1870s. Dick Geary has pointed to the significance of older craft-based organisations in furnishing the Social Democratic labour movement with both traditions of organisation and militancy, and a positive sense of the dignity of labour.[15]

Thomas Welskopp's *Das Banner der Brüderlichkeit* has underlined the extent to which the Social Democratic Party was a party of skilled workers with a craft-worker background in its early decades, leading up to the period of the anti-socialist law of 1878. Skilled workers with a craft background still represented a substantial proportion of the membership around 1900, even if workers who described themselves in terms of a specific trade or craft were increasingly employed in large factories or firms, and even if the numbers of less skilled factory workers in the party increased (as did numbers of members from other social strata).[16] This is not so surprising when one considers that out of just under 8.6 million workers in industry in 1907, approximately 4.9 million were classified as 'skilled'.[17] If, as Welskopp argues, the early Social Democratic labour movement grew partly out of a rejection of older guild forms of organisation in which the better-off masters were seeking to defend their relatively privileged position against the encroachments of capitalist industrial development, at the expense of smaller masters, apprentices and journeymen, the legacy of the consciousness of the craft organisational background of skilled workers remained a factor in the culture of the movement. Elsewhere, Welskopp has argued that the formulation in the first paragraph of the 1875 Gotha Programme – 'Work is the source of all wealth and of all culture', famously attacked by Marx for its conceptual imprecision in his critique of the programme – was not simply a residue of the compromise between the Eisen-

---

14 Evans 1989, especially pp. 41–61.
15 E.g. Geary 1984, pp. 31–47.
16 Welskopp 2000, pp. 212–13. See also Schmidt 2018.
17 Kelly 1987, p. 15.

achers and the Lassalleans, or a mark of theoretical obtuseness, but reflected the values of a party still dominated by journeymen and small master artisans.[18]

A revealing case study in the persistence of skilled craft-workers' attitudes to work in Social Democracy is provided by Social Democrats' responses to the debate over the alleged malaise of 'German work' that sprang up around the negative reviews of the German exhibits at the 1876 Philadelphia World Exhibition, where critics had referred to German products as 'cheap and nasty'. After Professor Franz Reuleaux, the German commissioner for the World's Fair, relayed these criticisms in one of his regular reports from Philadelphia for the *National-Zeitung*, the deplorable state of German manufacturing industry occupied the German newspapers for some weeks, with a great deal of blame being thrown around between different social groups and interest groups.[19] The bourgeois democratic *Frankfurter Zeitung* argued in response to conservative and national-liberal charges that the rise of the Social Democratic labour movement was responsible for the poor showing of German industry that Germany's best workers were in fact to be found in the ranks of the Social Democratic movement. As evidence, it cited the fact that textile products from Elberfeld and Barmen had been singled out as outclassing the foreign products at Philadelphia, and pointed out these were socialist strongholds, and had even returned a socialist deputy at the previous Reichstag elections (a reference to the Lassallean Wilhelm Hasselmann, who had won the Reichstag mandate for Düsseldorf 2 (Elberfeld) in the 1874 elections. As noted in previous chapters, Barmen and Elberfeld were early strongholds of the ADAV).[20]

The Social Democratic press hardly needed this friendly encouragement to defend the honour of German Social Democrats as skilled workers. Both the Lassallean *Neuer Sozialdemokrat* and the Eisenacher *Volksstaat* – which were soon to fold into the united party paper *Vorwärts* as a result of the previous year's party unification – argued that organised socialist workers were the most skilled and most intelligent producers of quality German work, and they cited

---

18   Welskopp 2010, pp. 55–6. The first sentence of the Gotha Programme reads in full: 'Work is the source of all wealth and of all culture, and since generally beneficial work is only possible through the existence of society, so the entire product of labour belongs to society, that is, all its members, according to the same right, to each according to his own reasonable needs, while there is a universal obligation to work'. Gotha Programme, in Dowe and Klotzbach 1973, p. 172. See also Welskopp 2000, pp. 60–97.

19   For the context and the wider debate, see Bonnell 2001, here especially pp. 211–12. Some of the following material is drawn from this article.

20   'Politische Übersicht', *Frankfurter Zeitung und Handelsblatt*, 186, 4 July 1876, Abendblatt; also quoted in 'Politische Übersicht', *Der Volksstaat*, 80, 12 July 1876.

numerous examples of firms praised for high-quality workmanship in which the workforce consisted of, or at least included, significant numbers of, organised Social Democrats.

For *Der Volksstaat*, it was beyond doubt that 'on average the socialist worker is a better worker than the nonsocialist'. The two decisive factors in a worker's personal performance were intelligence and pleasure in one's work. The socialist paper was convinced that 'socialist workers represent the intelligence of the working class', as the socialist workers were those who had displayed the capacity to analyse their disadvantaged class situation and to develop the corresponding consciousness: 'Only intelligent workers can be socialists, and every intelligent worker is a socialist or must become one'. The second factor, 'pleasure in one's work' (*Arbeitslust*), was more problematical, as the socialist worker could not develop any enthusiasm for wage labour as such. On the other hand, the intelligent socialist worker realised that, 'despite his hatred for the unjust distribution of labour and of the products of labour', work was a general social obligation, which needed to be fulfilled for the good of all. Workers who had not yet attained the heights of the 'socialist *Weltanschauung*' could, however, be forgiven for doing as little as their employer would let them get away with, as they were only acting in accordance with capitalists' own standards of conduct, but *Der Volksstaat* still found the distinction between this behaviour and that of socialist workers significant.[21]

Der Volksstaat backed up its case with a list of factories which had been considered successful in Philadelphia. Among makers of tools, instruments, and knives, the successful concerns were from Berlin (in one case), Solingen, Ronsdorf and Hagen, 'that is, places painted red thrice over with a core troop of socialist workers', and the Wellmann firm in Altona, whose workers were social democrats. Among the goldsmiths, those from Pforzheim and Hanau had distinguished themselves, and the goldsmiths were claimed to be the main supporters of the socialist labour movement in these towns. The socialists were not to blame for the '"Sedan" of German industry', but the bourgeoisie, and if anyone had saved the 'honour' of German work in the midst of the defeat, it had been the German Social Democrats.[22] Of the places named by *Der Volksstaat*, Solingen, the centre of Germany's knife-making, cutlery and metal utensils industry, deserves particular mention as a stronghold of Social Democracy in the 1870s, returning a Social Democratic Reichstag deputy (Moritz Rittinghausen) in the 1877 elections. Production and labour organisation

---

21   Ibid.
22   Ibid.

was still characterised in Solingen by skilled craft-work, with workers in small-scale production and home-based outwork still seeking to hold out against factory production and industry-level union organisation in the Deutscher Metallarbeiterverband well into the 1890s.[23] Ronsdorf had been one of the most celebrated sites of Ferdinand Lassalle's agitation in 1864, and had been an early stronghold of the ADAV before switching to the SDAP in 1869.[24] Hamburg and its close neighbour Altona were also Social Democratic strongholds, with the Reichstag electorate of Schleswig Holstein 8 (Altona) held by the Lassallean, Wilhelm Hasenclever, in 1876. In Hamburg and Altona, the Social Democratic Party membership in the 1870s also still consisted largely of skilled craft workers.[25] On a more modest scale, the social democrat newspapers were also justified in claiming that the Party was well represented among the goldsmiths of Pforzheim.[26]

The word 'honour' was again prominent in a subsequent report in *Der Volksstaat*, on 23 July, which commenced with the declaration: 'The socialist workers have saved Germany's honour in Philadelphia'. This time, *Der Volksstaat* drew its evidence from the reports in the *Neues Berliner Tageblatt*. The latter paper had singled out the jewellery (cufflinks, etc.) by the firm of Eduard Peine in Hamburg for praise. *Der Volksstaat* claimed that most of the workers in this firm were socialists. Likewise, the workforce of the firm of Heinrich Adolf Meyer, Hamburg, whose ivory products were praised at some length by the *Neues Berliner Tageblatt*, was said to consist almost entirely of socialists. When the *Neues Berliner Tageblatt* described the successful displays of A.W. Faber, from Stein near Nuremberg, and Schwanhäuser of Nuremberg, both makers of pencils and other writing and drawing materials, *Der Volksstaat* noted that these firms, too, employed mostly socialists. The same applied to Elberfeld textile manufacturers, Schlieper and Baum, and Gebhardt & Co., makers of high quality wares – 'the workers of these firms are almost without exception socialists', as were the workers of the firms F.E. Woller (Stollberg in Saxony, manufacturers of stockings of fine quality) and Heinrich Gulden (Chemnitz, makers of widely praised gloves). The Saxon lacemakers Dörffel Söhne and Hirschberg & Co., whose wares received honourable mention, had mainly socialist workers in their employment, and the socialist workers of the Eulengebirge district in Silesia, especially those of Emanuel Kohn, Wüstergiersdorf, were also said to

---

23   Boch 1985, reference to strength of Social Democracy, p. 257.
24   Offermann 2002, enclosed CD-Rom, pp. 551–2.
25   See Trautmann 1983, p. 169; Kutz-Bauer 1983, p. 186; Kutz-Bauer 1988, pp. 179–84.
26   See the report from Pforzheim under the rubric 'Correspondenzen', *Der Volksstaat*, 37, 29 March 1876.

have distinguished themselves. Finally, the *Neue Berliner Tageblatt* had found that the products of the mechanical weaving mill in Linden near Hannover 'deserve the highest praise in every respect [...]. Germany has every reason to thank the Linden mill for what it has achieved here'. For *Der Volksstaat*, this crowned a list of products and firms which proved that 'socialist workers, on average, were better workers than nonsocialist ones'.[27]

The Reuleaux controversy received equally intensive coverage from *Der Volksstaat*'s Lassallean sister-paper, and erstwhile rival, the *Neuer Social-Demokrat*. Even before *Der Volksstaat* took up the theme, the *Neuer Social-Demokrat* responded to Reuleaux' first letter from Philadelphia with the claim 'that it is socialist workers, who have saved the honour of German industry in the few better-quality branches', singling out the achievements of socialist Wuppertal (Barmen and Elberfeld) textile workers. The *Neuer Social-Demokrat* also claimed that most of the workers of Siemens & Halske, the Berlin electrical firm, which had been successful in the field of telegraph technology, were socialists, and that the 'world-renowned Krupp works in Essen', whose products, especially heavy artillery, dominated the German stand at the exhibition to what struck many observers as an intimidating or downright indecent extent, 'count among their workers a significant number of socialist-minded men'. For the *Neuer Social-Demokrat*, the exhibition demonstrated that politically active workers' determination to secure shorter working hours and adequate wages created conditions under which workers could apply more intelligence and care to their work – a strong argument against trying to boost the competitiveness of German industry by cutting wages and opposing organised labour.[28]

Like *Der Volksstaat*, the *Neuer Social-Demokrat* also claimed the cutlery and instrument manufacturers of Berlin, Solingen, Ronsdorf, and Hagen, the Wellmann factory in Altona, and the goldsmiths of Hanau and Pforzheim as successful examples of Social Democratic workforces.[29] The *Neuer Social-Demokrat* reproduced the full list of firms named by *Der Volksstaat* (on the basis of *the Neues Berliner Tageblatt*'s reports) in which Social Democrats could claim to have achieved success in Philadelphia. In slightly more colourful language than the other socialist newspaper, the *Neuer Social-Demokrat* wrote of how social democratic workers had 'saved the honour of German work': 'just as in

---

27 *Der Volksstaat*, 85, 23 July 1876.
28 'Leitartikel', *Neuer Social-Demokrat*, 75, 2 July 1876.
29 'Das deutsche Reich auf den internationalen Ausstellungen', *Neuer Social-Demokrat*, 77, 7 July 1876.

the midst of a wild, disorderly rout, a batallion of the old guard stands fast here and there and saves the flags'.[30]

It may seem surprising to see the Krupp firm listed as a socialist stronghold. The Krupp concern is best known for a combination of patriarchal rule within the firm, disciplining its workforce in order to suppress any irregular conduct or industrial unrest, and highly-developed company-based welfare measures to keep workers loyal to the concern.[31] In the mid-1870s, however, support for social democracy in Essen was growing appreciably, and did not stop at the factory gate of the Krupp works. In early 1877, the regional government authorities made their concern known to the Krupp firm over the extent of Social Democratic agitation among the Krupp workers, both in their residential colony and in the factory, where agitation was apparently tolerated by some supervisors. Alfred Krupp reacted to the increasingly open socialist activities of his workers with a wave of dismissals, chiefly among lathe operators (*Dreher*) and fitters (*Schlosser*) from the mechanical workshops, and with a formal proclamation to the workforce, exhorting them to behave virtuously and to resist the blandishments of social democracy, and reasserting the prerogative of the proprietor to dispose of the means of production as he saw fit.[32] The claim of the *Neuer Social-Demokrat* that the Krupp works 'count among their workers a significant number of socialist-minded men' as of 1876 was therefore justified.[33]

That German workers and artisans were themselves concerned about the Philadelphia debacle's consequences for their international reputation (and sense of 'honour') was illustrated by a report which *Der Volksstaat* took from the *Hamburg-Altonaer Volksblatt*, regarding a meeting by small *Handwerker* and wageworkers with the purpose of starting a subscription to support sending a delegation of German workers of various occupations to the World Exhibition.[34] The theme in this discussion of 'honour' reflects the place of that concept in the discourse of skilled craft-workers, as discussed in Andreas Griessinger's work on 'The Symbolic Capital of Honour'. The high value the craft worker put on his own skills and qualifications, manifested in the quality of his work, was a crucial component of the 'moral economy' of the German artisan, and was tied up with the discourses of 'honour' which characterised collective

---

30   'Die Social-Demokraten und die Welt-Ausstellung', *Neuer Social-Demokrat*, 83, 21 July 1876.
31   See Ritter and Tenfelde 1992, pp. 414–19.
32   Paul 1987, especially pp. 205–11, 219–29.
33   Twenty years later, the possible presence of Social Democrats in the Krupp works still concerned Friedrich Krupp and the Prussian authorities in the region. See Landesarchiv Nordrhein-Westfalen, Düsseldorf, Reg. Düsseldorf 9062, Bl. 55–76: correspondence between Krupp and the police authorities, 1897–98.
34   Quoted in *Der Volksstaat*, 87, 28 July 1876.

action on the part of artisans' guilds.[35] It is striking how often formulations such as 'the maintenance of the honour and material interests' appears in the statutes of Social Democratic workers' associations in Bavaria in the 1870s, when it came to specifying the purpose of the association or union.[36]

At the same time, can we trace an evolution away from exclusivist craft guild discourses of 'honour' to more inclusive language of 'solidarity' across the class of wage-earning workers? Reading *Der Volksstaat* from the first half of the 1870s, there is an increasing emphasis on the language of solidarity (encompassing terms such as 'comradeship' and unity). Where *Gesellen* in skilled trades had defended their 'honour' by enforcing the exclusion of outsiders from their organisations and workplaces, the Marxian-influenced Social Democratic press in the late 1860s and 1870s and subsequently cultivated a feeling of solidarity with workers engaged in industrial conflict both across different occupations and across different geographical areas, even internationally. This sense of solidarity with workers across borders was manifest both in the prestige of the International Workers' Association (First International) among German socialist labour movement circles in the 1860s (despite the International's paucity of material resources) and in practical acts of international solidarity between workers, as well as between different regions in Germany, such as raising strike funds (as discussed in Chapter 2 above). It might be worth analysing the language applied to industrial conflict to trace the way in which the emphasis on 'honour' was eclipsed by the value of 'solidarity', although the latter concept did not so much replace the idea of honour but subsume it: workers who exercised solidarity were honourable, those who did not, such as strike-breakers, forfeited any claim to be regarded as honourable. But the newer ethos of solidarity was potentially more inclusive than the older discourse of honour.[37]

There was growing recognition that the conditions of industrial capitalism required new forms of organisation. As a Saxon miner wrote in *Der Volksstaat* in 1876:

> The miners of today no longer, as they did in previous years, constitute an estate that is respected. Who is surprised at this, when the miner stands

---

35 Griessinger 1981, especially Ch. 8. Gabriel 2014 notes the prevalence of the language of 'honour' among Social Democrats in the 1880s, but relates it to the values of the aristocracy (p. 92) without acknowledging the antecedents of this discourse among artisans.

36 See the tabulated lists of banned Social Democratic associations in Bavaria in Bayrisches Hauptsstaatsarchiv Munich, M.Inn 66312, Bl. 10–112, 15–26.

37 For discussion of the lines of continuity, and differences, between older craft guild organisation and trade unions, see Schmidt 2018, especially pp. 298–9.

12–15 hours a day in the service of the capitalist, and is often employed in labour on Sundays and holidays as well? When he no longer feels at home in his family, and he feels the need of some stimulus to wake up his tired body and his dull spirit, even if only temporarily? The result of this is that the situation of the miners gets worse and more unfortunate year by year.

The writer concluded that only a new organisation for all miners in Saxony could remedy the plight of Saxon miners.[38] At the same time, the Allgemeiner deutsche Schneiderverein, the tailors' union, sought to combat the poor wages and conditions suffered by tailors whose lack of unity made them a prey to wage-cutting competition in the labour market by calling for greater unity and solidarity ('one for all and all for one') in a single organisation:

> To promote unity and to conduct a united struggle, the call goes out to all colleagues: join the Allgemeiner deutsche Schneiderverein! Also to those of you who still belong to local craft associations, we also call on you to join, as our association does not only work for local interests, but for the interests of all German tailors. Through local craft associations, you will never be in a position to rid yourselves of the least of the measureless evils that exist in our line of work, and to create something good that will last, for a single town is much too weak to achieve anything against the employers who are more and more acting in concert. That requires the unity of all colleagues. Our call also goes out to small masters, who are more and more being forced down into the position of wage labourers [...].[39]

One change from the older guild mentality concerned the status of proletarian women. The language of labour was inevitably gendered. How did Social Democracy deal with the tension between a view of women's wage labour as exploitative, and a challenge to the working conditions of male 'breadwinners', and an ideology that construed women's work as potentially emancipatory?[40] There was also the hostility expressed in the workplace by male workers towards women whose work they regarded as undermining men's wages and conditions. As one worker in the Berlin machine industry around 1910 was recorded as saying:

---

38   C. Ebert, 'Die Organisation der Bergarbeiter in Sachsen', *Der Volksstaat*, 13, 2 February 1876.
39   Fr. Holzhäusser, 'Allgemeiner deutsche Schneiderverein', *Der Volksstaat*, 16, 9 February 1876.
40   See Hausen 2010, pp. 73–92.

Women stab us in the back too much by pushing down our pay rates. The whole issue of wages suffers from that. If workers refuse to accept a reduction in piece-rates, the work is divided up and declared to be women's work ... Women's work undermines us, in the first place because women are cheaper, and secondly because they don't need as much as a man. The woman spends less overall und the married woman says, her husband earns money anyway.[41]

Jean Quataert has styled German Social Democrats in the period of the Second International as 'reluctant feminists', at the same time as she has characterised the German socialist women's movement as having developed 'the most far-reaching program for change' of any such movement at that time.[42] There was a tension between Clara Zetkin's theoretical demand for gender-blind labour legislation and the party's regular advocacy of protective labour legislation for women, particularly with a view to protecting the health of mothers and potential mothers.[43] In Zetkin's theory, wage work would provide women from the proletariat with a degree of economic independence and with the opportunity to share in the economic and political struggles of their male working-class comrades. In practice, the conditions working women had to endure were often cited as emotionally powerful indictments of the present capitalist order, including in August Bebel's *Woman and Socialism*, the best-selling German Social Democratic text (which went through 50 editions from 1879 to 1910). Critical exposés of women's working conditions could be found in Social Democratic periodicals and newspapers, including Zetkin's *Die Gleichheit*, and in the writings of the few women worker autobiographers and party activists, such as the seamstress Ottilie Baader and Adelheid Popp, who at an early age (from ten years old on) had to work as a servant, seamstress and factory worker, to the ruination of her health.[44]

One regularly occurring theme in Social Democratic discourse, a key focus of parliamentary reform efforts, and a regular topic in the party and union press, was what we would now call workplace health and safety. James Retallack has recently pointed out that industrial disasters were a focus of August Bebel's

---

41   Cited by Dora Landé, *Arbeits- und Lohnverhältnisse in der Berliner Maschinenindustrie zu Beginn des 20. Jahrhunderts*, Leipzig, 1910, cited in Homburg 1991, p. 182. Ellipsis in original.
42   Quataert 1979, p. 229.
43   Quataert 1979, pp. 40–1. See Zetkin's speech at the foundation congress of the Second International 1889, e.g. in Hervé 2008, p. 44. Zetkin conceded that an exception could be made for the case of pregnant women in the workforce, but otherwise stated that she did not recognise any 'women's question' or 'women workers' question'.
44   Baader 1979 [1921] and Popp 1978 [1915].

and Wilhelm Liebknecht's socialist agitation in its very earliest period (the late 1860s), for example, when a mining disaster in Liebknecht's own electorate of Stollberg killed 101 miners in July 1867, or when an explosion in a coal mine owned by a prominent Saxon Conservative grandee claimed 276 lives in August 1869.[45] Marx spoke of the statistical summaries of workplace accidents and resultant deaths and injuries as 'despatches from the battlefront, which add up the wounded and killed of the industrial army'.[46] Social Democratic papers ran regular rubrics with titles like 'from the battlefield of labour'.[47] Historians have commented critically on the tendency of Social Democrats to adopt a martial vocabulary, but the stress in this case was, in a quite anti-militarist spirit, on the senseless waste of human life that resulted from inadequate regulation of workplace safety. 'Victims of the Moloch' of capitalism was another frequent locution. That this was a pressing issue was illustrated by statistics showing between 9,000 and 10,000 fatal workplace accidents a year in Germany between 1906 and 1909 inclusive (up from 8,567 in 1900), with well over 100,000 accidents a year resulting in compensation claims. In the ten years from 1900 to 1909 inclusive, there were over 89,000 workplace deaths in Germany.[48] In a longer timeframe, from 1886 to 1913, the number of deaths from workplace accidents in a year rose from about 2,700 to 10,300.[49] Among the most dangerous industries was mining, with over 20,000 deaths in mining in the Ruhr alone between 1871 and 1913, with the annual death toll passing 1,000 in 1912 and 1913.[50] Writing in *Die Neue Zeit* in 1912 on the topic of 'Works accidents as a social mass phenomenon', J. Brod attributed the high number of

---

45   Retallack 2017, p. 94; see also *Demokratisches Wochenblatt*, 32, 7 August 1869, p. 361: 'Die Katastrophe in dem Burgk'schen Kohlenwerk'; *Demokratisches Wochenblatt*, 34, 31 August 1869, Beilage, p. 492: 'Eine Mahnung'.
46   *Das Kapital*, Vol. I, Ch. 13, in MEW, Vol. 23, pp. 448–9. Also cited in Brod 1911/12, p. 126.
47   E.g. 'Vom Schlachtfelde der Arbeit', *Volksstimme* (Frankfurt/M.), 17, no. 280, 30 November 1906, 2. Beilage, in this instance a description of the scene after an explosion in a chemical factory in Dortmund; 'Vom Schlachtfeld der Arbeit', *Rheinischer Volksfreund. Kalender 1900* [almanac-style publication for workers], copy in LA NRW Reg. Düsseldorf, 9063, Bl. 138–139.
48   Brod 1911/12, p. 126. While historians of Imperial Germany have become increasingly sensitive to examples of symbolic oppression and discrimination in the cultural sphere, this staggering industrial death toll goes unremarked in most historical accounts of the period. See, however, Ritter and Tenfelde 1992, pp. 372–89; for comparative perspectives, special issue of *Journal of Modern European History*, 7, no. 2 (2009), on 'Health and Safety at Work: A Transnational History'.
49   Schmidt 2015, p. 80. Schmidt notes that this was a relative decline in the proportion of insured workers, despite the increase in absolute terms.
50   Ritter and Tenfelde 2015, p. 377. For more details on workplace safety and deaths in Ruhr mining (in the period 1841–91), see Tenfelde 1981, pp. 225–8.

workplace deaths in Germany to the greater complexity and speed of operation of modern machinery, coupled with tired and overworked workers; the number of workers from rural backgrounds who came into factories without adequate training in the operation of machinery; the prevalence of piecework payment regimes; general negligence on the part of employers, all driven by the supremacy of the profit motive over all other considerations on the part of employers.[51] Workers themselves tended to agree on the importance of the last factor: the primacy of the profit motive on the part of capitalists, inadequately restrained by state regulation, was held responsible for workplace deaths such as those caused by mining disasters.[52]

∴

To what extent did the discourse on work within German Social Democracy internalise or develop Marx's insights into the alienation inherent in wage labour? How adequately did Social Democrats engage with these questions?

Work naturally occupied a central place in the programme and programmatic literature of the party. The proximate demands set out in the Erfurt Programme of 1891 included the eight-hour day, labour protection legislation including a ban on child labour (for children under 14 years of age), a ban on night work except where it was essential for technical reasons or the public welfare, an uninterrupted rest period of at least 36 hours in every week for workers, and a ban on the 'truck system' (payment in kind instead of money).[53]

The struggle for a greater share of the day to be self-determined time, and to reduce the hours during which the employer disposed of a worker's time and labour power, was a central defining issue for the labour movement. While the working-day was gradually shortened during the period from the 1870s, when it averaged about 12 hours a day, to the years 1909 to 1914, when it averaged 9.5 hours, the eight-hour day remained one of the most potent rallying calls of Social Democrats and the Free Trade Unions aligned with them.[54] Every May Day, the demand for the eight-hour day formed a central focus of Social Democratic agitation and festivities. The number '8' on a red flag or a poster sufficed

---

51 Brod 1911/12, p. 129.
52 See, for example, StAHH, 331–3, 5320 (Vigilanzberichte Schutzmann Mebus), reports of 17 and 26 November and 16 December 1908.
53 Dowe and Klotzbach 1973, pp. 175–80, here especially pp. 179–80. For explanatory glosses on these points, see the widely disseminated pamphlet by Kautsky and Schoenlank 1910, pp. 55–61.
54 On working hours, see Rüden and Koszyk, 1979, p. 41; Mühlberg 1985, p. 50.

to communicate the message that the workers were entitled to a fairer division of their own time: eight hours' labour, eight hours' recreation, and eight hours' sleep.[55]

Much has been written about the huge network of cultural organisations that grew up in the Social Democratic labour movement, and the apparent tendency of these organisations to replicate forms of dominant bourgeois culture. In a number of publications relevant to this topic, Dick Geary has taken issue with the easy assumption that such cultural organisations represented a mere attempt to replicate the cultural norms of the dominant social groups, an attempt to 'elevate the workers' to bourgeois standards. Geary has stressed the extent to which the creation of separate workers' leisure, sporting and cultural organisations was a political act, reaffirming the organisational autonomy of the Social Democratic labour movement from bourgeois political and social organisations.[56] However limited the success of such cultural organisations as far as the creation of an 'alternative culture' in some formal respects is concerned, they nonetheless constituted a sphere within which working-class solidarity, organisational autonomy and sociability could play out without direction from middle-class politicians or other outside authority figures. Furthermore, if one keeps in mind the centrality of the demand for the eight-hour day to Social Democrats' political consciousness, any activities in the sphere of self-determined leisure or cultural organisations take on an added significance, underlining the claims of Social Democratic workers for sovereignty over a greater share of their day. Such organisations helped to demonstrate that 'eight hours recreation' would be put to good use by class-conscious Social Democrats.

In terms of the development of socialist theory, one might find that during the period of the Second International little was done to deepen or elaborate on Marx's insights into the alienation that arose in wage labour under capitalism, or into the kind of 'freedom' that could be enjoyed by the notionally 'free' worker who had to live by selling his or her labour power. While Social Democratic periodicals such as the Marxian theoretical organ *Die Neue Zeit* sought to keep up with publications in the young social sciences that had a bearing

---

55 For graphic illustrations of the theme of the demand for the eight-hour day on May Day posters and other visual material for May Day, see Achten 1979, especially pp. 26, 27, 129, 130 (showing the eight-hour day as a milestone on the road to the dawn of socialism on the horizon), p. 132 (contrasting the life of the gluttonous and wasteful life of the capitalist class with the honest toil, rest from work, and hard-earned sleep of the workers, from *Süddeutscher Postillon*, 1894), pp. 134, 159, 164 (from 1914).

56 See especially Geary 2000, pp. 388–402. See also Chapter 7 below.

on labour conditions, or on the condition of the working class more broadly, innovative theoretical work on labour *per se* was largely missing from the literature. There were, however, attempts to engage with, to describe and analyse, new forms of labour relations under industrial capitalism, and to make sense of these new phenomena within the framework of Marxist theory.

For example, Richard Woldt's study *Der industrielle Grossbetrieb*, published by the Social Democratic Dietz Verlag in 1910, sought to analyse labour conditions in large factories.[57] The short book was greeted by a reviewer in *Die Neue Zeit*, Fritz Kummer, as a rare exception in a rapidly growing literature on the management of large firms: while most of this literature was written for managers with the intention of assisting them in the exploitation of their labour force, Woldt's book was intended to be of use to trade unionists in helping them to understand how large factories worked, and the ways in which the latter might be vulnerable during industrial disputes.[58] This constituted an alternative perspective to that of the modern 'professional expert in factory organisation', who, Woldt suggested, 'sees in the worker only a work-machine, a production factor like any other'.[59] Woldt described an increasingly mechanised production process, in which 'the worker becomes a mere servant of automatically working machines', while the search for ever-increasing productivity entailed increasingly refined methods of exploiting the worker's labour power at the same time as skilled workers were replaced by unskilled, 'and above all by the working woman'.[60] Woldt argued that the trend of mechanisation had verified Marx's and Engels' predictions that mechanisation would not free workers but would subject them to a 'labour of Sisyphus', and to a tiring and monotonous work regime.[61] New technical devices (such as various kinds of punch-clocks) assisted managers in the enforcement of time discipline among the workforce, and also assisted sophisticated calculation of piece-rates, to promote further work intensification.[62] Woldt's book reflected on the new methods of labour intensification increasingly practised in the United States and associated with the name of Frederick W. Taylor, 'the most fertile hatcher of schemes for surveillance of workers and for driving them on', as Kummer called him. Kummer noted in his review that while most of the new theories for

---

57 Woldt 1913 [1910]. Woldt also published an analysis of the new white-collar workforce of large firms, Woldt 1911, reflecting on the prospects of trade-union organisation among this section of the workforce.
58 Kummer 1910–11.
59 Woldt 1913 [1910], p. 4.
60 Woldt 1913 [1910], p. 7.
61 Woldt 1913 [1910], p. 23.
62 Woldt 1913 [1910], pp. 23–38.

intensifying the exploitation of labour 'sprang from Yankee brains' in 'Dollarland', his own observations of work in both Germany and the United States persuaded him that in general American workers did not suffer from greater labour intensification than their German counterparts already did.[63] However, Taylorism was on its way to Germany, where *The Principles of Scientific Management* was translated in 1913. Even prior to this, Woldt cited Taylor's work on *Shop Management* as outlining a more ramified and refined system of controlling workers on the shop-floor than the simple reliance on one foreman per group of workers, in order to maximise the manager's degree of power and control over the work process, increasing also the separation between physical and mental work.[64] Woldt also cited a 1910 article from the journal *Werkstatttechnik* that claimed that the 'Taylor system' had already been successfully tried out in one German machine factory.[65] This discussion of Taylor was just one of numerous references to American management experts and technical innovations in Woldt's book, which already noted the growing 'Americanisation of German firms'.[66]

On the very eve of the outbreak of the First World War, the Düsseldorf *Volkszeitung* published an article on 'The Taylor System of Working People to the Bone'.[67] The author, 'ap' (like Woldt), put the Taylor system into the context of a Marxist understanding of the evolution of capitalism as a system that was constantly seeking to achieve productivity increases through either improved technology or increased intensification of work, with Taylorism being an example of the latter tendency. 'ap' grasped the essence of Taylor's 'scientific management': where the worker had previously disposed of the skills and knowledge to control the actual execution of the labour process, leaving management to rely on incentives to increase productivity, Taylorism wrested this level of control from the worker, prescribing every single movement of the worker to the last detail:

> The mental and physical activity which in every labour process belong together inseparably as the half-instinctive, half-conscious application of an expert knowledge that has been handed down to the worker, is separated here; the mental part is transferred to the works management in the

---

63   Kummer 1910–11. On Frederick Winslow Taylor and 'Taylorism', see Kanigel 1999.
64   Woldt 1913 [1910], pp. 60–3.
65   Woldt 1913 [1910], p. 63.
66   Woldt 1913 [1910], p. 40.
67   ap, 'Das Taylorsystem der Abrackerung', *Volkszeitung* (Düsseldorf), 25, no. 173, 27 July 1914, Beilage.

form of scientific dissection and reconstruction of work actions, while the worker is left with the mindless physical, purely mechanical part of the work.

To 'ap', this process recalled Marx's characterisation in *Capital* of the original transformation from artisanal production to factory manufacturing: 'Just like that transformation, the Taylor system also means a degradation, an abasement of the worker'. The Taylor system even raised the future prospect of fully automated production. The elimination of any superfluous rests or motion, the assumption that the worker needed to be monitored constantly to ensure absolute efficiency, and the individualisation of incentives to undermine solidarity in the workplace were all perceived as threats to workers by the author of the Düsseldorf *Volkszeitung*, who recognised how difficult it would be to resist more advanced and productive methods of labour control.[68] The full implementation of Taylorist 'scientific management' techniques had to wait until after the First World War and the 'rationalisation' movement in German industry in the 1920s.

Arguably, such changes might have been better understood and better anticipated by Social Democratic theorists – it is unlikely, though, that the German labour movement, deeply divided after 1918, could have prevented changes driven by capitalist industry's innate drive for increased profit.

---

68   Ibid.

CHAPTER 4

Social Democracy and the Price of Bread: The Politics of Subsistence in Imperial Germany

In 1943, the economic historian Alexander Gerschenkron published *Bread and Democracy in Germany*. Gerschenkron's title pointed to the link between the economics of subsistence and the health or otherwise of political democracy in Germany. Gerschenkron described how Prussia's class of large aristocratic landowners, with estates East of the Elbe river (known to history as the Junkers), were able to leverage their privileged political position in the constitution and power structure of Prussia and thus also of the Reich to extract economic benefits at a succession of critical junctures: in the grain tariffs of 1879 as Bismarck shifted away from a coalition with National Liberals and towards a right-wing protectionist coalition of heavy industrial and large agrarian interests; in subsequent significant increases in the grain tariffs (1885 and 1887); and the increase of tariffs on wheat, rye, oats and malt barley under the Bülow government in December 1902 (along with increased import duties on meat and livestock).[1] The political position of the Junkers was buttressed by the three-class property-based franchise in Prussia, the powers of the Prussian upper house in a Reich constitution that afforded Prussia veto power over constitutional change, and the social power exercised by an aristocracy that retained disproportionate influence over the upper ranks of the army and the bureaucracy. Originally writing during the Second World War, Gerschenkron drew the conclusion the Junkers had not only succeeded in forcing higher bread prices on urban consumers to further their own interests, but in doing so, had 'delayed the development of democratic institutions in Germany'.[2] For Social Democrats in Imperial Germany, struggling against tariffs on grain and import restrictions on meat and livestock, as well as against indirect taxes on consumer goods, the connection between the price of food staples and the democratic deficit of the *Kaiserreich* was crystal-clear, and the insistence on this connection was a powerful theme in Social Democratic agitation.

The politics of subsistence and consumption in Imperial Germany demands closer analysis than it has received in recent literature (with a couple of excep-

---

1 Gerschenkron 1989 [1943].
2 Gerschenkron 1989 [1943], p. xxxvii.

tions, e.g. Christoph Nonn, Thomas Lindenberger),[3] especially in terms of an analysis of the thinking of Social Democratic Party members. The price of bread and other foodstuffs had a very direct impact on the everyday lives of the urban workers who were the party's main social base. As Gerschenkron perceived, the question of the price of bread was a highly politicised one, bringing together the cost-of-living pressures on workers and the political economy and fiscal system of Imperial Germany, in which the state relied heavily on indirect taxation, and the powerful landowning lobbies demanded tariffs on imported grain. What Social Democrats called 'bread usury' was one of the most electorally significant issues for the party. The nexus between the everyday experience of working-class families and the political economy of the Empire calls out for closer analysis, an analysis that also has to include the gender dimension.

The impact of government tariff policies on the cost of living of workers was compounded by the nature of Imperial Germany's financial system, with its heavy reliance on indirect taxes on everyday consumer goods (such as salt, tobacco, brandy, beer, and sugar) to supplement its customs duties and the so-called *Matikularbeiträge* (matricular contributions) – the contributions by the individual German states to the Reich treasury. *Marikularbeiträge* were set on the basis of population figures. They were, in effect, an indirect poll tax. (The individual states raised their own revenue, including through income tax, but the application of these taxes between the states was inconsistent. The national government did not levy an income tax.) The Reich also derived income from the postal and telegraph services, and the railways. When protective tariffs were introduced in 1879, the income from these and the tobacco tax was effectively capped by agreement with the Reichstag parties in 1879, with revenue over RM 130 million going to the states. (There was thus some fiscal churn of funds between the Reich and the states.) Large landed estates generally escaped municipal charges (being outside the jurisdiction of the *Gemeinden*, or municipal authorities). In general, then the fiscal system of Imperial Germany was both regressive and inefficient; it relied heavily on indirect taxation, which imposed a proportionally heavier burden on lower-income earners. The spending of the Reich government went overwhelmingly to defence, to the army, and from the late 1890s on, the rapidly expanding navy.[4] Indeed, in 1913, a full 90 per cent of the Reich's budgeted expenses were going on defence purposes. The

---

3   Nonn 1996 and 1994, and Lindenberger 1994.
4   The standard work on the financial system of Imperial Germany is Witt 1970. On 'matricular contributions' and the awkward fiscal federalism of the Reich, see Kruedener 1987. On taxation, see also Spoerer 2004 and Ullmann 2005, pp. 56–88. For an older account of the finance policy of the Social Democratic Party, see Calmann 1922.

navy's share of these expenses rose from 17.9 per cent in 1901 to over 26 per cent by 1909, dropping in relative but not absolute terms (compared with the army) with the massive increase in expenditure on the army in 1913.[5]

The Social Democratic Party made the cost of food a key theme of their agitation. Periodically, there were waves of agitation linking the rising cost of bread, meat, and other staples to the greed of the Junker landowners, who both dominated the agrarian lobby and held a disproportionate amount of political power. Campaigns over the cost of daily living thus led logically to the Social Democrats' campaigns for electoral reform, for example, the fight against the Prussian three-class franchise and its counterparts in other states and at the municipal level.

When the Social Democratic Party published a summary of its parliamentary activity in the first two decades of the existence of the German Reich, the topic of the effects of tariffs on foodstuffs and of indirect taxes on workers' standard of living was given prominence.[6] After an initially confused political response to the issue of protectionism,[7] the party campaigned against the grain tariffs of 1879, which increased the price of bread, and the increase of duties on grain and some other foodstuffs in 1887. It also opposed the tax on brandy and proposed state monopolies on brandy and tobacco.[8] Consumption taxes on brandy, coupled with generous rebates for producers, amounted to redistribution of money from working-class consumers to landowning agrarian interests. The same applied to the tax regime on beet-sugar, and the effect of import duties on grain.[9] Import restrictions on meat and livestock had a similar effect, as the Social Democrats argued.[10]

In May 1890, the parliamentary deputies of the still outlawed Social Democratic Party introduced a motion into the Reichstag that called for the abolition of tariffs or import duties on all grains, butter, meat, fish, herrings, salt, fats, eggs, and livestock, which was, of course, unsuccessful when it finally came to the vote in February 1892.[11] Despite the party's in-principle oppositional stance to the Reich government and invariable opposition to the government's budgets, the Social Democrats welcomed the trade treaties of the early 1890s,

---

5   Table in Witt 1970, pp. 380–1.
6   *Die Sozialdemokratie im Deutschen Reichstag* 1909, pp. 314–34.
7   Lidtke 1966, pp. 86–8.
8   Calmann 1922, pp. 91–3.
9   Witt 1970, pp. 41–54 (with detailed tables on revenue and rebates for these commodities).
10 *Die Sozialdemokratie im Deutschen Reichstag* 1909, pp. 331–4. For details on contemporary controversies over the German government's import restrictions on meat imports from the United States, ostensibly on health grounds, see Spiekermann 2010.
11 *Die Sozialdemokratie im Deutschen Reichstag* 1909, p. 462.

introduced by Bismarck's successor as Chancellor, Leo von Caprivi. (Treaties were concluded with Austria-Hungary, Italy, Belgium and Switzerland in 1891, followed in subsequent years by treaties with Serbia, Rumania and Russia.)[12] Social Democrats supported these trade agreements on the basis that they promised to put downward pressure on food prices at a time when these had been increasing, although the party complained that even after these treaties, grain tariffs continued to impose a significant burden on working class families.[13] As was usually the case in Bebel's Reichstag speeches on such issues, the party's electoral propaganda emphasised statistics that showed the impact on ordinary German workers:

> The grain tariff still imposes an annual burden of over 300 million Marks on the people, two thirds of which goes to benefit the large landowners. Even now [after Caprivi's trade treaties] a worker's family with three children, which consumes around 900 kilos of bread grain a year, is burdened to the extent of 30 to 32 Marks by the tariff, so that they have to devote 20 to 15 days of work to pay for this tariff, indeed just as in previous times a feudal obligation of two weeks' unpaid work was due to the feudal lord. Around 35 million inhabitants of Germany who live outside of the agricultural sector have to pay more for their bread as a result of this grain tariff, und every effort must be made to completely abolish it.[14]

While the Reich's financial measures following Caprivi's modest tariff reductions did not impose major new burdens on working-class consumers, the persistence of grain tariffs and other import duties, and the indirect tax system, combined with complaints over rising food prices, and the prospect that Tirpitz's proposed expansion of the German navy would require substantial new taxation measures, all provided the Social Democratic Party with campaign themes for the 1898 Reichstag elections. The handbook that was produced to inform the party's organisers and agitators during the election cam-

---

12 Burhop 2011, pp. 111–12. For a detailed account of the politics of the trade treaties, see Nichols 1958, pp. 138–53, 287–98. The second round of trade treaties, including the treaty with Tsarist Russia, would not have passed the Reichstag without the votes of the Social Democrats. For a more recent analysis of the Caprivi trade treaties, see Torp 2005, pp. 179–209.
13 *Die Sozialdemokratie im Deutschen Reichstag* 1909, pp. 462, 463; Calmann 1922, pp. 107–9.
14 *Die Sozialdemokratie im Deutschen Reichstag* 1909, p. 463; cf. August Bebel, speech to Reichstag on the Reich budget, 27 November 1893, in Bebel 1995–97, Bd. 3, pp. 413–20. ms [Max Schippel] 1891/92 noted that the benefits of the trade treaties would be limited, but saw them as a potential breach in the protectionist front between heavy industrial and agrarian interests.

paign focussed heavily on the themes of indirect taxes and tariffs, and their impact on the cost of living for workers. The indirect tax burden on the public had increased, according to the Social Democrats' election material, from 7 Marks a head annually in 1878 (the year before Bismarck's protectionist turn) to over 16 Marks a head twenty years later – or over 80 Marks annually for a family of five. The party's election guide also detailed exactly how much customs duties cost for basic commodities – from 3.50 Marks per 100 kilos for the staples rye and wheat (reduced from 5 Marks by the Caprivi administration) to 17 Marks for pork, 20 Marks for butter, 50 Marks for roasted coffee, and 80 Marks for cacao and chocolate (each per 100 kilos). The regressive effects of this indirect taxation were also spelled out in a table showing how much greater a proportion of a worker's income went on consumption taxes as opposed to a millionaire's.[15] The Social Democrats were also quick to link Tirpitz's Naval Bill with the threat of even greater indirect tax burdens on workers and their families: 'It is **working people**, who already have to contribute the main share of Reich revenue though *tariffs and indirect taxes*, who will once again have to pay the **costs** of the Naval Bill'.[16]

Records of party meetings during the 1898 Reichstag election campaign reflect the focus on these cost-of-living issues. For example, in early May 1898, the popular Berlin Social Democratic member of the Reichstag Paul Singer addressed a meeting of approximately 2,500 people (including a large number of women) in Keller's *Festsäle* in Koppenstrasse in Berlin's East End, in the Fourth Reichstag Electoral District. Singer recounted how the Social Democrats in the Reichstag had attempted to abolish the duties on grain, and complained that:

> The grain prices have risen higher today than they were even in the crisis year of 1891/92 and at the same time the prices for meat have reached a previously unheard-of level. We therefore demand the suspension of grain tariffs. [...] Out of 54 million inhabitants [of Germany] only 4 million have an interest in high grain prices. And on account of these 4 million, are the 50 million to have their daily bread made more expensive?

Vorwärts recorded 'tempestuous, long-lasting applause' for Singer's speech.[17] Simultaneously, at another meeting in Eastern Berlin, another Social Demo-

---

15 Sozialdemokratischer Parteivorstand 1898, pp. 239–47.
16 Sozialdemokratischer Parteivorstand 1898, p. 224 (bolding and emphasis in the original).
17 Landesarchiv Berlin (= LAB) A Pr Br Rep. 30, Nr. 14145, Bl. 153; *Vorwärts*, 106, 7 May 1898. On Singer, see Reuter 2006.

cratic Reichstag deputy, Franz Lütgenau, gave a similar speech, attacking the 'activities of the bread usurers', 'of the agrarians and their associates that were hostile to the people's interests, which ruthlessly made more expensive the most essential foodstuffs'.[18]

With Caprivi's trade treaties expiring ten years after their signing, the Bülow government prepared a new tariff law for 1902, which envisaged significant increases in tariffs on grain and meat. Under Chancellor Bernhard von Bülow, agrarian protectionism, covering both grain and livestock, meat and other animal products, became entrenched. It has been estimated that 3 per cent of the income of the German people was being redistributed from consumers to agricultural producers. As Social Democratic publicists did not tire of reminding the public, this included redistribution, through the hands of the state, from ordinary urban workers to large Junker landowners.[19]

The stage was thus set for food prices to become an election issue again in 1903, amidst political controversy and agitation by a range of lobby groups.[20] The Social Democrats were prepared for an election campaign around this issue.[21] Speaking again to the members of the party organisation for Berlin's Fourth Reichstag electoral district in September 1902, Paul Singer announced that the central issue for the 'Election Year 1903' would be tariffs and the campaign against the 'agrarian plague', which would also involve protests against militarism and the naval build-up.[22] As in Berlin, a series of meetings were held in Hamburg in October 1902 to protest against the 'usury on food, especially the meat shortage'.[23] The well-attended meetings were conspicuous for the high participation rate of women at a time when women were still legally excluded from participation in political organisation: out of 550 listening to Emil Fischer and Luise Zietz at Jacob's Tivoli at the Besenbinderhof, some 200 were women, and about 300 women were in the crowd of 800 listening to trade union leader Carl Legien at the Valentinskamp. There were similar numbers of women and men at a simultaneous rally in Eimsbüttel. Fourteen simultaneous meetings in Hamburg and its environs passed a common resolution condemning the tariff policy of the Bülow government and pledging those present to work to

---

18   LAB A Pr Br Rep. 30, Nr. 14145, Bl. 153; *Vorwärts*, 106, 7 May 1898.
19   Burhop 2011, p. 114 (citing Friedrich-Wilhelm Henning).
20   See Torp 2005, pp. 211–91.
21   Cornelius Torp stresses that the Social Democrats were already well prepared to organise around issues of food prices prior to the wave of price increases from 1905, which is stressed by Nonn as a key watershed in this respect. Torp 2005, pp. 246–7. See Sozialdemokratischer Parteivorstand 1903, pp. 82–141 (on tariffs) and 162–95 (on indirect taxes).
22   LAB A Pr Br Rep. 30, Nr. 14146, Bl. 13; *Vorwärts*, 213, 12 September 1902.
23   Staatsarchiv Hamburg (= StAHH), 331-3, 7949-2UA1.

strengthen Social Democracy's representation in both the Reichstag and the Hamburg city-state parliament (the *Bürgerschaft*), in the interests of an economic policy that would serve the people's interests.[24]

The 1902 Party Congress in Munich was told of 'thousands of meetings in all parts of the Reich' protesting against the planned tariff increases, or as the party leadership put, 'the planned robbery of the people'.[25] The party also made increasing use of printed propaganda, preparing flyers against the threatened increase in food prices, and distributing them 'in millions of copies, into the furthest villages of the Reich'.[26] Even in small towns in rural parts of Hessen, electorally unpromising terrain for socialism, pamphlets on 'The Taxation of Hunger', with simple and effective graphics illustrating how much everyday commodities were taxed and what the money was spent on (army, navy, imperial adventures in places like China, royal courts, etc.) were distributed by Social Democrats.[27] Social Democrats were also starting to make a practice of saturating the working-class precincts of Berlin with cheaply produced one-page flyers whenever they ran a political campaign. In just one Berlin electoral district (the Fourth), eleven flyers totalling 1.5 million copies were distributed from October 1902 to the end of 1903.[28] There was something of a pamphlet war on the question of food prices: agrarian lobbyists hit back against Social Democrats' agitation against 'bread usury', pleading for priority to be given to the interests of depressed small farmers, while bourgeois social reformers sought to demonstrate that workers could ameliorate their condition by more rational diet planning.[29] Research into how to calculate the minimal nutritional requirements of

---

24 Reports in ibid (file not consistently foliated).
25 *Protokoll über die Verhandlungen des Parteitages der Sozialdemokratischen Partei Deutschlands*. Abgehalten zu München vom 14. bis 20. September 1902, Berlin, 1902, p. 12; cf. also Torp 2005, p. 249.
26 *Protokoll* München 1902. See also reports on the circulation of a flyer 'Fort mit dem Brodwucher' in Düsseldorf, Elberfeld, Barmen and other towns in February 1901, Landesarchiv Nordrhein-Westphalen (= LA NRW), Reg. Düsseldorf, 9064, Bl. 85, 89, 90 (copy attached, Bl. 86).
27 Hessisches Staatsarchiv Marburg, 165, 706/4, Bl. 450 ff., September 1901. The same pamphlet was distributed in large quantities in the region around Düsseldorf, LA NRW, Reg. Düsseldorf, 9064, Bl. 269–270. *Vorwärts*, 182, 7 August 1901 (on petitions against 'bread usury', and distribution of flyers in Berlin).
28 *Vorwärts*, 25, 30 January 1904, report on meeting of party organisation in the Fourth Berlin electoral district.
29 Siebertz 1901; Rademann n.d. [ca. 1889]. For a clear summary of the Social Democratic position, see *Lebensmittelwucher und Warenteuerung*, Berlin 1910 (= Sozialdemokratische Flugschriften VI); also *Die indirekten Steuern und Zölle. Wer sie zahlt und wem sie nützen*, Berlin 1911 (= Sozialdemokratische Flugschriften VIII).

workers to maintain their labour power had been a flourishing field of scientific work in Central Europe since the 1870s.[30] The Social Democrats' emphasis on the cost of living, and the negative impact of tariffs and indirect taxes on it, proved successful in the 1903 election. Christoph Nonn attributes the party's gain of nearly a million (from 2.1 million in 1898 to just over 3 million) votes to the campaign against 'bread usury' and higher tariffs.[31]

Workers benefitted from a gradual rise in living standards between 1871 and 1914, as far as nutrition is concerned. Available statistical evidence shows that workers' consumption of meat and protein in general was increasing over the period, in large part because of the success of workers' industrial organisation, including waves of strike activity, in improving the bargaining power of workers in the labour market. However, while workers' expectations of a diet that included regular meat consumption increased, the tightness of workers' household budgets rendered them vulnerable to price increases, and they then found themselves having to resort to the cheapest and least favoured kinds of meat.[32] After a long period of relative stability between 1871 and about 1900, wholesale prices for meat began to climb significantly after 1902, with an increase of close to 50 per cent by 1913 compared to 1901 prices.[33] By 1905, the combination of the 1902 tariffs and import restrictions on meat and cattle were resulting in widespread unhappiness at the rise in meat prices, in particular, while the price of bread also increased significantly.[34]

That this dissatisfaction with rising meat prices was acutely felt by the Social Democrats' core working-class constituency is reflected in the police reports on Hamburg pub conversations from this period (and it was also very evident in the reports from the years 1901–02). In February 1905, one of a group of workers complained that food was too expensive, especially meat. 'This comes from the high tariffs and the ban on the import of meat', he stated. The government was clearly not concerned with the plight of workers, instead: 'The suffering agrarians have to be supported'.[35] In July, another group of Hamburg workers discussed the same topic, with one worker complaining that with food prices, especially meat, rising so much,

---

30 Kučera 2016, Ch. 1.
31 Nonn 1996, p. 139.
32 Ritter and Tenfelde 1992, pp. 507–11; see also table on per capita meat consumption in Hohorst, Kocka and Ritter 1975, p. 120. On workers' industrial organisation and strike action in the period, see Tenfelde and Volkmann 1981.
33 Hohorst et al. 1975, p. 122.
34 Nonn 1996, p. 147; Barkin 1970, pp. 253–70.
35 StAHH, 331–3, 5288 (Vigilanzberichte Schutzmann Hinz), 27 February 1905.

it was impossible for him, with his family of eight persons, to eat meat more than once a week. Every day they have potatoes twice, mostly without anything else. And on top of that he had to work hard to earn his pay of 21 Marks a week. He and his friends didn't get much out of life, and at most occasionally visited a pub to forget his sorrows with a shot of schnapps and a glass of beer.[36]

A few days later, the same Hamburg constable eavesdropped on another conversation between workers on the price of meat:

One said, 'With the high food prices it would hardly be possible at all now for a family to get by, meat was now so expensive that a worker could no longer afford it'. [...] Hereupon another [worker] said: He still eats meat nearly every day, but that was horse-meat. But even this has recently gone up in price and has become relatively expensive.

'Yes, it is not at all unlikely that we workers will soon have to eat dogs and cats, but it is only the fault of the damn agrarians and capitalists. These have to be fattened by our hunger'.[37]

The following month, policeman Hinz heard similar complaints from workers on his rounds:

It really sounds like mockery when the agrarians claim there is no meat crisis. That may be true among those gentlemen, but they should look into the workers' kitchens for once; then they'd find the opposite is true. Meat has gradually become a luxury item for the worker and at most he can only afford this on Sundays. Every other day there are potatoes and on this diet he has to do the heaviest work. The agrarians aren't satisfied with sucking the marrow out of the workers' bones through heavy workloads, they now want them to starve as well.[38]

Also in August 1905, another Hamburg policeman heard the same accusations levelled, blaming the landowning interests for the price of meat:

It is outrageous that them up there don't want to admit that there is such a thing as a meat crisis at all. Everyone can see that the Junkers are run-

---

36 StAHH, 331–3, 5288 (Vigilanzberichte Schutzmann Hinz), 27 July 1905.
37 StAHH, 331–3, 5288 (Vigilanzberichte Schutzmann Hinz), 31 July 1905.
38 StAHH, 331–3, 5288 (Vigilanzberichte Schutzmann Hinz), 23 August 1905.

ning the whole show. It can't be because of disease that the borders are closed, because the Danish cattle are much healthier and better than the cattle here.[39]

A week later, workers on Constable Kramer's beat were drawing conclusions:

'Right now you can see how much those at the wheel care about the well-being of the people. No devil from this lot cares a bit about the high price of meat'. [...] 'If we didn't get active and start to get some attention by agitation, we would have to starve before this gang would do anything about it'.[40]

As if on cue, the Social Democratic Party in Hamburg staged a series of public protest meetings on the question of the rising price of meat from 2 to 5 September 1905. 22 meetings were advertised for Hamburg, with another five in the close environs of the city.[41] The size of the meetings ranged from audiences of under 100 to up to 2,000 in the case of the main gatherings of the three Hamburg electoral districts: on Sunday 3 September, Lily Braun spoke to a packed Hammonia Variety Theatre in St. Georg (1,500 to 2,000 present) in Hamburg's first electoral district; in the second district, Ernst Fischer spoke to between 1,200 (including 200 women) and 2,000 people on the Monday night, the 4th; and other meetings on the same night also attracted between 1,000 and 2,000 (or more, according to both the Social Democratic *Hamburger Echo* and a couple of 'bourgeois' newspapers).[42] The meetings all endorsed a common resolution, placing the blame for the 'present shortage of cattle and the consequent rise in the price of meat', principally on the 'measures taken to benefit the agrarian interest, the tariffs on cattle, meat and fodder, and above all in the blocking of imports of cattle and meat from abroad'. The resolution deplored the effects that these measures were having on the standard of living and health of the working class.

The protest meetings were the subject of subsequent discussion among Hamburg workers. A week after the meetings, one worker was overheard expressing doubts as to whether the protest meetings would achieve anything: 'Bülow won't care about them'. One of his companions disagreed: he thought

---

39   StAHH, 331–3, 5288 (Vigilanzberichte Schutzmann Kramer), 24 August 1905.
40   StAHH, 331–3, 5288 (Vigilanzberichte Schutzmann Kramer), 2 September 1905.
41   *Hamburger Echo*, 2 September 1905, Beilage.
42   See reports in StAHH, 331–3, 7949-2UA2, Fleischverteuerung – Öffentliche sozialdemokratische Versammlungen am 2., 3., 4. u. 5.9.1905; *Hamburger Echo*, 5 and 6 September 1905.

that 'the meetings will be of some use. The people had to become aware of its power'.[43] The fact that workers in pubs were discussing the issue, and doing so in terms that echoed the Social Democrats' links between the cost of food and the need to break the political power and privilege of the landowning elite, suggests that the agitation was at least getting traction within the party's social base of support.

Similar protest meetings on the topic of the 'meat crisis' (*Fleischnot*) were held around the country, and the Social Democratic press continued to campaign vigorously on food prices, and the cost of meat in particular. To take one example at random, one can follow the coverage of this issue in the Frankfurt (am Main) *Volksstimme*, bearing in mind that several dozen party newspapers around the country were carrying similar messages.

In November 1905, the Frankfurt *Volksstimme* dramatised the issue of the meat crisis with a front-page story from the Saxon state parliament, describing the appeals of Social Democratic representatives calling on the government to address it and the hollow and unconvincing replies of the government – the state with the most industrialised population was thus shown to be still incapable of acting against the interests of a 'handful of agrarians'.[44] News reports on the meat crisis followed two days later, including a report on Saxon official statistics which showed cattle-raising in Saxony lagging behind population growth in the state (strengthening the case for relaxing import restrictions).[45] News reports the next day continued the theme of rising food prices: the prices at the Frankfurt livestock market threatened to transform the 'butcher's trade into a wild stock-market speculation', and to make things worse, the government was acceding to the agrarian lobby's demand to ban the importation of milk from Denmark.[46] Later in November, more news reports dealt with further statistics on the inadequacy of German cattle stocks, and it was reported that demand for rabbit meat was rapidly increasing in Berlin, for lack of higher-quality alternatives.[47] The Frankfurt *Volksstimme* also provided its readers with a simple graphic illustrating the impact of indirect taxes on the consumption of beer and essential foodstuffs.[48]

---

43   StAHH, 331–3, 5288 (Vigilanzberichte Schutzmann Hinz), 14 September 1905.
44   'Fleischnoth und sächsische Kammer' (Leitartikel), *Volksstimme* (Frankfurt/M.), 16, no. 265, 11 November 1905, p. 1.
45   'Zur Fleischnoth', *Volksstimme* (Frankfurt/M.), 266, 13 November 1905, Beilage.
46   'Zur Lebensmittelvertheuerung', *Volksstimme* (Frankfurt/M.), 267, 14 November 1905, p. 1. Beilage.
47   'Zur Fleischnoth', *Volksstimme* (Frankfurt/M.), 276, 25 November 1905, p. 1. Beilage.
48   'Der Konsum der wichtigsten Nahrungsmittel', *Volksstimme* (Frankfurt/M.), 278, 28 November 1905, p. 2. Beilage.

The *Volksstimme* began the month of December 1905 with another leading article on the meat crisis, this time focussing on the Reichstag debate on the question, led by Philip Scheidemann for the Social Democrats.[49] The same issue highlighted the government's new taxation plans, using a graphic that showed the size of indirect taxes and other sources of revenue on the one hand and the proposed government expenses on the other (dominated by the army and navy budgets).[50] A column later in the month described the differing impact of the meat crisis on rich and poor Berliners.[51]

The *Volksstimme* continued to pursue the topic of the impact of taxes and tariffs on the cost of living for workers into 1906. In January 1906, the paper reported on Reichstag debates in which conservatives defended tax increases on tobacco and beer with a full front-page leading article on the 'Hunger Tax', which set the proposed increases in their wider context of the pressures on workers' standard of living.[52] In March 1906, the *Volksstimme* marked the anniversary of a tariff increase on meat, reviewing the effects of the 'meat crisis' of 1905, noting a decrease in consumption of rice, fruit and herrings, and a stagnation in the consumption of coffee, which the paper attributed to the greater share of household budgets that was required for the purchase of meat. The *Volksstimme* suggested that butchers' shops should display posters which clearly outlined the impact of high duties and import restrictions – and the 'ruinous policies of the agrarians' – on meat prices.[53]

In August 1906, the *Volksstimme* turned its attention to the tax increases on beer, that 'humble refreshment and enjoyment' of the workers, 'which furthermore limits the more dangerous consumption of schnapps'. This was the first tax increase on beer since the founding of the Reich in 1871.[54] The parties responsible – the Catholic Centre, the conservatives, and the National Liberals – were pilloried for their indifference to the welfare of the workers. Also to blame were the large and increasingly organised breweries which sought to exercise their market power in order to push up prices.[55] A series of meetings were called by the Frankfurt Social Democrats to protest against the large brew-

---

49 'Die Fleischnoth im Reichstage', *Volksstimme* (Frankfurt/M.), 281, 1 December 1905, p. 1.
50 'Reichshaushalt und neue Steuern', *Volksstimme* (Frankfurt/M.), 281, 1 December 1905, p. 3. Beilage.
51 'Berliner Freßkultur im Zeichen der Fleischnoth', *Volksstimme* (Frankfurt/M.), 281, 1 December 1905, 297, 20 December 1905, p. 3. Beilage.
52 'Eine Aushungerungs-Steuer', *Volksstimme* (Frankfurt/M.), 17, no. 21, 23 January 1906, pp. 1–2.
53 'Wirkungen der Fleischteuerung', *Volksstimme* (Frankfurt/M.), 70, 23 March 1906, p. 1.
54 Roberts 1984, p. 96.
55 'Bierkrieg?', *Volksstimme* (Frankfurt/M.), 17, no. 180, 4 August 1906, pp. 1–2.

eries passing increased brewing tax onto consumers, and linking the beer tax to the effects of the policy of indirect taxes in general: seven simultaneous meetings were held in different parts of Frankfurt.[56] The *Volksstimme* claimed that all of these meetings were well-attended, with all the venues full. The crowd was said to be in good spirits despite abstaining from beer as a sign of support for the boycott of the large breweries. By now, the *Volksstimme* was calling on its readers not to buy beer at the new high prices. The speakers at these meetings, who included Wilhelm Dittmann, once again linked the beer tax question to the broader context of the Reich's reliance on consumption taxes to fund the expansion of the army and navy.[57]

After negotiations between representatives of the Social Democratic Party and trade unions on the one hand, and the breweries, and between breweries and publicans, the 'beer war' was declared to have ended in an agreement (which the *Volksstimme* called on readers to enforce by continuing to avoid overpriced beer).[58] This was neither the first nor the last 'beer war' or beer boycott in Imperial Germany. For most of 1894, the Berlin trade union movement and Social Democratic Party organisation had been locked in a dispute with the cartel (or *Ring*) of Berlin's big breweries which started with a dispute over coopers taking the day off on May Day, but which involved wider conflicts over labour relations in the industry, and which resulted in a boycott of the '*Ring*' breweries from May until the end of 1894, when a compromise settlement was reached.[59] During the summer of 1909, there was another 'beer war', with protests not only in Frankfurt, but in cities all over North Germany and elsewhere. For example, in Braunschweig, a crowd of between 6,000 and 7,000 workers resolved not to drink beer at the increased prices. According to James S. Roberts, the protests, along with negotiations with local brewers and distributors in some places, were successful in restraining the increases, at least temporarily.[60] Boycotts imposed some pressure on working-class consumers, especially when they involved such staples as beer (or bread, during

---

56   Advertisement: Protest-Versammlungen gegen Biersteuer, *Volksstimme* (Frankfurt/M.), 181, 6. August 1906, p. 4.
57   'Frankfurter Arbeiterschaft und Bieraufschlag', *Volksstimme* (Frankfurt/M.), 183, 8 August 1906, Beilage.
58   'Zum Bierkriege von Frankfurt und Umgebung', *Volksstimme* (Frankfurt/M.), 189, 15 August 1906, Beilage, also in *Volksstimme* (Frankfurt/M.), 196, 23 August 1906, Beilage; 'Vom Ende des Bierboykotts', *Volksstimme* (Frankfurt/M.), 216, 15 September 1906, p. 1. Beilage.
59   Turk 1982.
60   Roberts 1984, p. 97. For beer boycotts in Hamburg in 1904 (over industrial dispute involving brewery workers) and 1906 (over the 'beer war' involving price increases and conflict between large breweries and publicans), see also Wyrwa 1990, pp. 214–20.

industrial disputes with the owners of bakeries), but could achieve some measure of success. A beer boycott was perhaps particularly challenging for Social Democrats given the extent to which the party made use of venues such as pubs and beer halls for meetings. (During the 1894 Berlin beer boycott, the 'Ring' breweries retaliated against organised labour by trying to deny the Berlin Social Democrats any meeting venues.)[61] Consumption of beer increased during the last decades of the nineteenth century at the expense of brandy, schnapps, and other hard liquor, a trend promoted by the Social Democratic Party, not only on health grounds, but because the schnapps industry was regarded as the domain of the Junker landowning class.[62] The Hamburg party organisation was happy to exempt cognac – for those who could afford it – from the 1909 schnapps boycott, called in protest against the 1909 tax increases, as it was not produced by Junkers.[63] However, attempts to organise boycotts of schnapps encountered resistance from an influential constituency within the Social Democratic Party – the party publicans, who provided the venues for the monthly dues-paying evenings as well as for many other party-related activities. They complained that the schnapps boycott risked hitting them harder, as small-scale distributors catering to organised workers, than the Junkers who produced the schnapps for wider consumption, or the larger commercial liquor outlets.[64] Women party activists, on the other hand, praised the beneficial effects of a schnapps boycott on workers' family lives.[65]

It may be noted here that for the working class drinking was not uncommon even in the workplace in the late nineteenth century – building workers would receive mugs of beer for their breakfast break, for example. By 1900, there were concerted efforts by employers and the state to restrict drinking at the workplace to non-alcoholic beverages.[66]

While the 1906 'beer war' was still raging, the Frankfurt *Volksstimme* was also raising concerns about the rising price of milk,[67] and gearing up for another

---

61 Turk 1982, p. 390; see also Wyrwa 1990, pp. 202–8, on the pub as a 'bulwark of freedom' for the labour movement.
62 Ritter and Tenfelde 1992, pp. 511–16; Roberts 1984, pp. 83–108; Wyrwa 1990, pp. 232–4.
63 Wyrwa 1990, p. 232; on the 1909 schnapps boycott, see also Hübner 1988, pp. 205–13.
64 LAB A Pr. Br. Rep. 30, Nr. 14153, Bl. 225, 226; 249–50.
65 LAB A Pr. Br. Rep. 30, Nr. 14153, Bl. 254–255.
66 Roberts 1984, pp. 110–12; see also Wyrwa 1990, pp. 173–83; Hübner 1988, pp. 79–102.
67 'Zur Milchverteuerung' (report from the North-Rhine/Westphalian industrial region, but conditions in Frankfurt said to be similar), *Volksstimme* (Frankfurt/M.), 17, no. 189, 15 August 1906; 'Teure Zeiten', *Volksstimme* (Frankfurt/M.), no. 198, p. 1. Beilage, 23 August 1906; 'Nach dem Bier die Milch!', *Volksstimme* (Frankfurt/M.), no. 202, 30 August 1906, pp. 1–2.

round of protest meetings over the rising cost of foodstuffs, this time addressed principally at women. On 8 September 1906 (a Monday evening), six simultaneous public meetings for women, albeit all addressed by male speakers (women were not yet allowed to engage in political activities under the Prussian law of association, although Social Democratic women frequently tested the limits of this law) were held in different parts of Frankfurt and its environs, on the topic of 'Rising beer prices, rising milk prices and the role of women in the current struggles'.[68] The meetings, according to the party press, were strongly attended, with predominantly female audiences, a change from the usual party meetings, where women often made up 10–15 per cent of those in attendance. At venues such as Frankfurt's trade union building, there was reportedly standing room only. In addition to condemning the rising price of necessities such as milk, the meetings passed a resolution strongly endorsing the beer boycott, which, as noted above, was called off a few days later following concessions by the breweries to the publicans.[69]

Concerns about high food prices, especially meat, continued to be near the forefront of the concerns of Frankfurt's Social Democrats, however.[70] In the autumn of 1906, the rising cost of food, and of meat in particular, was a regular lead story on the front page of the Frankfurt *Volksstimme*. The *Volksstimme* regularly published statistics documenting the rising price of meat, and it also stirred up outrage among its readers by quoting conservative attempts to play down the problem, for example by suggesting that workers must be better off than they used to be if they now expected to eat meat regularly, or the agrarian lobby's efforts to justify the high prices as objectively necessary.[71] In an attempt to counter the rising cost of foodstuffs more generally, women party comrades (specifically, the '*Hausfrauen*' among them) were increasingly encouraged to

---

68   Advertisement: Große öffentliche Frauen-Versammlungen, *Volksstimme* (Frankfurt/M.), 210, 8 September 1906, p. 2. Beilage.
69   'Frankfurter Angelegenheiten. Protest der Frauen gegen die Lebensmittelverteuerung', *Volksstimme* (Frankfurt/M.), 212, 11 September 1906, Beilage.
70   E.g. 'Die Lebensmittelverteuerung in statistischer Beleuchtung', *Volksstimme* (Frankfurt/M.), 215, 14 September 1906, p. 1, Beilage.
71   On meat prices: 'Der "Fleischnotrummel"', *Volksstimme* (Frankfurt/M.), 216, 15 September 1906, p. 1; 'Vom Steigen der Fleischpreise', *Volksstimme* (Frankfurt/M.), 221, 21 September 1906, p. 1; 'Die Fleischteuerung', *Volksstimme* (Frankfurt/M.), 226, 27 September 1906, pp. 1–2; 'Zur Fleischteuerung', *Volksstimme* (Frankfurt/M.), 17, no. 229, 1 October 1906, p. 1, Beilage. On the impact of tariffs and taxes on food prices more generally: 'Vom Lebensmittelwucher', *Volksstimme* (Frankfurt/M.), 232, 4 October 1906, p. 1, Beilage; 'Vom Lebensmittelwucher', *Volksstimme* (Frankfurt/M.), 236, 9 October 1906, p. 1, Beilage; 'Wirkungen des Zoll- und Landwuchers', *Volksstimme* (Frankfurt/M.), 238, 11 October 1906, p. 1.

join the consumer co-operatives endorsed by the party.⁷² At this time, a ribbon of large bold print ran along the bottom of the local news section of the *Volksstimme*, with the appeal: 'Housewives! Support the consumer association in its struggle against milk usury!'.

On 6 November 1906, the Frankfurt Social Democrats organised another coordinated set of public meetings to protest against rising food prices. This time, ten simultaneous meetings in and around Frankfurt were organised, with the topic for all meetings announced as 'What does the people demand from the Reichstag against the policies of price rises and hunger?'. The protest meetings were timed to take place a week before the opening of the next Reichstag session. Again, all meetings passed a common resolution, which condemned protectionism and rising food prices, for which the agrarian lobby was blamed, as both harmful to the health and well-being of the people, and against the interests of German industry. The *Volksstimme* emphasised the increasing participation of women in these meetings.⁷³

In the following weeks, the Frankfurt *Volksstimme* kept up a regular coverage of the issue. A week after the round of protest meetings, the front page carried a leading article entitled: 'On top of meat scarcity – the rising cost of bread!', highlighting the findings of a new publication examining the effects of tariff increases on grain and bread prices.⁷⁴ The price of meat was front-page news again on 4 December, with a very lengthy and detailed article filled with figures on the meat crisis and with a detailed refutation of agrarian defences of tariffs and non-tariff barriers to imports.⁷⁵ A few days later, the *Volksstimme* turned its attention to rising milk prices.⁷⁶ Meat prices returned to the front page of the paper the next day, as the Social Democratic Reichstag deputies prepared to launch a parliamentary debate on the topic.⁷⁷ On 12 December, the *Volksstimme* reported on the Social Democratic Party's Reichstag motion on the 'meat crisis'.⁷⁸ On the next day, the Reichstag was dissolved, as the Bülow gov-

---

72   'Vom Lebensmittelwucher', *Volksstimme* (Frankfurt/M.), 232, 4 October 1906, p. 1, Beilage.
73   [Meeting notice:] 'Auf zum Protest gegen den Lebensmittelwucher!/[…]/Zehn Volks-Versammlungen', *Volksstimme* (Frankfurt/M.), 259, 5 November 1906, Beilage; 'Der Massenprotest gegen den Lebensmittelwucher', *Volksstimme* (Frankfurt/M.), 261, 7 November 1906, pp. 1–2, Beilage.
74   'Zur Fleischnot noch Brotverteuerung!', *Volksstimme* (Frankfurt/M.), 266, 13 November 1906, p. 1.
75   'Zur Fleischnot', *Volksstimme* (Frankfurt/M.), 283, 4 December 1906, pp. 1–2.
76   'Zur Milchverteuerung', *Volksstimme* (Frankfurt/M.), 286, 7 December 1906, p. 2, Beilage.
77   'Gegen die Verschleppung der Fleischnot', *Volksstimme* (Frankfurt/M.), 287, 8 December 1906, p. 1.
78   'Die Fleischnot im Reichstage', *Volksstimme* (Frankfurt/M.), 293, 12 December 1906, p. 1.

ernment sought early elections, ostensibly on the grounds of the refusal of the Social Democratic and Centre Party deputies to approve more funds for the war against the Herero and Nama peoples in South-West Africa.[79]

The early and unusually short election campaign took the Social Democrats by surprise. One indication of this is the party's election handbook, which in previous Reichstag elections had been a well-prepared and thoroughly fact-filled pocket-sized hardback. For the election held on 25 January 1907, the party only had time to put out a relatively slim, paper-bound volume. The election handbook focussed strongly on the issue of food prices, and the associated questions of agricultural tariffs and indirect taxes, stating:

> This politics of increasing prices, which is carried out at the expense of the vast majority of the people for the advantage of an agrarian minority, is not a temporary, but a permanent and growing phenomenon. It is quite impossible for German agriculture to satisfy the rapidly growing demand for foodstuffs of all kinds given a fast growth-rate of the Reich population of about a million people per year.
>
> The maintenance of the current tariff and agricultural policies therefore means **growing hunger prices for the masses of the population, who have to buy food, and increasing wealth for the agrarian minority.**
>
> **The fight against these tariff and agrarian policies is therefore a vital necessity for the great majority of the people.**
>
> **Undernourishment, increased incidence of cases of death and disease, reduction in the number of marriages, reduction in the number of men fit for military service, rising costs of support for the poor and orphans, increased budget expenses for both municipal and state governments for the support of the inmates of all manner of institutions, the provision of personnel in the army and navy, higher fodder prices and finally an increasing tax burden are the inevitable effects of this policy.**
>
> Hand in hand with the rising prices for the most essential requirements of life for the great majority of the people as a result of our tariff and agrarian policy, go the **higher rates and proliferation of indirect taxes** on the necessary requirements of life, as resolved in particular by the last Reichstag in the spring of 1906. And their proliferation and increased rates will continue to grow, in view of the enormous increases in the

---

79 On the 1907 elections, see Crothers 1968 [1941]; Sperber 1997, pp. 240–54.

costs especially of the army, navy and colonies unless the people manages to ensure a different majority to the one present in the Reichstag previously.[80]

The Frankfurt *Volksstimme* kept up the focus on food prices during the short election campaign, publishing a concise statistical compilation on 'Germany as the Land of Hunger', which compared average wages and spending on food in the United States, Britain, France, Belgium, Switzerland and Germany to depict Germany as the 'country of the lowest wages and the highest food prices'.[81] In the week before the elections, the *Volksstimme* published another front-page piece on 'The Significance of Reduced Meat Consumption for the Worker', discussing the nutritional implications of a lower protein intake.[82]

Unfortunately for the Social Democratic Party, the government succeeded in fighting the election campaign on so-called 'national' issues, mobilising large numbers of previous non-voters in a 'khaki' election campaign in support of German troops in South-West Africa, earning the election the nickname of the 'Hottentot elections'. The intensive voter mobilisation by the government parties and nationalist pressure groups temporarily checked the electoral advance of the Social Democrats at the national level: while the party gained just under 250,000 votes compared with the 1903 elections, the number of Reichstag seats won dropped from 81 in 1903 to 43 in 1907. Chancellor Bernhard von Bülow appears to have realised that the reprieve for the 'parties of order' was only temporary. Writing to the conservative sociologist Gustav Schmoller, Bülow stated:

> Like you, I see an important gain of the election campaign in that it has removed the feeling of hopelessness *vis-à-vis* Social Democracy that had beem so widespread [...].
>
> At the same time we cannot deceive ourselves as to how far away in the distance the separation of the labour movement from the embrace of Social Democracy lies. Here, the nation, especially the sciences, faces the most difficult paedagogical task.[83]

---

80   Sozialdemokratischer Parteivorstand 1907, pp. 9–10 (emphasis in original).
81   'Deutschland als Hungerland', *Volksstimme* (Frankfurt/M.), 18, no. 10, 12 January 1907, p. 2.
82   'Die Bedeutung des verminderten Fleischgenusses für den Arbeiter', *Volksstimme* (Frankfurt/M.), 13, 16 January 1907, p. 1.
83   Reich Chancellor von Bülow to Gustav Schmoller, 12 February 1907, Geheimes Staatsarchiv, Berlin-Dahlem, VI, HA, Nachlass Schmoller, No. 199a, Bl. 70.

In May 1908, as a concession to Bülow's liberal coalition partners, a liberal reform of the laws of association came into force, which allowed women to take part in political organisations and activities (although they remained excluded from the franchise). While the Social Democrats had long sought to involve women in their activities to the extent permissible by the law, the new *Reich* law, replacing more repressive state legislation in Prussia and elsewhere, now permitted the formal membership of Social Democratic women in the party and its organisations, and removed the restrictions that had previously allowed police to shut down meetings on political topics if women took part in them. The number of women in the party grew from 29,000 in 1908 (out of some 600,000) to nearly 174, 754 (out of 1,085,000) by 1914.[84] At the same time, as argued by Richard Evans, the incorporation of the previously existing separate women's organisations into the mainstream party organisation also enabled the more radical women's organisations in cities like Berlin and Hamburg to be brought under the control of the centrist party executive.[85] The issue of food prices became a natural focus of agitation by and among Social Democratic women (as previously seen in the case of Frankfurt and elsewhere). Women came to the fore in the protest meetings against the indirect tax increases that were associated with the 'Reich finance reform' of 1909.

In July 1909, after long and bitter parliamentary wrangling that broke up Chancellor Bülow's government coalition, a Reich finance reform bill passed the Reichstag against the opposition of the Social Democrats. The finance 'reforms', which were intended to cover an annual Reich budget deficit of 500 million marks, which was 'the bill for the ruinous naval arms race with England',[86] resulted in increased indirect taxes on a number of common commodities, including brandy, beer, tobacco and coffee. There were also a number of new duties on financial transactions, and taxes on newspaper advertisements, electricity and gas, but the commodities consumed daily by the masses made up the lion's share of new revenue.[87] The prices of these commodities rose appreciably, triggering a temporary reduction in consumption of these goods, showing a degree of consumer sensitivity to the price rises, and contributing to the failure of the reform to meet its fiscal objective of eliminating the budget

---

84 Fricke 1987, Vol. 1, pp. 308, 439 (membership figures based on annual reports of the party executive to the party congresses).
85 Evans 1979, pp. 172–5.
86 Kroboth 1986, p. 34.
87 Witt 1970, Ch. 4. See also the detailed handbook produced by the Social Democratic Party on the 'reform', Sozialdemokratischer Parteivorstand 1910.

deficit.[88] At the same time, a national inheritance tax, which the Social Democrats advocated, was rejected, in a tax package that once again favoured landed property while increasing the indirect tax burden on ordinary consumers.

The Social Democratic Party responded to the Reich finance reform and the government's renewed attack on the workers' standard of living, or what it called the 'Great Robbery Raid on the Pockets of the People', with a coordinated protest campaign. In each of the six Berlin electoral districts, simultaneous mass protest meetings were held during the Reichstag's deliberations and in the month after the passage of the reform through the Reichstag, led by women speakers. In Moabit, in the Sixth Electoral District, *Genossin* Agnes Fahrenwald addressed 200 women and about 50 men in the Kronen-Brauerei on the topic of women and the finance reform. Fahrenwald linked the attack on the workers' pockets to the lack of political power for women: if women had the vote, she argued, the national household would be in better order. As it was, the military on land and sea was to blame for the 500 million marks that the state wanted to extract from ordinary Germans, while the '*Schnaps* bloc' of Junker landowners rejected an inheritance tax.[89] In the Second Electoral District, Mathilde Wurm spoke to this theme before an audience of 550 women and 50 men in the Hasenheide, stressing the need for men and women to 'work together in the struggle against the ruling classes'. Like many other women speakers, she supported her rhetoric by using figures to prove the extent to which the workers were burdened by the government's reliance on indirect taxes, and rejected the use of the money for militarism and warships. Also in the Second District, Agnes Fahrenwald spoke again, to a simultaneous meeting attended mostly by women in Kreuzberg.[90] In the Third Electoral District, Martha Hoppe spoke on the effects of the new taxes, attacking the role of the Catholic Centre Party for its role in the reforms, putting the blame on that party for the 'raid on the pockets of workers and the less well-off'. Like Fahrenwald in the Moabit meeting, Hoppe coupled her critique of the finance reform with a call for women's suffrage: 'If women sat in the Reichstag, such a tax bill would never have been passed'. The speakers at these meetings also called on women to join the party organisations and become active, if they were not already members.[91]

---

88   Witt 1970, pp. 311–12.
89   LAB, A Pr Br 030, Nr. 14153, Bl. 127–128, police report, 8 July 1909.
90   LAB, A Pr Br 030, Nr. 14142, Bl. 230–231.police report, 18 August 1909; 'Aus der Frauenbewegung', *Vorwärts*, 192, 19 August 1909, p. 1, Beilage.
91   LAB, A Pr Br 030, Nr. 14144, Bl. 319–320, police report, 18 August 1909; 'Aus der Frauenbewegung', *Vorwärts*, 192, 19 August 1909, p. 1, Beilage.

Hamburg's political police recorded the immediate reaction of rank-and-file workers to the Reich finance reform: 'The less well-off will suffer most' [...] 'It was foreseeable that the agrarian gents would push the whole tax burden onto working people. But none of us could have dreamed that it would happen to the extent that it actually has'.[92] The negative reaction of the Social Democrats' support base to the 1909 finance reform and the associated tax increases was one important factor in the unexpectedly strong showing of the Social Democratic Party in the October 1909 Landtag election in Saxony, despite a carefully calculated plural voting system designed to contain the Social Democrats' electoral strength.[93]

One response to the increasing cost of food was the encouragement of Social Democratic workers to join consumer cooperatives – women played a prominent role in this agitation. The consumer cooperatives affiliated with the Central Association of German Consumer Cooperatives increased their combined membership from 570,000 in 1903 to 1.7 million in 1914, by which time the affiliates and the central organisation themselves employed 30,000 people and boasted a turnover approaching 700 million marks.[94] If some in the Social Democratic Party, especially on the party's Left, viewed the consumer cooperatives with scepticism, especially in view of the overly sanguine belief of some revisionists and reformists that these could 'hollow out' capitalism from within,[95] it is possible to see the consumer organisations as contributing another dimension to the overall Social Democratic subculture: class-conscious workers could join the party, be organised in one of the Free Trade Unions, subscribe to socialist newspapers, spend their leisure time in Social Democratic Party-affiliated associations, and they and their families could shop in consumer cooperatives.

The growth in consumer cooperatives notwithstanding, the Social Democratic Party continued to make food prices and the associated issues of tariffs and indirect taxes a central plank of their platform in the lead-up to the 1912 elections, and continued to link cost-of-living concerns with the undemocratic power structure of the German Reich. This became a major theme of the Social Democratic election campaign for the Reichstag elections due in January 1912.

---

92 StaHH 331–3, S5319: report of Schutzmann Buse of 13 July 1909.
93 Retallack 2017, Ch. 12. The Social Democrats gained the votes of an absolute majority of voters taking part in the election, with a result of 25 seats out of 91 – more than the architects of Saxony's plural franchise system had anticipated.
94 Fricke 1987, Bd. 2, pp. 1043–55, figures cited from p. 1048. See also Prinz 1996, pp. 242–73.
95 Fricke 1987, Bd. 2, pp. 1049–50.

Even before the 1912 elections, there was a dress rehearsal with the by-election in the Fourth Berlin electoral district in March 1911, following the death of the popular Social Democratic Reichstag deputy Paul Singer. Flyers were circulated decrying the impact of indirect taxation on working people: 'The finance reform of the *Schnaps* bloc has inflicted burdens of hundreds of millions on the people'.[96] The finance reform, along with the expenditure of the revenues on militarism, was a major theme of the numerous meetings held in the Fourth electoral district, culminating in an address by Arthur Stadthagen on the eve of the by-election in the Friedrichshain Brauerei, in which he 'spoke about the criminal finance reform, the taxation policy which sucks the marrow out of working people, and the militarism and navalism which swallow up millions'.[97] Hermann Molkenbuhr spoke at one of the several parallel meetings held at the same time, also attacking the finance reform and warning that more indirect tax increases could be expected from the Reichstag, which would primarily burden the working population, 'for the agrarians and capitalists are there to approve it, as long as it happens in a form that will mainly be at the workers' expense'.[98]

The campaign for the January 1912 Reichstag elections was opened in September 1911 by the Social Democratic Party leadership, who published a manifesto in *Vorwärts* which among other things pilloried the way in which 'the distress of the working class has reached an intolerable degree due to the rising prices of all necessities'.[99] Unlike the rushed campaign of 1906–07, the Social Democrats had plenty of time to prepare for the 1912 elections, reflected in the size of the party's election handbook, which reached nearly 800 pages, with a central focus given to the 1909 finance reform, indirect taxes, and trade and tariff questions, although the handbook also provided a comprehensive treatment of other policy areas as well.[100] Less weighty flyers were mass-produced, with titles such as 'Rising prices and hunger crisis', proclaiming 'because the rich don't want to pay, the poor must go hungry', and distributed in Berlin and elsewhere.[101] On 17 October, to coincide with the commencement of the session of the outgoing Reichstag, a co-ordinated set of no fewer than 78 meetings took place all over Greater Berlin, in which the topic of the day was the rising price of food. The Berlin police counted over 24,000 people, a third of them

---

96   LAB, A Pr. Br. Rep. 30, Nr. 14149, Bl. 212, 244, 250.
97   LAB, A Pr. Br. Rep. 30, Nr. 14149, Bl. 253–4.
98   LAB, A Pr. Br. Rep. 30, Nr. 14149, Bl. 265.
99   *Vorwärts*, 224, 24 September 1911.
100 Sozialdemokratischer Parteivorstand 1911.
101 LA Berlin, A Pr. Br. Rep. 30, Nr. 15985, Bl. 9, 11, 24, 26.

women, in attendance in 26 meetings held in Berlin's city limits (therefore not counting the populous suburbs where over 50 other meetings were held). At several venues, police declared the meeting hall full and banned any further attendees to prevent overcrowding. It is worth noting, as a sign of how comprehensive the party's organisation and efforts at mobilising its mass base had become, that the Berlin meetings even included a special meeting for the deaf, which was attended by 90 men and 10 women.[102] The meetings all passed a common resolution, which demanded the removal and immediate abolition of all tariffs on foodstuffs; the abolition of the import permits which 'only benefitted the rapacious agrarian lobby'; the abolition of import restrictions on meat and livestock; and the organisation of mass supply of essential staple foodstuffs such as potatoes, fish and vegetables by local governments.[103] It is worth noting in passing that these co-ordinated mass protest meetings triggered a concerted mobilisation of Berlin's police to contain the protests: all leave was cancelled, mounted units were held in readiness, major government buildings were heavily guarded, and a command post of the Police President located in the basement of the royal palace in Berlin was to receive regular reports on the state of the streets.[104] This kind of concerted mobilisation of the police would be repeated for subsequent episodes of mass protest by the Social Democratic Party, notably for the anti-war demonstrations in July 1914.

These meetings were not confined to Berlin: mass meetings, or co-ordinated series of meetings, took place in Frankfurt, Magdeburg, Hamburg, Leipzig, Munich, and many other cities and towns. In Frankfurt, on 1 October 1911, between 4,500 and 5,000 people took part in an open-air protest meeting against rising food prices in the Tivoli Garden (addressed by Eduard Bernstein), despite bad weather.[105] In Magdeburg, on 8 October, Dr Klara Weyl spoke at a public meeting on 'The Hunger Year and the Task of Women'.[106] In Hamburg and its environs, 21 simultaneous women's meetings were scheduled for 10 October 1911. The *Hamburger Echo* reported that all meetings were very well attended, including some that were full to capacity.[107] On Sunday 22 October,

---

102 LA Berlin, A Pr. Br. Rep. 30, Nr. 15985, Bl. 60–7 (meeting for the deaf, Bl. 67); reports in *Vorwärts*, 244, 18 October 1911.
103 LA Berlin, A Pr. Br. Rep. 30, Nr. 15985, Bl. 55.
104 LA Berlin, A Pr. Br. Rep. 30, Nr. 15985, Bl. 68–9.
105 'Eine Massenkundgebung gegen die Lebensmittelteuerung', *Volksstimme*, Frankfurt a/M., 230, 2 October 1911, clipping in LA Berlin, A Pr. Br. Rep. 30, Nr. 15985, Bl. 14.
106 *Volksstimme*, Magdeburg, 232, 4 October 1911, clipping in LA Berlin, A Pr. Br. Rep. 30, Nr. 15985, Bl. 15–16; report of the 'extremely well-attended' meeting in *Volksstimme*, Magdeburg, 237, 10 October 1911.
107 *Hamburger Echo*, 239, 12 October 1911, Beilage: 'Der Frauenprotest gegen die Teuerung'.

a mass open-air meeting (again defying grey autumn weather) filled Leipzig's Messplatz, demonstrating against rising food prices and passing a resolution condemning the government's tax and tariff policies. The *Leipziger Volkszeitung* estimated 70,000 participants, supporting this claim with photographs illustrating the scale of the protest meeting. When the crowds left the Messplatz, they took an hour to pass through Leipzig's Frankfurter Strasse.[108]

In her study of the politics of the Düsseldorf working class, Mary Nolan summed up the issue's salience in the 1911–12 election campaign: 'Nothing revealed the unreformed and unreformable nature of the German economy and state more clearly than tariffs, the issue that dominated the 1911–12 Reichstag contest as it had the 1903 one'.[109]

The 1912 elections did not, of course, put an end to the Social Democratic agitation against tariffs and indirect taxes, and the impact of these on workers' cost of living. In August–September 1912, there was a renewed round of co-ordinated national agitation on this theme, with protest meetings in Berlin (with 28 simultaneous meetings), Leipzig, Hamburg, Stuttgart (seven meetings), and other cities, along with renewed mass circulation of flyers on the theme of the ironically named 'Dear Fatherland', attacking rising food prices and tariffs.[110]

Christoph Nonn has presented Social Democracy as a mobilisation of consumer interests, reflecting the interest of urban consumers in lower food prices. However, as Torp has pointed out, the party's self-image and organisation as a workers' party pre-existed its adoption of consumer agitation as a strategy.[111] The party was thus well-placed to overcome the traditional obstacles that face consumer protest movements, which are often diffuse and weakly organised. Not only did the Social Democratic Party consistently and effectively voice the interests of its members as consumers; it also successfully framed the issue as one that was tied to its core political demands, and integrated agitation around food and commodity prices into its broader political and social programme. Rank-and-file Social Democrats clearly drew the connections between the high cost of bread and meat, the political power of the agrarian lobby that was able to defend its interests through tariffs and the indirect taxation system, and the need to democratise the Imperial German system of government.

---

108   'Das Volksgericht', *Leipziger Volkszeitung*, 246, 23 October 1911, p. 3, Beilage. On the Munich meetings, see *Münchener Post*, 244, 20 October 1911, 'Münchener Angelegenheiten'.
109   Nolan 1981, p. 219; for the case of Saxony, see Retallack 2017, p. 567. The Social Democrats won 55 per cent of the vote in Saxony (Retallack 2017, p. 574).
110   See the collection of material in LA Berlin, A Pr. Br. Rep. 30, Nr. 15985, Bl. 81–126.
111   Nonn 1996; Torp 2005, pp. 246–7.

The question of the relationship between the price of bread and the state of German democracy exemplifies what has been called the 'fundamental politicisation' of society in Imperial Germany.[112] Everyday questions of subsistence and the cost of commodities in everyday use inevitably led to critical reflection on the political power structures of the German Reich, and on the social groups whose interests were served by these structures. Whenever workers bought a kilo of meat, or a loaf of rye bread, or reached for a beer after the day's shift, they had good cause to reflect on the *Kaiserreich*'s democratic deficit.

---

112   Ullmann 1995, pp. 126–37.

CHAPTER 5

Reds in the Ranks: Social Democrats in the Kaiser's Army

Stig Förster has characterised the militarism of Wilhelmine Germany as double-sided: directed both externally against real or presumed external enemies, and internally against the 'enemies of the Reich' – above all the Social Democratic Party.[1] When, not long after the founding of the Reich, the elder Moltke declared that the army was the school of the nation, he was repeating a formulation of the Prussian Minister of War Hermann von Boyen from as far back as 1816, who stated that the standing army should be not only 'a school of the nation for war, but also a school for all the virtues of the citizen that are necessary for it'.[2] In the age of the 'nationalisation of the masses', the notion that military service had a particular role to play in this process was of course by no means unique to Germany, as Eugen Weber's classic study *Peasants into Frenchmen*[3] illustrates for the case of the Third Republic. However, in Imperial Germany the extent to which antagonism towards a particular political party helped to shape the role, conduct, and even recruiting practices of the army was particularly pronounced. Already in 1871, the same Moltke who saw the army as the 'school of the nation' was warning against the dangers of socialist agitation in the army's ranks.[4]

Clearly, large numbers of German Social Democrats had to perform military service in the Kaiser's army before 1914. However, historians of the German labour movement have not often paused to consider what effect, if any, this experience might have had on them.[5] How did German Social Democrats experience military service, and did it have a significant impact on them? The sources for an investigation of this question include the memoirs of Social

1   Förster 1985.
2   Moltke 1892, pp. 69–72; Boyen, cited in Frevert 2001, p. 100.
3   Weber 1976.
4   'Das Militär und die socialistische Agitation' (Leitartikel), *Neuer Social-Demokrat*, 1, no. 25, 27 August 1871, p. 1.
5   See, however, Kitchen 1968, Ch. 7: 'The Army and Social Democracy'. The scope of Kitchen's book is broader than suggested by the title. There is some relevant material in Höhn 1961–69, but Höhn's work should be used with some caution given his background as an officer in the Nazi SS/Sicherheitsdienst and his post-war career as a director of a private management academy.

Democratic workers and functionaries (obviously a small, and self-selecting, sample) and reports in the Social Democratic Party press of the experiences of army recruits. At the same time, numerous German state archives document the efforts of the authorities to screen Social Democratic recruits and to monitor and check any Social Democratic anti-militarist agitation that might have an influence on serving soldiers.

Among autobiographical works by Social Democrats, there are two books that deal specifically with the authors' experience of military service, and they come from two different generations of Social Democratic leaders: books by Wilhelm Hasenclever and August Winnig. While other Social Democratic and working-class autobiographies include accounts of military service (and are referred to in what follows), these are considered separately here, as military experiences constitute the principal focus of their memoirs.

As mentioned in Chapter 2, Hasenclever, an early leader of the ADAV, had served in the Franco-Prussian War of 1870–71 as an ordinary soldier. The son of a tanner, Hasenclever had managed to attend a *Gymnasium* in Arnsberg, Westphalia, and qualified as a 'one-year volunteer' for his service in a Westphalian infantry regiment, commencing in April 1857. When this finished, he went on his period of travelling as a journeyman craftsman, until he was called up for another half-year of service in 1859, which he performed in Cologne and Düsseldorf. In 1862/63, the young tanner began his political activity, editing the democratic *Westfälische Volkszeitung* in Hagen. In summer 1864, he was called up again during the German-Danish War. When this term of duty was over, he published an article in the *Rheinische Zeitung* which resulted in a sentence of six weeks' imprisonment for *lèse-majesté*, which he successfully appealed against. He subsequently joined the recently founded ADAV. In 1866, he was called up again, for the Prusso-Austrian War, then again in 1870–71. He thus performed no fewer than five stints of army service, including in all three of Bismarck's wars of unification. His memoir *Erlebtes* deals principally with his military experience.[6]

In his military memoir, Hasenclever began by claiming that he had always had an aversion to the life of a soldier: volunteering as a 19-year-old *'Einjähriger'* had been an attempt to dispose of his obligation to serve as early and quickly as possible.[7] His memoir describes the usual routines of military life: the fear of the tyrannical *Unteroffizier*, the daily drills for three to four hours in hot

---

6 Hasenclever 1987 [n.d. (1877)] (first published in serial form in *Die Neue Welt. Illustriertes Unterhaltungsblatt für das Volk*, 1877).
7 Hasenclever 1987 [n.d. (1877)], pp. 3–4.

sun – about-turns, presenting arms, marches.[8] In Hasenclever's regiment, the attitude of recruits from the Rhineland or Westphalia towards officers from the Eastern provinces of Prussia was fraught, even more than the soldier's usual dislike of officious superiors.[9] The memoirs contain the typical veteran's humorous anecdotes about how these superiors were sometimes outwitted, but they also testify to the frequency of mistreatment of recruits. Hasenclever described how at the end of his year as a 'one-year volunteer', he and some of his friends did their best to fail their exams for the rank of '*Landwehr*-Lieutenant'. He summed up the 'mad year' as one in which 'one learned nothing sensible, only played "silly pranks", a year that would have been just the heart's desire for a frivolous little son of the bourgeois estate'. Hasenclever was glad to escape 'the stink of the barracks, the coarse behaviour of the *Unteroffiziere*', to go back to the peaceful life of a journeyman craftsman, only to have his wanderings through Austria interrupted by his call-up in 1859.[10] Hasenclever sympathised with Garibaldi, and found himself called up to the Prussian colours in the event that Prussia had to support the Austrian empire that was denying Italy its freedom.[11] He found low morale widely prevalent in the mobilised regiments in and around Cologne, a state aggravated by enduring pointless marches and parades in hot summer sun, which exacted its own toll of casualties.[12]

In 1864, Hasenclever, now involved in a *Turnverein* after a stint editing a democratic newspaper in Westphalia, received another call-up order, this time for the war against Denmark. Hasenclever's unit remained in Westphalia. He recounted that it was around this time that his aversion to militarism was reinforced by his study of socialism, especially the ideas of Lassalle.[13] Thus, when Hasenclever was called up again, for the campaign against Austria in 1866, his political views and activities were known in his unit, and he was singled out for punishment for a minor offence.[14] Hasenclever was transferred to another regiment, carrying a letter that warned his new commander that he was a Social Democrat. However, to his good fortune, his new company consisted of recruits from his hometown and he found himself among friends.[15]

---

8   Hasenclever 1987 [n.d. (1877)], p. 5.
9   Hasenclever 1987 [n.d. (1877)], pp. 6–7.
10 Hasenclever 1987 [n.d. (1877)], pp. 22–3.
11 Hasenclever 1987 [n.d. (1877)], p. 25.
12 Hasenclever 1987 [n.d. (1877)], pp. 28–32.
13 Hasenclever 1987 [n.d. (1877)], p. 59.
14 Hasenclever 1987 [n.d. (1877)], p. 69.
15 Hasenclever 1987 [n.d. (1877)], pp. 69–88.

In 1870, Hasenclever, now a social democratic member of parliament, found himself called up to serve in a war after he had voted against its continuation in the North German Reichstag. He still had the rank of a corporal in the *Landwehr*. His account of this campaign makes a point of stressing the distress of the wives and children many reservists left behind them, contrasting it with the official myth of the 'Spartan mother' commanding her son to return with his shield or on it.[16] Only after his Brandenburg *Landwehr* regiment arrived in France did Hasenclever realise the extent to which he was a marked man: a group of some eight officers ordered him to stand on the public marketplace of Vitry while they stared at him for several minutes, in order to discover what a traitor and ally of French republicans looked like.[17] Hasenclever subsequently realised that he was never assigned to transport duty and he learned that for some time his regiment had to supply weekly reports on his conduct.[18] He took care not to attract any adverse notice from his superiors. Subsequently, Hasenclever's regiment was stationed in Spandau, guarding French prisoners of war, with whom he fraternised.[19] Such fraternisation was not unique: in August 1871, the *Neuer Social-Demokrat* quoted the *Paris-Journal* as reporting on gatherings involving both French socialists and Prussian soldiers, including non-commissioned officers, on the outskirts of Paris in St. Denis and Nogent-sur-Marne. The *Neuer Social-Demokrat* observed that many Lassalleans were currently stationed before Paris, and claimed that 'during the war the socialist principle has spread to no small degree in the army'.[20] Finally, Hasenclever was formally released from his service in autumn 1871, and invited to collect his meritorious service buckle, which he never did. His memoirs conclude with a reassertion of his 'thorough aversion' to military life after his five terms of service.[21]

Not all Social Democrats who served in the Franco-Prussian War attracted the kind of adverse attention that the prominent party leader Hasenclever experienced. The shoemaker Josef Belli, who had already been an activist for the SDAP in Heidelberg, served in a Badenese regiment, not a Prussian unit (which may have made a difference). He found that at most he and the several other Social Democrats in his unit were considered odd – 'back then they didn't understand what it was about' in the army. They were able to receive their

16   Hasenclever 1987 [n.d. (1877)], pp. 92–3.
17   Hasenclever 1987 [n.d. (1877)], pp. 115–22.
18   Hasenclever 1987 [n.d. (1877)], p. 123.
19   Hasenclever 1987 [n.d. (1877)], pp. 127–31.
20   *Neuer Social-Demokrat*, 21, 18 August 1871, 'Politischer Teil'.
21   Hasenclever 1987 [n.d. (1877)], p. 132.

copies of *Der Volksstaat* without any hindrance. Belli's sergeant even betrayed a certain sympathy for what he jocularly called the 'decimal-sociocraten' and Belli was excused potato-peeling duty.[22] Such indulgence would become rare later in the newly established *Reich*, as the military sought to enforce a harder line against Social Democrats in the ranks.

August Winnig (1878–1956), a full generation younger than Hasenclever, was born in Blankenburg/Harz, one of 12 children of a gravedigger. He took up an apprenticeship as a bricklayer (1892–95), after which he began to be active in the Social Democratic Party and the building workers' union. In 1899, he was sentenced to gaol for a few months for hitting a strike-breaker during a building workers' strike in Blankenburg.[23] In October 1900, Winnig was drafted for two years' military service in the 46th Prussian Infantry Regiment, stationed in the fortress of Posen.[24] In 1904, he started working on the union newspaper *Grundstein*, which he subsequently edited. As a union official, he was involved in organising a large building workers' strike in 1910, which ended unsuccessfully. However, Winnig continued to progress through union and party posts, becoming chairman of the Building Workers' Federation in 1912 and being elected to the Hamburg *Bürgerschaft*, the parliament of the city-state, in 1913. His collection of recollections of his military service, *Preussischer Kommiss. Soldatengeschichten*, some of them possibly partially fictionalised for literary effect,[25] was published in 1910 by the party publisher, Buchhandlung Vorwärts, and was dedicated to the party leader August Bebel, 'the brave and meritorious friend of the German soldiers'. Winnig's first chapter began with an account of a conversation on a troop train which Winnig held with an old sergeant about Bebel. Winnig praised Bebel for his concern for ordinary soldiers, which the sergeant apparently took to refer to Bebel's parliamentary interventions on the mistreatment of soldiers. Some time later, Winnig was about to be subjected to abusive treatment by another NCO, when the sergeant stepped in, warning the other NCO that Winnig was a Social Democrat, so there might be political complications. Winnig wrote that he escaped mistreatment thereafter. He witnessed cases of mistreatment, however, and related how soldiers' rights to complain of abuse were blocked or circumvented by superior officers. He referred at one point to the 'thousandfold barbarism of the military penal code',

---

22 Belli 1978 [1912], p. 82.
23 Ribhegge 1973, pp. 38–9.
24 Ribhegge 1973, p. 41.
25 Winnig 1910. The story about the suicide of 'Gimm' includes dates that do not coincide with Winnig's period of military service, suggesting liberties with chronology at the least.

in relation to arbitrary and disproportionate punishments being meted out for relatively minor infringements.[26] In response to these experiences, Winnig and a comrade wrote a letter to the Social Democratic newspaper *Vorwärts* (copies of which were completely unavailable in their East Prussian garrison town), detailing cases of mistreatment in their regiment. A few weeks later, their captain called them together for a tirade against the *Schweine*, who were spreading lies about the regiment. Winnig and his ally managed to remain undetected, and they took some comfort in the fact that cases of abuse diminished for a while.[27] Winnig described instances of chicanery and arbitrary treatment of recruits, and recruits' attempts at passive resistance, such as deliberately failing to shoot accurately in regimental contests (on this occasion, the recruits' efforts were frustrated as the officers successfully contrived to cheat in the contest anyway, substituting corporals who were experienced marksmen for the raw recruits). When Winnig became involved in a pub brawl, his six-week sentence for his breaches of army discipline was harsher because of the previous offence of hitting a strike-breaker.[28] In a chapter on his time in the 'bastion', Winnig related that he helped a long-time inmate to escape.[29] He elsewhere described how recruits with enough experience developed a facility for 'passive resistance', carrying out commands 'but in a tempo that largely defeats the purpose of the tormenting'.[30]

Winnig's account betrays some ambivalence towards aspects of his military service, for example in his account of the conventional reservist portraits prepared before the end of service. While Winnig disparaged the 'patriotic arabesques' with which they were often ornamented, he wrote: 'It is the best souvenir of the friendships, which one once made, friendships for our common defence and defiant solidarity against the manifold hostile powers facing us'.[31] Winnig here leaves room for ambiguity over whether the enemies were external or within Germany, or within the Prussian army, for that matter, but still reveals some nostalgia for the camaraderie of army life. Winnig and his comrades angered their commanding officer by arranging to have their year-class group photo taken without any officers or NCOs, resulting in tougher drills for all of them.[32] In the last chapter, or story, of Winnig's book, he gives a long

---

26 Winnig 1910, p. 90.
27 Winnig 1910, chapter, 'Zwei Beschwerden', pp. 7–19.
28 Winnig 1910, pp. 43–4.
29 Winnig 1910, chapter 'Auf Festung'.
30 Winnig 1910, p. 79.
31 Winnig 1910, p. 74.
32 Winnig 1910, chapter 'Das Reservebild'. Kirn 2009 has referred to the widespread prevalence of such *Reservistika*, writing that 'the feeling of belonging together with the com-

and circumstantial account of a 'Kaiser manoeuvre', stressing the way in which soldiers had to be drilled to spontaneously cheer the monarch in the correct fashion: he states that the Kaiser was feared by his troops, but not loved.[33]

After becoming something of an expert on military affairs, giving talks on military topics to the Hamburg party organisations,[34] Winnig was among those Social Democratic functionaries who was later to internalise the patriotic 'experience of August', and became a staunch nationalist. At the end of the war, Winnig was despatched to the Baltic region to help to keep Bolshevism at bay there, seeking both to protect the interests of the German population of the region and to promote the independence of Latvia and Estonia as bulwarks against revolution. Appointed *Oberpräsident* of East Prussia, Winnig continued to cultivate links with *Freikorps* and to oppose revolutionary unrest. He was among the Prussian officials dismissed for supporting the rightist Kapp Putsch in March 1920. In the following years, he engaged in nationalist and *völkisch* politics, writing such books as *Vom Proletariat zum Arbeitertum* (1930) and *Das Reich als Republik* (1929). Winnig welcomed the advent of the Nazi regime, but after 1933 moved towards more Christian-conservative positions. In 1945, he was part of the founding cohort of the Christian Democratic Union and received the *Bundesverdienstkreuz* in 1955, the year before his death.[35]

In 1932, Winnig revisited his period of military service in another memoir, *Der weite Weg* (epigraph: '*Alles Deutsche meint das Reich*'). Here, the theme of mistreatment of recruits is no longer so prominent. Rather, Winnig was at pains to put his youthful political views, including his preoccupation with Social Democratic complaints against the mistreatment of recruits into perspective: he was an impetuous young person, and at the time there was much criticism of military institutions, and he was affected by this. However, he balanced the negative sides of his experience of military service with the more positive themes of comradeship within the ranks of his regiment. He stressed that as time went by, he came to understand the justification for many military practices, especially as he became entrusted with some clerical tasks, and had to transcribe his officer's instructions. Here, Winnig's military experience, and his youthful

---

rades of a barrack or company remained mostly unaffected by experiences with superiors, whether they beat the troops or were more friendly' (p. 113).

33 Winnig 1910, p. 110.
34 *Hamburger Echo*, 116, 19 May 1911 (lecture to Second Hamburg electoral district on 'Militarism as a social phenomenon'); 120, 25 May 1912 (lecture on the growth of the army, stressing that the army as an instrument of class rule was still a long way from becoming the 'genuine people's army, worthy of a cultured state'); and 154, 5 July 1914 (speaking on militarism and the workers).
35 See Ribhegge 1973.

reactions against it, become subsumed into a right-wing nationalist *Bildungsroman*, in which military service made a positive contribution to his maturation, and to his gradually awakening national consciousness.

How is one to interpret the different accounts of military experience given by Hasenclever and Winnig? To some extent, they may reflect different generations in the German labour movement.[36]

Perhaps part of the differences between Hasenclever and Winnig reflected the generational change from the founding generation of Social Democrat leaders who were revolutionary people's tribunes, and who experienced the persecution of the anti-socialist law, to the 'Ebert generation' of functionaries, for whom, as Robert Michels insisted, the party offered increasingly secure employment and even upward social mobility.[37] Winnig's evolution also reflects the shock of the First World War, which propelled a number of Social Democrats from positions on the political left to the nationalist right (while it further radicalised others). And then there were the individual factors of personality and biography (stressed by Ribhegge in his work on Winnig).[38]

These accounts provide a convenient entry point into the topic of Social Democrats' experiences of the military, but a broader approach drawing on a wider range of sources is needed for a fuller picture. To begin with, it is useful to consider how the German authorities sought to deal with the potential dangers of reds in the ranks, and sought to combat Social Democratic subversion of the army and militarism.

Moltke's notion of the army as a school was reiterated in 1891, not long after the expiry of Bismarck's anti-Socialist law, in a pamphlet purportedly by an active officer, entitled 'What does our army accomplish as an educational institution?' The author wrote: 'We need to train men's convictions, and their convictions again and again, for what is the use if we teach a man the finest parade march, and later as a reservist and *Landwehr* member he becomes a Social Democrat?'[39] The campaign against Social Democracy by and in the military took many forms. Soldiers were banned from attending pubs which were known to be used by Social Democrats for meetings, or which were known to be frequented (or owned) by Social Democrats.[40] In 1913, the list of banned

---

36 Schönhoven and Braun 2005.
37 However, throughout the 1890s and into the early 1900s, editorship of a party newspaper, to name one kind of party office, still carried with it the high risk of a period of imprisonment.
38 Ribhegge 1973.
39 Quoted in Opitz 1995, p. 23.
40 Kitchen 1968, p. 160.

pubs in Berlin named 293 as off-limits to the troops.[41] In addition to seeking to quarantine soldiers from the socialist contagion, this military boycott served the broader fight against Social Democracy by denying the movement meeting places. If pubs in proletarian quarters of Berlin could survive such boycotts, it was a grave threat in smaller garrison towns. Even in the small Hessian university town of Marburg, a Social Democratic meeting in a pub was swiftly followed by the military ban.[42] This practice was not confined to Prussian territory: in 1904 the number of pubs banned by the two Saxon army corps combined reached 413.[43] This led to concerted lobbying of the authorities by the Saxon hospitality industry, which complained of being caught between the threat of an effective boycott by the working class (given the power of the Social Democratic Party in Saxony, which had won 22 out of 23 seats in Saxony in the June 1903 elections, and that party's alleged willingness to engage in 'terrorism'), and a military ban barring all men in uniform on the other. The army saw no need to change its policy, however.[44] Soldiers found in blacklisted pubs could be arrested and handed over to military authorities for disciplining. Bans were also applied to barber shops and tobacconists frequented by Social Democrats. The weapon of the boycott also extended to industry: in 1895, the press published a decree of the War Minister, Bronsart von Schellendorf, which ordered that firms that worked for the military must immediately dismiss any worker who was in any way linked to a Social Democratic organisation, and that if managers of firms were unsure if a worker was a Social Democrat, they had to make inquiries, calling on the assistance of the police if necessary.[45] *Konsumvereine*, the consumers' co-operative shops linked to the Social Democratic Party, were also declared off-limits to soldiers.[46]

The struggle against Social Democracy also helped to form the army's recruiting patterns. In 1911, just over 64 per cent of army recruits came from rural districts, even though by this time the rural population of Germany was down to 42 per cent. A further 22.3 per cent of recruits came from small towns.

---

41 Frevert 2001, p. 264.
42 *Vorwärts*, 263, 10 November 1894; for Marburg, Hessisches Staatsarchiv Marburg, MR, 180/752, report by Fuss-Gendarm Trott, Ockershausen, 28 May 1903, order by Bezirks-Kommando Marburg attached.
43 Ulrich, Vogel and Ziemann 2001, p. 152.
44 Sächsisches Hauptstaatsarchiv Dresden (= SHStAD), 11250, Sächsischer Militärbevollmächtigter in Berlin, Nr. 3 (unfoliated), letter from Saxon Minister of War to von Salza, Dresden, 27 September 1904; report of Saxon Ministry of War, 11 April 1908, and other documents in this sequence.
45 *Vorwärts*, 48, 26 February 1895. See also *Vorwärts*, 53, 3 March 1895.
46 Kitchen 1968, p. 161.

Urban workers were regarded as less trustworthy recruits than peasants, especially peasants from East Elbian Prussian estates, who were more accustomed to the patriarchal authority of the Junker landowners.[47] (There were also concerns about the health and general condition of urban workers, given their living conditions.) By 1911, the army leadership had mixed feelings about the prospect of expanding the army, because of the number of socialist elements that it might have to assimilate.[48] Particular care was taken with the recruiting of the non-commissioned officer class, which was recruited overwhelmingly from rural or petit bourgeois backgrounds (the less educated the better). As the cohort most directly responsible for enforcing discipline and obedience in the barracks, loyalty to authority was the cardinal virtue sought in this stratum of the army, and gratuities and preferential recruitment into state employment at the end of the period of military service were designed to reinforce it.[49]

With the Social Democratic election successes in 1890, and the collapse of the anti-Socialist law the same year, the anxiety of the authorities over possible socialist infiltration of the army grew. Even before the anti-Socialist law, in the mid-1870s, the Saxon Minister of War had been worried about what was said to be 'alarmingly rampant' Social Democratic agitation in the army.[50] In the mid-1880s there was concern about the amount of Social Democratic election propaganda getting into barracks.[51] For Saxon Minister of War General Alfred von Fabrice, even when Social Democrats were relatively quiet in army ranks and keeping a low profile, this was worrying in itself: clearly, they were 'waiting to spot the moment for a massive revolutionary outburst'.[52] In March 1890, the Prussian Interior Ministry instructed all *Oberpräsidenten* in charge of the administration of Prussia's regions to exercise police surveillance over recruits to ascertain their political allegiances, a measure that proved to be of limited success in practice.[53] This measure accompanied an order from the War Ministry to commanding generals to exercise similar surveillance over their areas.[54] In 1894, the Minister of War modified this earlier decree to limit its effect to the 'leading and committed elements of Social Democracy', ignoring mere passive

---

47   Wehler 1985, p. 160; see also Förster 1985, p. 21; Frevert 2001, pp. 260–1.
48   Brose 2001, pp. 173–4.
49   Förster 1985, p. 21.
50   Retallack 2017, p. 114.
51   Frevert 2001, p. 264.
52   Fabrice in 1883, quoted in Retallack 2017, p. 167.
53   Förster 1985, p. 27.
54   Kitchen 1968, p. 155.

followers of the party. The former category, along with anarchists, were also to be excluded from service in the Guards.[55]

Every year, local authorities were reminded to get reports from their local police or gendarmerie on known Social Democrats among that year's potential army recruits, and were instructed to report on these to the local draft boards or to higher regional authorities.[56] Screening potential recruits for 'leading and committed elements of Social Democracy' proved to be not a simple matter, however. The factory towns of Hessen-Nassau, for example, furnished a regular crop of Social Democrats whose names had to be sent forward to the provincial government authorities in Kassel. As early as 1885, during the anti-Socialist law, the Wiesbaden Landrat's (county administrator) office was pointing to difficulties in identifying them: it was assumed that the factory towns of Biebrich, Griesheim and Schwanheim contained numerous Social Democrats, but it was difficult to prove which individuals were supporters of the party.[57] Nearly three decades later, the police in Biebrich still complained that, even though most of the workers in the factory town were known to be Social Democrats, potential army recruits were often too discreet to allow themselves to be identified as such:

> In response to the above instruction, we report that the recruits enlisted here have not been active politically, especially in a Social Democratic way. They do not at all get to this point, even if they belong to Social Democracy by conviction or association, because the leaders do not allow the young people to get active prior to their military service, in their interest. Hereabouts there are a great many Social Democrats among those who have completed their service, which is already evident from the various political elections. Those troops who belong to the working class, and in part also to the lower middling estate, are overwhelmingly to be counted among the ranks of Social Democracy.[58]

---

55 Decree published in *Vorwärts*, 122, 28 May 1895.
56 For examples, see Państwowe Archiwum w Poznaniu, Landrats-Amt Graetz 112; ibid, Landrats-Amt Posen-Ost 133, 137; Hessisches Hauptstaatsarchiv Wiesbaden (Hess. HstAW), Abt. 422. Kgl. Landrats-Amt Wiesbaden. Nr. 41. Spezial-Akten betr. Sozialdemokratische Militärpflichtige 1885–1916; Państwowe Archiwum we Wrocławiu, Magistrat Glatz 518; Sächsisches Staatsarchiv Leipzig 20030, Amtshauptmannschaft Rochlitz Nr. 143. The district of Graetz, comprising villages in the countryside around Posen, never found any Social Democrats, whereas they were quite numerous in Rochlitz, near Leipzig, in the heart of 'Red Saxony'.
57 Hess. HstAW, Abt. 422. Kgl. Landrats-Amt Wiesbaden. Nr. 41, Bl. 1 (verso).
58 Ibid, Bl. 270.

Following the army's 1894 decree on monitoring the recruitment of known Social Democrats, the navy also sought to screen and exclude Social Democratic recruits, especially among the volunteers.[59] In the army, wealthier individuals could gain the status of one-year volunteers and serve a shorter time on active duty if they had qualified for matriculation to university, could furnish their own equipment, and meet their own living expenses. In the navy, professional seamen, skilled machinists, harbour-pilots, and other personnel with important maritime skills could get their active service period reduced from three years to one year, in recognition of their useful skill base.[60] As the navy expanded, under Tirpitz's ambitious naval ship-building plans in the late 1890s, anxiety also rose about the potential for Social Democratic influence on the navy. In 1899, the command of the Baltic fleet in Kiel expressed its concern:

> The great masses of workers in Kiel, Gaarden and Friedrichsort, who overwhelmingly belong to the Social Democratic Party, and the proximity of Hamburg and Neumünster, where large meetings are frequently held, give cause for concern over the possibility of the infiltration of Social Democratic doctrine in the navy.[61]

Surviving admiralty files contain numerous cases of sailors being refused enlistment into, or dismissed from, the navy on the grounds of their Social Democratic political affiliations.[62]

Rudolf Wissell, then a young Social Democrat and a machinist in Kiel, found himself called up for army service in 1891 a few days after a court case in which he had challenged the dissolution of a metalworkers' association meeting by the police, despite the fact that in two previous *Musterungen* his service had been deferred for a year (despite his height and good health). Wissell suspected, but could not prove, that there had been a connection between the deferments and his political activities, as he was now known to the authorities as a 'black sheep'.[63] Wissell was stationed in Posen, well away from his comrades in Kiel. Of course, some young Social Democrats also sought to evade military service, like Eugen May, a turner from Württemberg, who hated the prospect of it, and who would leave his job to go wandering whenever the call-up season came around. According to May, his fellow workers, some of whom had served their time

---

59 Bundesarchiv Militärarchiv (BA-MA), Freiburg, RM 31/660, Bl. 15, 16.
60 *Deutsche Wehrordnung vom 22. November 1888* 1904, p. 21.
61 BA-MA RM 31/660, Bl. 11 (Kiel, April 1899).
62 BA-MA RM 31/660 and 2291.
63 Wissell 1983, pp. 46–7.

with the army, all approved of his conduct.[64] Not all Social Democratic workers were keen to avoid military service, however. For many it can have seemed little worse than their normal employment, and indeed could have been seen quite positively as 'the longest, most complete and most shining change from the desolate monotony of factory life' (according to the observer of working-class life Paul Göhre).[65] Moritz Bromme seems to have been quite chagrined at having been passed over twice on his call-up because he failed his physical,[66] and, from an older generation, Carl Fischer was devastated by the shame of being found unfit, and miserable at the prospect of having to continue at his ordinary job.[67]

If known Social Democrats were called up, despite official efforts to comb out known activists from recruitment, officials were instructed to ensure that they were posted well away from centres of socialist agitation, or dispersed to avoid any significant concentration of Social Democrats in a unit.[68] There are plenty of indications that known Social Democrats quickly became marked men in the army. In a pub conversation reported by Hamburg political police in 1895, a Social Democratic worker told of how he had only been in the army for a week when his regiment was notified that he had spoken in a public meeting the day before he had joined up, with the result that he had a tough time thereafter.[69] When the then editor of the *Sächsische Arbeiter-Zeitung*, Georg Gradnauer, was called up for service as a an *Unteroffizier* in the reserve in 1893, his newspaper reported that his officers warned the troops against this dangerous individual, but that despite this, Gradnauer had managed to win over to socialism many of his fellow soldiers. The authorities read this newspaper report as an admission that Gradnauer had been conducting socialist agitation in the barracks. When this charge failed to stick, they charged Gradnauer with insulting the army on the basis of these and other comments in the newspaper.[70] Wilhelm Liebknecht's comment on this affair in the Reichstag was reported back to the Saxon War Ministry:

---

64   Excerpt from May, 'Mein Lebenslauf (1889–1920)', in Kelly 1987, pp. 380–1, 387.
65   Göhre 1891, p. 122.
66   Bromme 1971 [1905], pp. 184, 189, 209.
67   Excerpt from Fischer's autobiography in Ulrich et al. 2001, pp. 57–8.
68   Prussian Interior Minister Herrfurth to Oberpräsident, Westfalen, 31 March 1890, in Ulrich et al. 2001, pp. 150–2. See also Kitchen 1968, p. 159.
69   Evans 1989, p. 388. See also the case of Heinrich Reuter, Wehrheim in Hesse, in Hess. HstAW, Abt. 420, Kreis Usingen, No. 269, unfoliated, reports of 28 October, 7 November 1905.
70   See the file SHStAD, 11250, Nr. 5 (unfoliated), including *Sächsische Arbeiter-Zeitung*, 230, 4 October 1893; and 11250, Nr. 121, Bl. 115.

The Social Democrats aren't as stupid as to conduct socialist propaganda during their army service time. They don't need to, as the recruits are already socialists when they enter the army. That the army believes the former is a characteristic sign of its nervousness regarding Social Democracy.[71]

Military courts imposed draconian sentences on soldiers suspected of Social Democratic activities. Even a conversation in a barrack room about a past strike in which a soldier had been involved as a civilian worker could be heavily punished, with stiff sentences handed out for 'incitement'.[72] In 1894, *Vorwärts* cheerfully reported an officer in Saalfeld informing his men on parade that singing Social Democratic songs, discussing matters pertaining to Social Democracy or reading Social Democratic newspapers were offences that would be punished by 14 days imprisonment.[73] Not long afterwards, news broke of a *Landwehr* man in Dresden who was reported to have been arrested for the very offence of singing Social Democratic songs.[74] When news of this (or perhaps another, similar, case) reached the superior military court in Dresden, the presiding officer expressed serious doubts as to whether 14 days was a sufficient punishment for the offender, who had also played the 'Socialists' March' on a mouth harmonica.[75] The authorities were alert to the dangerous charms of subversive music: investigations were also conducted during subsequent weeks into reports that soldiers had been breaching the military ban on certain dance locales frequented by Social Democrats and had been seen dancing the polka to the 'Socialists' March' or the 'Workers' *Marseillaise*'.[76] In another case in Saxony, in 1893 a soldier called Robert Gräf received a sentence of two years' imprisonment for raising his rifle while he was cleaning it and shouting: 'Long live Social Democracy!'[77] Another Saxon soldier, called Karl Otto Bachmann, was found guilty of multiple offences: verbal propaganda for Social Democracy among his fellow soldiers, trying to encourage them to visit a banned socialist pub with

---

71 SHStAD, 11250, Nr. 121, Bl. 126, report of Major Graf (Paul) Vitzthum, 1 December 1893.
72 For an example from an East Prussian regiment from 1891, see Fritz Kunert, *Die heilige Vehme des Militarismus*, cited in Ulrich et al. 2001, pp. 153–6.
73 *Vorwärts*, 81, 8 April 1894, p. 1, Beilage.
74 *Vorwärts*, 139, 19 June 1894.
75 SHStAD, 11250, Nr. 3 (unfoliated), Oberkriegsgericht v. Gottschalch, Dresden, 20 January 1894.
76 Ibid., clipping from *Berliner Tageblatt*, 18 February 1894; memo of Saxon Army Corps court martial, 3 March 1894.
77 SHStAD, 11250, Nr. 4 (unfoliated), transcript of War Ministry memorandum dated 21 November 1893. Minister of War von der Planitz to Major Hügel, 24 February 1894.

him, singing a socialist song, *lèse-majesté*, and telling his comrades that if it came to war he would sooner fire on his superior officers than on the enemy. He was sentenced to five years in prison.[78] A Saxon pioneer, Eduard Woldemar Fehmlich, under arrest for 10 days for drunkenness 'and other disciplinary offences', received a sentence of three years' imprisonment for writing graffiti in his cell which included Social Democratic slogans.[79] Another soldier who also wrote socialist graffiti in a cell while under arrest (verses beginning: 'The Kaiser shoots at socialists, let the flags fly red ...') was comparatively fortunate to get away with a five-month sentence.[80]

The Social Democratic Party responded to the difficulties of conducting agitation within the army by focussing on preparing young workers for the rigours of military service, and giving them a good grounding in socialist ideas before they were enlisted. At the party congress in Jena in September 1905, it was resolved that young men should be given factual information about their legal rights and responsibilities as army recruits (including especially their right to lodge complaints against ill-treatment), and that every year, immediately before the commencement of that year group's military service, farewell parties should be held for them as the most appropriate venue for that instruction.[81] Occasionally, local authorities in industrial regions expressed concern about Social Democrat and Free Trade Union festive farewells for draftees, even when they had no hard evidence that draftees had been systematically informed of their 'rights as soldiers'.[82] This resolution seems to have alarmed the Prussian war ministry, which initiated inquiries in federal states about the form in which this 'education of the recruits' was taking place. The Prussian Interior Ministry also expressed concern at the prospect of Social Democratic and anarchist anti-militarist propaganda around the commencement of the annual enlistment round, and instructed all police authorities to pay particular attention to anti-militarist agitation and to use whatever legal means possible to confront it. However, as the festivities were classified as private functions, which were not

---

78   Ibid, court martial of 32nd Division to Saxon Ministry of War, 23 December 1893.
79   Ibid, memorandum of Ministry of War, Dresden, 18 October 1894, quoting sentence of Dresden court martial, 26 September 1894. The offending text: 'Long live liberty, equality, fraternity. I have so loved unto death, our flag, which is red. 10 days medium arrest, Pioneer, Batallion No. 12, 11. Company, Landwehrmann Fehmlich, year class 82, pissed 1894'.
80   Ibid, court martial of 3rd Division to Ministry of War, 21 November 1896.
81   *Protokoll über die Verhandlungen der Sozialdemokratischen Partei Deutschlands*. Abgehalten zu Jena vom 17. bis 23. September 1905, Berlin, 1905, pp. 283–5. A more radical form of the resolution, promoting anti-militarist agitation more broadly, which was sponsored by Karl Liebknecht, was withdrawn on Bebel's advice.
82   Linton 1991, pp. 133, 267n51.

generally subject to formal police surveillance, and as the Social Democratic Party was careful to confine its advice to army recruits to verifiably accurate information about military law and recruits' rights under it, there was little scope for official intervention into these events.[83] The mass-produced flyers addressed to military recruits and widely distributed, which exhorted recruits to make use of their rights to complain of ill-treatment in order to combat the prevalent abuse of recruits and called on them to avoid the conservative patriotic veterans' associations (*Kriegervereine*) after their service, and the small handbook which the party published as a guide to recruits, were carefully factual in content and avoided inflammatory rhetoric sufficiently to avoid legal penalties.[84] The ever-vigilant Leipzig police, for example, ruled that the handbook's text was 'unobjectionable': it did not attack the military, but contained 'only the most important legal determinations and regulations which might interest the recruit or the currently serving soldier as well as the recently discharged soldier'.[85]

The spirit in which this adherence to legality was carried out in practice by some Social Democrats is suggested by a Leipzig police report from 1906. At a farewell party to mark the call-up of members of the Social Democratic Gymnastics Association 'Vorwärts', a member of the association was reported to have said words to the effect of:

> You who are now about to fall into the hands of the Moloch militarism, make sure that none of you gets yourselves punished. Show that you can do it, and that you are organised workers, and if it ever happens – which

---

[83] Staatsarchiv Hamburg (= StAHH), 132-I: 3403 Senatskommission für die Reichs- u. auswärtigen Angelegenheiten. Beeinflussung der Militärpflichtigen durch die Sozialdemokratie, Verunglimpfung des Heeres und seiner Einrichtungen 1906–1909; 331–3, 3300 Sozialdemokratische Presseartikel gegen das Militär – Aufklärung der Rekruten; Hessisches Staatsarchiv Darmstadt (= Hess.StAD), G15 Erbach Q4 Acten des Großherzoglichen Kreisamtes Erbach betreffend: Secrete Verfügungen, Bl. 23–24, 27. Landesarchiv Berlin (= LAB), 30 A Pr. Br. Nr. 8809, Bl. 223: instruction of Ministry of the Interior, Berlin, 27 September 1908. For investigations into the Social Democratic recruits' farewell events in Düsseldorf, Essen, and elsewhere in the Ruhr, see Landesarchiv Nordrhein-Westphalen, Düsseldorf (LA NRW), Reg. Düsseldorf, 9064, Bl. 309–319. For a police description of a farewell party held in Leipzig in 1898 by a Social Democratic gymnastics association, see Stadtarchiv Leipzig, Polizeiamt 15, Bl. 1–2, and the Leipzig police's response to the queries about recruit farewells in 1906, Bl. 7–8.

[84] Schröder, *Führer für die Wehrpflichtigen*, Berlin, 1904 (copy in LA NRW, Reg. Düsseldorf, 9064, Bl. 321–350, also in other archives).

[85] Stadtarchiv Leipzig, Polizeiamt 15, Bl. 5, Polizeiamt Leipzig, 18 September 1905 with file note of the same date.

we certainly don't wish for – that you have to fire on your parents, brothers and sisters, don't hang back, just take good care that not too many bullets hit the target so that you don't have anything to reproach yourselves for afterwards.[86]

The speaker was alluding to one of the Kaiser's most notorious speeches to army recruits, when he told them that they had to be prepared to fire on their own family members if they disobeyed the Kaiser. The need to 'enlighten' young workers before their recruitment into the armed forces, along with the obstacles in the way of conducting agitation among them once in the barracks, were reflected in Karl Liebknecht's insistence that anti-militarist agitation required more effective organisation of working-class youth.[87]

The scope for chicanery against individual soldiers once they were enlisted was enormous: surveillance of mail, repeated intrusive searches of personal effects, transfers to more unattractive postings. A former army captain in Alsace-Lorraine wrote: 'Frequent locker searches injure the feeling of honour of a sensitive musketeer. If there is a theft somewhere in the barracks, or a report on the presence of Social Democratic literature is due, all lockers of the other ranks are subjected to a detailed search'.[88] Social Democratic newspapers and journals regularly pilloried the army's arbitrary and harsh discipline, and the degrading effects of what Social Democrats used to refer to as 'Kadavergehorsam': corpse-like obedience.[89] Such experiences were of course not confined to Social Democrats, nor were they necessarily politically motivated, but they always could be. This does not include the informal, unofficial, but apparently endemic acts of physical abuse, acts that in armies everywhere are known under terms such as 'bastardisation' or 'hazing'. As Hartmut Wiedner has pointed out, the mistreatment of army recruits was a constant theme in public debates over the army in Imperial Germany, and was regularly raised in parliaments and in the press. Only partial statistics of recorded cases of ill-treatment that came before military courts are available, and it would be reasonable to assume that a very large number of cases never came before military courts and remained uncounted, but it seems safe to speak of many thousands of cases between 1890 and 1914.[90] Abuse of recruits may well have

---

86   Ibid, Bl. 11, undated report of Wachtmeister Müller, referring to a function held on 29 September 1906.
87   Liebknecht 1907, also in Liebknecht 1958, Bd. 1, pp. 247–456.
88   Pommer 1914, p. 131.
89   See account of Franz Bergg in Kelly 1987, pp. 90–6.
90   Wiedner 1982, on statistics, esp. pp. 175–6; Hall 1977, p. 126.

been a contributing factor to high suicide rates in the army, compared with the general population.[91] The thought that uncontrolled mistreatment of army recruits could turn out to be counterproductive did not escape the authorities. In 1892, the Social Democratic Party newspaper *Vorwärts* succeeded in obtaining and publishing a secret decree of Duke Georg of Saxony, commander of the 12th (Saxon) Army Corps that, without mincing words, ordered a crackdown on cruelty and brutality against recruits. The Duke expressed the fear that instead of resisting 'the subversive doctrines of Social Democracy', the army might turn into a cheap recruiting school for the party on account of such excesses.[92]

The long-running political controversy over the mistreatment of army recruits culminated in the celebrated court case against Rosa Luxemburg in 1914. In a speech in Freiburg in March 1914, Luxemburg, who had only just been sentenced to a year's imprisonment for inciting disobedience to the law in a previous speech against war, spoke out against abuse of soldiers in the army, citing cases in which this was believed to have led to suicides, and speaking of 'the countless dramas that happen in German barracks, day in, day out, and where the groans of the tormented only seldom reach our ears'.[93] This speech resulted in the Prussian minister of war, General von Falkenhayn, getting the Berlin state prosecutor to charge Luxemburg with insulting the army (more precisely, 'the entire corps of officers and non-commissioned officers' of the German army). The case proceeded with the approval of the Reich Chancellor Bethmann Hollweg.[94] Shortly before the trial against Luxemburg commenced in Berlin at the end of June 1914, *Vorwärts* published an appeal calling for witnesses to come forward to testify to the existence of mistreatment of soldiers in the army.[95] A few days later, *Vorwärts* reported that witnesses had turned out in droves to notify Luxemburg's lawyers of their experiences of abuse in the military. On the second day of the court proceedings, Luxemburg's lawyers, Kurt Rosenfeld and Paul Levi, introduced statements from over forty witnesses, and announced that they had so far received word from another 922, with more coming in

---

91 Durkheim 2002 [1897] discussed this phenomenon (pp. 186–99), although his comparative national data, including Prussia, Württemberg, and Saxony, do not extend past 1890. Durkheim classified suicide in the army as a form of 'altruistic' suicide. For a fuller discussion of this topic, see Bonnell 2014.
92 Wiedner 1982, pp. 165–6, citing *Vorwärts*, 31 January 1892, order dated June 1891, also pp. 187–8. Text of order excerpted in Ulrich et al. 2001, pp. 73–5. See also Reichstag debates 15–17 February 1892.
93 *Rosa Luxemburg im Kampf gegen den deutschen Militarismus* 1960, p. 99.
94 *Rosa Luxemburg im Kampf gegen den deutschen Militarismus* 1960, pp. 135–6.
95 *Vorwärts*, 170, 25 June 1914, reprinted in *Rosa Luxemburg im Kampf gegen den deutschen Militarismus* 1960, pp. 138–9.

constantly. Publicly, Paul Levi spoke of 30,000 cases of mistreatment that the defence would be able to cite.[96] Faced with the prospect of an unending procession of witnesses testifying to abuse in the military, the state prosecutor adjourned the case indefinitely.[97] Shortly after Luxemburg's victory in court, numerous Social Democratic Party newspapers carried a compilation of statistics prominently on their front pages, documenting abuse and suicides in the army.[98] Ironically, these articles appeared just a few weeks before mobilisation for the First World War swept into war service thousands upon thousands of readers of Social Democratic newspapers.

Restrictions on political activity in the army were strenuously enforced, especially as far as the distribution of contraband written material was concerned. In 1894, the Prussian Minister of War decreed that 'any activity observable by third parties that indicates revolutionary or Social Democratic sentiments, in particular through corresponding appeals, songs or other demonstrations', was forbidden, as were the keeping or distribution of Social Democratic writings in the barracks.[99] Even prior to this, there were cases such as that of a Saxon soldier and 'notorious supporter of Social Democracy', Gustav Hermann Zschaler, in barracks in Zittau, who was sentenced to six months' gaol after a search of his belongings uncovered two issues of a Social Democratic newspaper.[100] In an 1897 Reichstag debate, the Social Democrat Karl Frohme cited the case of an NCO dishonourably discharged and sentenced to six years imprisonment for having taken Social Democratic newspapers into his barracks and showing them to soldiers.[101] Frohme did not name the offending soldier in parliament, but this may refer to Karl Zinne, sentenced to six months in November 1895, for encouraging recruits to 'spread Social Democratic views among the soldiers' and distributing 'revolutionary' literature.[102] This was by no means an isolated case, even if the penalty in this instance was even more draconian

---

96   *Bremer Bürger-Zeitung*, 30 June 1914[?], in SAPMO NY4002/63 [Bl. 42–46]. See also Levi 1914.
97   *Rosa Luxemburg im Kampf gegen den deutschen Militarismus* 1960; SAPMO NY4002/63. Unfortunately, Luxemburg had already been convicted in a trial in Frankfurt earlier in 1914 for incitement to disobedience in speeches given in late 1913.
98   Among them, *Chemnitzer Volksstimme*, 151, 4 July 1914; *Schwäbische Tagwacht*, 156, 9 July 1914; *Vorwärts*, 186, 11 July 1914; *Volkszeitung* (Düsseldorf), 163, 15 July 1914.
99   Frevert 2001, p. 264.
100 SHStAD, 11250, Nr. 4 (unfoliated), copy of judgement against Zschaler [January 1904].
101 *Vorwärts*, 295, 18 December 1897, p. 1, Beilage, also cited in Hall 1977, p. 129.
102 Kitchen 1986, p. 153. The Zinne case was widely publicised: copy of the judgement rejecting Zinne's appeal on 28 April 1896 in Hess. StAD G24 Generalstaatsanwalt, Nr. 230 (unfoliated).

than usual. In Breslau, in 1907, a Social Democratic former candidate for the city council, the apprentice tailor Otto Koszig, was sentenced to two months in prison for sending clippings from the local party newspaper, the *Volkswacht*, to a musketeer called Golling in the barracks of the 22nd Infantry Regiment.[103] Party leaders therefore warned Social Democrats to exercise caution, and to refrain from exposing army recruits to risk of severe penalties or less formal kinds of mistreatment by sending them printed materials.[104] Reporting to a mass meeting in the 4th Berlin electoral district on the proceedings of the 1907 party congress, Heinrich Ströbel attacked militarism, defining the military in its present form as a weapon to defend the propertied classes, but warned against agitation among soldiers 'through pamphlets in the barracks – as it would rain huge prison sentences – for we are in Germany, not France'. Instead, the emphasis should be on agitation among the youth before they were called up, 'so that these don't one day "fire on their father and mother"' (another allusion – which would have been readily understood by Ströbel's listeners – to the Kaiser's inflammatory address to army recruits).[105] A decree of the War Ministry in 1902 reiterated the ban on 'any manifestation of revolutionary or Social Democratic sentiments by NCOs and enlisted men', as well as the possession or distribution of Social Democratic writings.[106]

Sometimes soldiers were able to get around these restrictions. Rudolf Wissell was able to make contact with the Social Democratic *Vertrauensmann* in Posen, Gustav Niendorf.[107] Wissell was even able to take part in an informal May day celebration in 1893, when he was out patrolling the pubs with an NCO, who stopped to meet some friends, giving Wissell the chance to get together with Niendorf and a few comrades.[108] Soldiers who clandestinely attended Social Democratic meetings had to reckon with the likelihood of a period of 'close arrest' if detected, however.[109]

The purpose of such measures was not simply to enforce ideological conformity for its own sake. Army leaders like General von Waldersee firmly believed that they would one day have to order their soldiers to turn their guns

---

103 *Der Reichsbote*, 30, 3 February 1907, clipping in LAB, A Pr. Br. Rep 30 Berlin C Polizei-Präsidium, Nr. 8809, Bl. 8.
104 E.g. LAB, A Pr. Br. Rep 30 Berlin C Polizei-Präsidium, Nr. 14145, Bl. 129 (meeting in Fourth Berlin electoral district, October 1897). Likewise, the comments of Daniel Stücklen on 13 August 1907 in LAB, A Pr. Br. Rep 30 Berlin C Polizei-Präsidium, Nr. 14147, Bl. 33–34.
105 LAB, A Pr. Br. Rep 30 Berlin C Polizei-Präsidium, Nr. 14147, Bl. 10–11, meeting on 16 July 1907.
106 *Reichs-Anzeiger*, 22 August 1902, copy in Hess. HStAW, Abt. 407, no. 166, Bl. 12.
107 Wissell 1983, p. 54.
108 Wissell 1983, p. 56.
109 Kitchen 1968, p. 151, see also pp. 156–7.

on socialists and give the order to 'shoot down the rabble'.[110] As Martin Kitchen writes, the 'determination to fight Social Democracy was common to officers of all political persuasions'.[111] The military sought to maintain surveillance over known Social Democratic leaders in their garrison districts.[112] In case of civil strife, a state of siege would be declared, and the local Social Democrat leaders would be rounded up, including Reichstag deputies whose parliamentary immunity would be disregarded. These contingency plans were periodically updated throughout this period.[113] Troops also had to be kept in readiness to be deployed as strike-breakers, or to be used to help quell unrest among striking workers, as occurred in the Mansfeld copper-miners' strike of 1909 or the great Ruhr miners' strikes of 1905 and 1912.[114] In a characteristically belligerent statement, Kaiser Wilhelm II once telegrammed his military cabinet in July 1898 with the order:

> The army corps are instructed that in the event that in the course of the summer unrest breaks out as a result of large-scale strikes, requiring the deployment of troops, it is to be stressed to those troops and those requesting their aid, that they must *not* make use of the *bayonet*, but are *immediately* to make use of *firearms*.[115]

Wilhelm was also eager for firearms to be used in defence of strike-breakers in the military intervention in the 1912 Ruhr miners' strike: '*Vor allem Schutz der Arbeitswilligen in der energischsten Form. Scharfschießen!*': 'Above all, most vigorous protection of those willing to work: fire with live ammunition!' Four workers were killed.[116]

The army's attempts to stop soldiers from becoming involved with socialist politics were of course facilitated by the fact that recruits were generally

---

110 On the 'political general' Alfred Graf von Waldersee, see Kitchen 1968, pp. 64–95, 148.
111 Kitchen 1968, p. 150.
112 BA-MA, PH1/22.
113 Förster 1985, p. 21; Kitchen 1968, pp. 166–8; Vollert 2014. See files in BA-MA PH 1/23: Acta des Kgl. Militär-Cabinetts betreffend das Eingreifen der bewaffneten Macht bei Unterdrückung von Unruhen, 1822–1918.
114 See BA-MA, PH1/22, Bl. 111–115, on plans for the call-up of reservists as strike-breakers on the Prussian-Hessian railways, 1907; on strike-breakers on the railways, see also PH 1/23, Bl. 95 (secret order of the ministry of war, 6 June 1904). Kitchen 1968, pp. 162–3; Grebing 1985, pp. 33–5; Vollert 2014, Ch. 5. See also Johansen 2004.
115 BA-MA PH 1/23, Bl. 85: Foreign Office copy of Kaiser's telegramme to the military cabinet, 22 July 1898 (underlining in original).
116 Vollert 2014, p. 121.

well below voting age (25 years old – a franchise measure that was inherently biassed against the working class, given the latter's age structure and workers' life expectancy in the nineteenth century). Thus, some working-class memoirists like Heinrich Georg Dikreiter and Nikolaus Osterroth relate their experiences in the army before they tell of their introduction to socialism.[117] Serving members of the military were in any event barred from any party-political activity. By 1914 the growth of Social Democracy was such that the military authorities started to press for further educational measures for young workers before they reached the safely patriotic surrounds of the barracks, such as compulsory gymnastics and open-air physical exercise for all youths from the age of 14 on, in order to promote 'fear of God, feeling for one's homeland and love of the Fatherland', and to counter 'anti-military influence' on young workers who were growing up 'in an antistate, unpatriotic and anti-military spirit'.[118]

The church worked hand in hand with state and military authorities in the attempt to combat socialist influences on the troops.[119] The *Christliche Zeitschriften-Verein* (CZV) was partly active from 1885 on in seeking to distribute religious papers and tracts in the garrison and regimental libraries and the barracks of NCOs and the other ranks, explicitly in order to counter the 'poison' of Social Democratic propaganda. The CZV sought to promote 'fear of God and patriotic sentiments' alike.[120] However, whether the army chaplains' hearts were not in the job, or whether it was simply beyond them, their efforts seem to have had little success: an inquiry in 1899 evaluated their influence as 'virtually nil'.[121]

Religion played a part in everyday discipline. One of the first exercises for recruits was to practice their swearing-in. In Rudolf Wissell's case, a Lieutenant called on Evangelicals to step forward, then Catholics, then Jews, and was baffled when Wissell remained back on his own – Wissell had resigned from the state church just before he was called up. The officer made sure that Wissell stood in the front rank during the oath-taking, where he could be observed.[122] Being *konfessionslos*, Wissell had to report to the divisional chaplain for conversations about religion every week. Wissell found these chats agreeable enough, as the discussions (over a glass of beer followed by a cigar) over topics such as David Friedrich Strauss's *Life of Jesus* (which Wissell had

---

117   Dikreiter n.d. [1914], pp. 125–55; Osterroth 1980 [1920], pp. 100–8.
118   Hall 1977, p. 125; Linton 1991, p. 189.
119   Kitchen 1968, pp. 168–74.
120   Saul 1972, p. 341.
121   Messerschmidt 1979, p. 266.
122   Wissell 1983, p. 480.

read 'several times' in Kiel) made a pleasant break from barrack duties, and he remained exempt from church parade. These privileges were openly resented by Wissell's sergeant, however.[123] Wissell was once called a *Schweinehund* by a lieutenant when he described himself as having left the state church,[124] but he reported that most of his officers treated him decently, his superior officer Lieutenant Hoffmann failing to bother to search Wissell's locker (which presumably was suspected of containing contraband socialist writings).[125] Wissell had some trouble with NCOs, but found his officers mainly treated him well.[126] Wissell kept his nose clean and was promoted to corporal after his first year of service. Socialists without a religious affiliation were not the only ones who could come under pressure in the army. During the *Kulturkampf*, Catholic recruits in the Prussian army were also exposed to aggressive anti-Catholicism.[127]

Paul Göhre, a clergyman and advocate of social reform, who later joined the Social Democratic Party (on its revisionist right wing), described his experiences of three months of living and working alongside factory workers in Chemnitz in an 1891 book. Göhre described a Social Democratic stonemason's apprentice who looked back on his time in a Thuringian batallion particularly fondly, showing himself impressed by fine uniforms and well-turned out officers. In the factory, Göhre found, everyone liked to think back on his time of military service:

> Whenever we were standing together and the conversation somehow got onto the topic, there was an enthusiasm for it. They told stories about the hardships of the service with some satisfaction, of the hot summer days on the parade grounds and the cold winter nights on sentry duty. And many were particularly proud of their regiment. And yet they were all Social Democrats, old and young, who spoke like that.[128]

Göhre found particular nostalgia for the army among veterans of the 1870 war against France (unlike the veteran Hasenclever, apparently). He also noted the popularity of prints showing soldiers and military subjects among the workers. At the same time, some complained of officers 'who had handled them all too

---

123 Wissell 1983, pp. 49–50.
124 Wissell 1983, p. 51.
125 Wissell 1983, pp. 52–3.
126 Wissell 1983, pp. 52–3, 58.
127 Ulrich et al. 2001, pp. 80–1.
128 Göhre 1891, p. 118.

roughly'. One worker expressed particular hostility to the military, but Göhre was not surprised by this, as the man in question was 'a rabid "elite Social Democrat"', which suggests that Göhre expected to encounter strongly anti-militarist sentiments among particularly committed socialist activists.[129] Another contemporary social researcher, Adolf Levenstein, discovered that the workers he surveyed, like the Saarland miner Peter Klein, reported painful memories of routine brutality from their time of military service. Klein referred to the military as a 'system to annihilate one's humanity just as it was unfolding' [*System* [...] *um die blühende Menschheit zu vernichten*].[130]

Richard Evans' study of political police reports from workers' pubs in Hamburg, largely frequented by Social Democrats, found, in general, strongly negative attitudes to militarism and the existing standing army among Social Democratic workers, findings which our own research in these reports confirms.[131] At a Social Democratic meeting in the Hamburg suburb of Wandsbek in 1892, the speaker, a comrade Block, gave a talk on the military, drawing on his own experience of army service. He characterised the military as 'a breeding ground of immorality and brutality. Militarism carries the mark of the class state on its brow', serving the economic interests of the ruling classes, who resorted to bayonets against the claims of the workers, and whose sons enjoyed easier conditions of service than the sons of workers. Block's remarks were rewarded with copious applause and a discussion followed in which the party member Rospitzky spoke along similar lines to Block.[132] Similarly, when Reichstag deputy Fritz Zubeil spoke to a gathering in Berlin's Fourth electoral district in February 1904 on the topic of the mistreatment of soldiers – taking two and a quarter hours to deal with the topic – he was met with thunderous applause.[133] In a Hamburg pub conversation in 1902, workers discussed the prevalence of mistreatment of soldiers, which they believed to be increasing, with one soldier commenting on the frequent practice of forcing a soldier's comrades to take part in the abuse of the victim.[134] The harshness and injustice of the military penal code and of military courts was a common topic of complaint, especially when the Social Democratic press publicised egregious cases in which

---

129 Göhre 1891, pp. 120–1.
130 Levenstein 1909, p. 110; see also p. 16.
131 Evans 1989, pp. 384–6.
132 StAHH, 422–15 Ea1, Wandsbek Polizeibehörde, Versammlungsbericht, Wandsbek, 13 Dezember 1892 (unfoliated).
133 LAB, A Pr. Br. Rep. 30, Nr. 14146, Bl. 76, 26 February 1906.
134 StAHH, 331–3, S5286 (Vigilanzberichte Schutzmann Hinz), report of 19 February 1902 (unfoliated). A report of 25 September 1902 in the same file also records workers' belief that abuse of recruits was increasing. See also report of 30 October 1902.

soldiers received excessive punishments while officers and non-commissioned officers who mistreated soldiers were treated leniently.[135] The general tenor of such recorded conversations about life in the army reveals a consensus that abuse and chicanery were highly prevalent, with such assertions going unquestioned by other workers present. In one 1909 conversation, in a group of seven workers talking in a pub, one worker commented on officers who mistreated their subordinates, saying: 'If it comes to a campaign, the tormenters will get it worse than in [18]70/71, for in the last war they discovered that most officers had been shot dead from behind, and that was already 38 years ago'. One of his comrades concurred, boasting that if he were called up, he would take the opportunity of getting revenge on the officers who had abused him.[136] In his autobiography, the rural worker Franz Rehbein wrote of his military service: 'If I hadn't already been wholly a Social Democrat – I would have become one there. One would have to become one there, entirely of one's own volition, without any agitational activity, just from using one's common sense'.[137]

Despite Social Democrats' ideological antagonism to militarism, and the army's intense opposition to socialism, Wilhelm Deist has suggested that the practical experience of the army by 1914 was that Social Democrats actually made quite adequate soldiers.[138] A Bavarian War Minister even declared that Social Democrats could be found among the best soldiers: 'thanks to the discipline that rules in the Social Democratic Party', there was 'no cause for complaint'.[139] In 1895, the naval artillery section in Friedrichsort reported to the commander of the Baltic fleet that it had ten sailors who had been identified as Social Democrats, but that they all had records showing consistent 'very good' or 'good' conduct – despite the common practice in the navy of screening out Social Democratic recruits. The artillery unit testified that one sailor, called Taube, who had been identified (by the local infantry brigade) as having had a 'leading role' in the party, or as being a committed socialist,

---

135 E.g. StAHH, 331–3, 5288 (Vigilanzberichte Schutzmann Hinz), report of 7 July 1905; 5302 (Vigilanzberichte Schutzmann Kramer), reports of 18 January and 15 July 1905. Comments in July 1905 concerned a case of military 'justice' in Altona that was given great publicity by the *Hamburger Echo* (153, 6 July 1905: 'Ein Exempel statuiert!' and articles in subsequent issues of the paper).
136 StAHH, 331–3, S5315 (Vigilanzberichte Schutzmann Zerulli), report of 27 February 1909.
137 Rehbein 1985 [1911], p. 293; see his account of his experiences in a dragoon regiment, pp. 168–209.
138 Deist 1974, p. 466.
139 Frevert 2001, p. 279. See *Mitteldeutsche Sonntags-Zeitung*, 50, 13 December 1903: 'Die Tüchtigkeit sozialdemokratischer Rekruten'.

had a record of constant 'immaculate conduct', and had never given the least occasion for complaint.[140]

Some historians have commented on the tendency of Social Democrats' language to become militarised: May Day rallies were commonly called 'the army parades of the proletariat'. Brigitte Emig has pointed to the emphasis in Social Democratic discourse on values such as discipline, which would ultimately bring victory.[141] Despite the party's pro-feminist programme, its rhetoric emphasised masculine comradeship in language often redolent of the barracks. Military metaphors were perhaps not surprising in a party that saw itself engaged in constant struggle, although the fact that so many members of the party had once performed military service may have made the metaphors more concrete than might otherwise have been the case. On the other hand (as noted in Chapter 3), when Social Democratic newspapers wrote of the 'Battlefield of labour', they were trying to dramatise, and condemn, the frequent maimings and fatal accidents in the workplace, the very opposite of seeking to glorify loss of life.

Any generalisation about Social Democrats' experiences of the German military will be fraught with difficulty. While the party continued to level vigorous criticism against the brutal excesses of army life and the bundle of phenomena comprehended under the term 'militarism',[142] and continued to include in its programme the demand for a people's militia to replace the hierarchical standing army, by 1907 at the latest there was a wide spectrum of opinion within the party on military issues. Bernhard Neff has diagnosed an increasing ambivalence in the Social Democrats' critique of militarism in the years leading up to the First World War, with a growing emphasis on reform of the antiquated aspects of aristocratic militarism in the interests of greater efficiency (not least out of a concern for the health and safety of ordinary soldiers).[143] The spectrum of views on militarism within the party went from Karl Liebknecht on the radical left to Gustav Noske on the 'social chauvinist' right. Karl Liebknecht, incidentally, served in a Prussian Guards regiment (as a 'one-year volunteer'); Gustav Noske, contrary to what is sometimes assumed, never actually performed military service.[144] Remarkably, Karl Liebknecht's anti-militarist agitation in 1907 came under attack from none other than Franz Rehbein, who would articulate such forthright criticisms of the army's treatment of recruits in his mem-

---

140 BA-MA, RM 31/660, Bl. 22, 23 (Friedrichsort, 27 February 1895).
141 Emig 1980, pp. 232–5.
142 Stargardt 1994.
143 Neff 2004.
144 Trotnow 1980, p. 25; Laschitza 2007, pp. 51–2; Wette 1987, p. 66.

oirs (which were posthumously published in 1911, following his death in 1909). Rehbein raised the charge that neither Liebknecht nor the Berlin radical Georg Ledebour would have taken the same radically anti-militarist position that they did if they had served in the army. While Rehbein had initially held anti-revisionist views, by 1907 he seems to have moved to the party right, taking a position with the General Commission of Trade Unions, and appearing as a frequent outspoken critic of the left radicals in the party in party meetings in Berlin over the course of that year (to the point that the left-leaning Sixth electoral district tried to expel him from the party).[145] Liebknecht took to *Vorwärts* to refute Rehbein's criticism, writing that: 'I have been a soldier, and have drunk this bitter cup to the very bottom. It is precisely my experience of the military that forms an essential part of the basis for my anti-militarist views'.[146]

As is well known, Social Democrats dutifully went to war in August 1914. But over half a million supporters of the party participated in anti-war demonstrations across Germany in the last week of July, before mobilisation put an abrupt end to anti-war activity. Large sections of the Social Democrats' rank and file, serving in the army or the fleet, were also willing to revolt against the monarchy by November 1918.

---

145 Biographical details by Urs J. Diederichs and Holger Rüdel, in Rehbein 1985 [1911], pp. 341–5. For Rehbein's criticisms of the party left during 1907, see LAB A Pr. Br. Rep. 30, Nr. 14151, Bl. 44–5, 182–5, 197–8, 199–200, 233–4, 272–3; *Vorwärts*, 69, 22 March 1907; 88, 11 April 1907.

146 *Vorwärts*, 209, 7 September 1907.

CHAPTER 6

Reading Marx

On 31 October 1894, the following advertisement appeared in the classified advertising pages of the German Social Democratic Party's main newspaper, *Vorwärts. Berliner Volksblatt*, which also doubled as the local paper for party comrades in Berlin:

> **Karl Marx**. We wish to form a small, informal society for the purpose of common thorough study of Das Kapital. Gentlemen, not too young, with the necessary basic knowledge in this area may leave addresses under G.S. in the newspaper's office.[1]

A perusal of subsequent issues of *Vorwärts* has failed to uncover any evidence of the success or otherwise of this *Capital* reading group. Did it share the fate of so many *Capital* reading groups since, of breaking up after an enthusiastic start after ploughing through the first couple of chapters on commodities and money? It is tempting to think of a dedicated circle of Berlin Social Democrats persevering with the task, and continuing until they grappled with Volume 3, which appeared shortly after this advertisement. Yet, the absence of further signs of life, as far as this author has been able to tell, is not encouraging. The existence of a Reading Club named after Karl Marx in Berlin in 1891–92, at which discussions over socialist theory took place, is documented, however.[2]

It is widely accepted among authorities on the German Social Democratic Party in Imperial Germany that the workers who made up the rank and file of the party did not actually read much Marx, despite the party's adherence, in theory, to a rigorously Marxist party programme. The important, and deservedly influential, work by Hans-Josef Steinberg, *Sozialismus und deutsche Sozialdemokratie*, first published in 1967 and repeatedly revised for subsequent editions, set a pattern for later authorities in this area. Steinberg cited Marx's comment in the afterword to the second edition to the effect that: 'The understanding which *Capital* has rapidly met with among broad sections of the Ger-

---

1 *Vorwärts*, 254, 31 October 1894, p. 1, Beilage.
2 Landesarchiv Berlin (= LAB), A Pr. Br. Rep. 30, Nr. 14169, concerning the arrest of a worker called Adalbert (also referred to as Max) Weber for 'insulting the army' during a discussion in the club (in July 1891) in which Weber spoke of the prospects of revolution in Germany. The club's meetings were clearly subject to police surveillance.

man working class is the best reward for my work'. Steinberg found, on the contrary, that 'the assumption that Marx's *Capital* was received and understood by the social democratic workers is simply absurd'. In support of this finding, Steinberg cited party theorist Karl Kautsky's memoirs: 'Only few had read [*Capital*] and even fewer were those who understood it'. Steinberg also pointed to Marx's correspondence with his publisher, Otto Meissner, who regularly complained about how hard it was to get the first edition (of 1,000 copies) of *Capital* off his hands (at least until 1871).[3]

Steinberg's discussion of the early (non-)reception of *Capital* among German rank-and-file Social Democrats might also have referred to the first congress of the Social Democratic Workers' Party in Stuttgart in 1870. At the start of the congress proceedings, Bruno Geiser requested that he be relieved of the task of giving a presentation on Marx's *Capital* as he had not been given sufficient notice to prepare it. Geiser's request was granted 'after a brief discussion'.[4] Clearly, no-one among the Social Democratic Party delegates was able to step in at short notice and speak with authority about Marx's work. (On the other hand, one might think it particularly noteworthy that a fledgling workers' party should feel the need to include in its party congress a discussion of a demanding work of economic theory.) *Capital*, along with other works by Marx classified as essentially 'scientific', escaped being banned under Bismarck's anti-Socialist law, to the vexation of some policemen who pointed to passages that justified revolution.[5] In October 1880, the Prussian Police Presidium in Berlin was informed that 'Marx's *Capital* is only very weakly disseminated here and it circulates nearly exclusively in scholarly circles'.[6] This classification as academic did not save the book from being banned in the Austro-Hungarian Empire, however.[7]

Steinberg demonstrated the extent to which German Social Democrats in the 1870s were influenced by a highly eclectic body of socialist theory, at least until the publication of Engels' *Anti-Dühring*. (Engels' polemic against Eugen Dühring, intended to dispel Dühring's influence among supporters of socialism, was originally published in series in the party's 'central organ', the newspaper *Vorwärts*, in 1877 and 1878, appearing then in book form.) Even the process

---

3 Steinberg 1979, p. 21, including quotations from n. 51.
4 *Protokoll über den ersten Congreß der social-demokratischen Arbeiterpartei zu Stuttgart, 1870* (Leipzig, 1870; Reprint Glashütten/T., 1971), p. 1.
5 LAB, A Pr. Br. Rep 30, Nr. 14740, Bl. 2 (escaping ban), and Bl. 5 (for a vexed policeman, 11 May 1879).
6 LAB, A Pr. Br. Rep 30, Nr. 14740, Bl. 8.
7 LAB, A Pr. Br. Rep 30, Nr. 14740, Bl. 12, 13.

of ideological clarification that took place during the anti-Socialist law (1878–90), and the subsequent adoption of the Marxist party programme at Erfurt in 1891, left some room for doubt as to how deeply Marxism penetrated into the thinking of the party's rank and file during the period from 1890 to 1914. Steinberg sought to demonstrate the limits of Marx reception among Social Democratic workers by analysing the available records of workers' libraries. Drawing on surveys of the borrowings of members of Social Democratic and trade union libraries conducted and published during the period 1890–1914, Steinberg concluded that even among those workers with a particular interest in books of a scientific, scholarly, or theoretical nature, whom he views as an elite minority among the trade union and party members, there was little interest in Marxism: 'the majority of socialist workers had absolutely no connection with the theory of socialism and showed no interest in the scholarly literature of the party'.[8]

As Dick Geary has recently pointed out, the fact that even the minority of workers who were active users of social democratic or trade union libraries 'rarely borrowed works of Marxist theory' (with the exception of August Bebel's *Die Frau im Sozialismus*, translated into English as *Woman under Socialism*, and to a lesser extent, Karl Kautsky's presentation of the *Economic Doctrines of Karl Marx*) does not mean that working-class reading habits did not reflect a worldview distinct from the bourgeois reading public, with an evident interest in socially critical fiction (Zola), and radical history (Zimmermann's *Peasant War* or the anti-clerical compilations of Otto von Corvin) proving congenial to a socialist outlook.[9] Even the evidently highly popular *Count of Monte Cristo* by Alexandre Dumas can be seen not only as escapist entertainment, but also as an indictment of a corrupt and unjust social order. The popularity of popular scientific books, history, and utopian novels or science fiction all contributed to the formation of a socialist outlook that made claims to be based on a scientific worldview (or was at least secular and anti-clerical), and reflected a desire for a better and more just society.[10] Nor were the two exceptions noted above insignificant: Bebel's best-selling *Woman under Socialism* – it reached its 50th edition in 1909, by which time 197,000 copies had been printed[11] – incorporated into its successive editions material from Engels' work on *The Origin of the Fam-*

---

8   Steinberg 1979, pp. 129–42, quotation p. 141. Cf. Fülberth 1972, pp. 110–14; Langewiesche and Schönhoven 1976; Lidtke 1985, pp. 180–91.
9   Geary 2000, pp. 390, 393.
10 Bonnell 1993, pp. 249–50.
11 Bernstein, 'Vorwort zur Jubiläums-Ausgabe', in Bebel 1980b (reprint of 1929 jubilee edition), p. 15.

ily, Private Property and the State and other works by Marx and Engels (albeit mixed in with ideas from Johann Jakob Bachofen, among others), while Kautsky's *Economic Doctrines of Karl Marx* was a faithful enough chapter-by-chapter condensed version of *Capital*, Volume 1.

Clearly, as Hans-Josef Steinberg points out, it would be unrealistic to expect an overly sophisticated understanding of socialist theory from the million Social Democratic Party members (by 1914), 'class-conscious, willing to make sacrifices, and filled with the spirit of solidarity' as they were.[12] However, the analyses based on library lending statistics might usefully be set against the context of other potential avenues of reception of Marxian ideas: firstly, the large volume of pamphlet literature produced by the Social Democratic Party; secondly, the communication of Marxist ideology in the Social Democratic press; thirdly, oral communication, in party meetings and public speeches.

From the early years of Social Democratic Party organisation in Germany, party newspapers carried advertisements for cheap political pamphlets for agitational purposes, commonly priced around 25, or even as low as 10, Pfennigs. During the anti-Socialist law of 1878–90, such pamphlet literature was smuggled into Germany along with the banned party newspaper, *Der Sozialdemokrat*. Looking back over the period of the anti-Socialist law, August Bebel referred to some 1,200 printed works, not counting the party press, which had been banned, 'including our entire, very considerable, pamphlet literature'.[13] With the lifting of the anti-Socialist law in 1890, and the party's electoral breakthrough of that same year (winning over 1.4 million votes), the party publishing house Buchhandlung Vorwärts was founded. The Buchhandlung Vorwärts joined the Dietz Verlag of Stuttgart as major publishers of socialist literature in Germany. Heinrich Dietz's publishing house produced the Internationale Bibliothek (International Library), which focussed on Marxian theory, popular science and history: its first two titles were Edward Aveling's book on Darwinism, and Kautsky's *The Economic Theories of Karl Marx*, in hard-bound volumes which usually sold for two or three Marks, as well as the theoretical journal *Die Neue Zeit*.[14] The Buchhandlung Vorwärts, on the other hand, aimed at producing the largest possible quantity of cheap pamphlet literature. At the 1890 party congress, Bebel predicted that 'so great is the demand from all sides' for

---

12 Steinberg 1979, p. 142.
13 *Protokoll über die Verhandlungen des Parteitages der Sozialdemokratischen Partei Deutschlands. Abgehalten zu Halle a.S. vom 12. bis. 18. Oktober 1890*, Berlin, 1890 (hereafter cited as *Protokoll*, place, year), p. 30. See also the compilation by Atzrott 1971 [1886].
14 On the Dietz Verlag, see Graf 1998, and the bibliographical reference work Graf, Heidemann, and Zimmermann 2006.

party literature, that he expected that no future party pamphlet would appear in an edition smaller than 20,000 to 30,000.[15]

By the end of June 1891, the Buchhandlung Vorwärts boasted a turnover of 66,000 Marks in the previous nine months, for some 300,000 copies of party publications (not including the mass-produced May Day celebration pamphlets). Even Eduard Bernstein's three-volume edition of Ferdinand Lassalle's writings was published in cheap instalments (20 Pfennigs an instalment), which, in the words of the party executive's report for 1891, 'allows even the most impoverished comrade to acquire these splendid writings'. The fact that there was a reasonably strong demand for Lassalle's works in this form is reflected by the fact that the Buchhandlung Vorwärts reported a slight dip in turnover when the serialisation of the edition was completed, and they did not have an equivalent serialised work to follow it with.[16] It was further claimed as 'shining testimony to our comrades' yearning for education' that the smallest editions in which agitational pamphlets appeared were of 10,000 copies: 'A whole series of these printings have already sold out within weeks and had to be reprinted. The Proceedings of the Party Congress in Halle, for example, sold 40,000 copies'.[17]

The protocol of the next congress, at Erfurt in 1891, at which the party adopted its Marxist programme, saw 30,000 copies produced by the time of the following congress.[18] The programme itself was printed in half a million copies, and 120,000 copies of the brochure explaining the programme were distributed.[19] These publications were also among the 40,000 copies of brochures distributed gratis in the previous year.[20] Other brochures to be produced in 1891–92 included reprints of such tried and tested agitational pamphlets as Wilhelm Bracke's *Nieder mit den Sozialdemokraten* (Down with the Social Democrats), Wilhelm Liebknecht's *Hochverrat und Revolution* (High Treason and Revolution), Bebel's *Christentum und Sozialismus* (Christianity and Socialism), and Engels' *Entwicklung des Sozialismus von der Utopie zur Wissenschaft* (Development of Socialism from Utopia to Science). Other brochures served practical

---

15 *Protokoll*, Halle, 1890, p. 36.
16 *Protokoll*, Frankfurt a.M., 1894, p. 33. The serialisation of Lassalle's works took advantage of the established working-class practice of buying serialised fiction from colporteurs. See Fullerton 1976–77; Fullerton 1978–79. On efforts to make use of the colportage trade for Social Democratic agitation, see Groschopp 1985, pp. 107–13.
17 *Protokoll*, Erfurt, 1891, p. 49.
18 *Protokoll*, Berlin, 1892, p. 44.
19 Ibid.
20 *Protokoll*, Berlin, 1892, p. 45.

ends: cheap editions of social legislation, such as the sickness insurance law, or copies of the laws of association.[21] Even parliamentary proceedings could be turned into successful pamphlet literature: the Reichstag debates of February 1893 over the shape of the socialist 'state of the future' were turned into a brochure of which 100,000 copies were produced within a few weeks.[22] (Parliamentary speeches also had the significant advantage of benefitting from parliamentary immunity from censorship.) By 1896, despite noting a certain 'overcrowding in the socialist book market', the Buchhandlung Vorwärts reported that its 18 new publications and 13 reprinted works amounted between them to a total of a million copies (well over 900,000 of which were the new items).[23] By the 1913 Party congress, the Buchhandlung Vorwärts could boast that in the nine months from 1 July 1912 to 31 March 1913, it had experienced a turnover of 623, 245 Marks, compared with 790,709 Marks in the previous full year.[24] In nine months, this amounted to well over a million items, not counting newspapers, periodicals, or May Day pamphlets.[25] The range of publications ranged from brochures on health issues (from 'Occupational Illnesses of Book Printers' to 'Sexual Intercourse and Venereal Diseases'); to the series *Sozialdemokratische Flugschriften* (Social Democratic pamphlets) in which the anti-militarist titles 'The Horrors of War' and 'War against War' were the biggest sellers (220,000 and 95,000 copies printed respectively); the 'Women's Library' series, from 'Women in Local Politics' to 'Child Labour, Child Protection and the Child Protection Commission'; practical guides offering information on the law; literary works and socialist commentaries on literature, and agitational staples such as *Grundsätze und Forderungen der Sozialdemokratie* (Principles and Demands of Social Democracy, in 75,000 copies), the much-reprinted commentary on the Erfurt Programme by Kautsky and Bruno Schoenlank, which constituted something of a handy primer on Marxism in 60 pages.[26]

William Guttsman has referred to the 'pragmatic and topical character' of much of the party's propaganda literature.[27] There is clearly much validity in this assessment, especially, as one would expect, when it came to material put

---

21 *Protokoll*, Berlin, 1892, p. 44.
22 *Protokoll*, Köln, 1893, p. 46.
23 *Protokoll*, Gotha, 1896, p. 30. This seems to include the May Day celebratory newspaper, of which 320,000 copies were distributed.
24 *Protokoll*, Jena, 1913, p. 33.
25 Calculated from *Protokoll*, Jena, 1913, pp. 32–3.
26 Ibid.
27 Guttsman 1981, p. 173.

out by regional and local party organisations during election campaigns, when the price of commodities and the mechanics of parish-pump politics naturally came to the fore. But more theoretical literature, even in simplified form (as in Kautsky and Schoenlank's commentary on the Erfurt Programme) continued to be produced in significant quantities, even if much of it could be seen as dated or overly eclectic in approach. Bebel's 1870 *Unsere Ziele* (Our Goals) continued to be reprinted, as were Wilhelm Bracke's phenomenally popular *Down with the Social Democrats* (first published in 1876 and still being reprinted 30 years later) and works by Lassalle.

Selected titles and print runs (where available) are as follows:[28]

Engels, *Entwicklung des Sozialismus von der Utopie zur Wissenschaft*

1892	reprint, no number given
1904	7,000
1908	11,000
1912	11,000

Marx/Engels, *Communist Manifesto*

1894	no number given
1895	6,000 (= 3 editions of 2,000 each)
1898	3,000
1899	reprint, no number given
1901	2,000
1903	2,000
1904	3,000
1906	5,000
1907	22,000
1908	10,000
1909	11,000
1913	11,000

Engels, *Internationales aus dem Volksstaat*

1894	no number given

---

28   Compiled from *Protokoll*, 1892–1913. Years given refer to report year (i.e. numbers as of 30 June, at end of financial year, or 31 March in case of 1913).

Lafargue, *Kommunismus und Kapitalismus*

1894	no number given
1895	reprint, no number given
1899	" "

Plekhanov, *Anarchismus und Sozialismus*

1894	no number given
1905	3,000
1911	5,000

Marx, *Class Struggles in France*

1895	3,000
1911	3,000

Marx, *Lohnarbeit und Kapital* (Wage Labour and Capital)

1907	6,000
1908	5,000
1909	5,000
1913	6,000

Kautsky/Schoenlank, *Grundsätze und Forderungen*

1892	120,000
1893	reprint, no number given
1894	" "
1895	10,000
1897	reprint, no number given
1898	7,000
1899	reprint, no number given
1900	5,000
1903	12,000
1904	5,000
1905	105,000 (new, revised edition)
1906	50,000
1907	100,000
1908	91,000

1909   55,000
1910   91,000
1911   121,000
1912   100,000
1913   75,000

Kautsky, *Die soziale Revolution*, I and II

1903   7,000
1905   (Part I: 20,500, Part II: 1,400)
1907   4,000
1911   5,000

Kautsky, *Die historische Leistung von Karl Marx*

1908   11,000

Kautsky, *Der Weg zur Macht*

1909   26,000
1911   5,000

Luxemburg, *Accumulation of Capital*

1913   2,000

On the basis of these incomplete figures, it seems reasonable to assume that 80–100,000 copies of the *Communist Manifesto* were printed from 1890 to 1914, and a million or more copies of Kautsky and Schoenlank, *Grundsätze und Forderungen*. It also seems reasonable to allow for a certain multiplier effect, with pamphlets possibly being read by more than one reader per copy.

The party's Central Educational Commission (*Zentralbildungsausscchuss*), set up in 1906 to co-ordinate the party's educational activities, sought to guide the party's large and growing network of organisations in the establishment of workers' libraries, recommending model libraries to fit a wide range of budgets. For the smallest budget, from 1 to 10 Marks, ten pamphlets were recommended, which included Marx's *Wage Labour and Capital* (for 95 Pfennigs) and the *Communist Manifesto* (at just 70 Pfennigs). For a library of up to 25 Marks, recommendations included Marx's *Civil War in France* (50 Pfennigs), and a brochure by Kautsky on Marx's 'historic achievement'. The next step up (75 Marks) included Engels' *Origin of the Family*, and a 100 Mark collection might include Engels on the *German Peasant War*, Kautsky's digest of Marx's *Economic Doctrines*, and Marx's *Class Struggles in France*. A library had to get up to 150 Marks and several dozen titles before it might stretch to Engels' *Anti-Dühring* (3 Marks) and the first volume of *Capital* (a daunting 11 Marks).[29] Whether these recommendations were followed or not, the implied progression from cheaper pamphlets and brochures to more demanding – and expensive – tomes, is interesting to note.

In his analysis of workers' reading habits, Steinberg considers the possibility that Social Democratic Party members may not have borrowed much socialist theoretical literature from libraries because they already owned cheap copies. However, he suggests that the fact that August Bebel's *Woman under Socialism* was not only a socialist bestseller, but also the socialist work most frequently borrowed from workers' libraries might indicate that borrowing figures could also be a good indicator of the popularity of socialist pamphlet literature.[30] But this overlooks a few key considerations: firstly, Bebel's immense personal popularity. It is quite likely that if workers bought only one hard-bound socialist classic, it would be Bebel's most celebrated work.[31] It also overlooks the cheapness of the pamphlet literature, which could be acquired for as little as 10 Pfennigs (and was sometimes even distributed gratis), compared to, say, 2.50 Marks for a hard-bound copy of *Woman under Socialism* (over half a day's wages for most workers). Thirdly, the sheer volume of pamphlet literature produced by the party puts the relatively modest lending figures for workers' libraries in the shade.

Next to the party's prodigious output of pamphlet literature, the role of the party press in disseminating Marxian ideas and vocabulary needs to be considered. Rosa Luxemburg may once have suggested that the leading articles of the party newspaper *Vorwärts* were only good for house-training her pet rabbit, Mimi.[32] But regular readers of *Vorwärts*, and there were 165,000 subscribers by 1912,[33] had a certain amount of exposure to Marxian thought, both directly and

---

29 LAB A Pr. Br. Rep. 30, Nr. 9267, Bl. 74: model catalogues for workers' libraries, Berlin, 1908.
30 Steinberg 1979, p. 138.
31 Such was Bebel's personal prestige that from time to time he had to take out notices in the party press requesting local party organisations not to advertise him as a speaker until they had his express agreement to appear. It was not unknown for party organisations, whether out of optimism or calculation, to advertise Bebel as a speaker prematurely, ensuring good attendance at meetings.
32 Rosa Luxemburg to Luise Kautsky, end of July 1904, in Luxemburg 1982–84, Vol. 2, p. 60.
33 Fricke 1976, p. 421.

indirectly, and the fact that party newspapers were available in pubs frequented by party members lends support to the assumption that the readership was much larger than the number of subscribers.

During 1891, to take just one year as an example, *Vorwärts* was frequently occupied with the issue of the formulation of the new party programme, which was eventually adopted at the Erfurt party congress. When the party's (relatively low-circulation) theoretical journal, *Die Neue Zeit*, printed Marx's *Critique of the Gotha Programme*, *Vorwärts* responded (in February 1891) by acknowledging it as a useful contribution to the debates about the party programme, but characteristically stressing that theoretical debates should not be allowed to sow division in the party: 'the German Social Democrats are not Lassallean and not Marxian – they are Social Democrats'.[34] Despite this rather equivocal acknowledgement of Marx's ideological influence, the following month the first page of the issue on the eighth anniversary of Marx's death was devoted to a tribute to him.[35] As noted in Chapter 1, above, while they have sometimes been overshadowed by commemorations of Ferdinand Lassalle, Karl Marx memorial celebrations were also held, and were reported in *Vorwärts*. Another month later, the leading article on the front page was devoted to a refutation of criticism of Marx raised by the bourgeois social reformer Lujo Brentano.[36] The leading article of the May Day issue did not mention Marx by name, but invoked Marxian language, referring to the dependence of workers on capital, the role of class-conscious workers, and the international organisation of labour, albeit in an article justifying why Social Democratic workers would not be striking on May Day, but demonstrating on the following Sunday. It closed, nonetheless, with the slogan 'Workers [*Proletarier*] of the world unite!' which was to become the catchphrase for May Day celebrations.[37] During the second half of the year, the debates around the adoption of the Marxian Erfurt Programme regularly took up space in *Vorwärts*.

A more consistently Marxist diction was, however, found in the Social Democratic women's newspaper, *Die Gleichheit*, under the editorship of Clara Zetkin, even if it did not really reach a mass audience until after about 1905. But Zetkin seems to have seen the newspaper's role in the 1890s as providing a political schooling for cadres of functionaries in the party's women's organisations, and seems to have counted on these functionaries to disseminate the paper's the-

---

34   'Der Marx'sche Programm-Brief', *Vorwärts*, 37, 13 February 1891.
35   *Vorwärts*, 62, 14 March 1891.
36   'Brentano und Marx', *Vorwärts*, 92, 21 April 1891.
37   'Der 1. Mai', *Vorwärts*, 100, 1 May 1891.

oretical content to wider audiences.[38] *Die Gleichheit* consistently used Marxian concepts to differentiate the socialist women's movement from bourgeois feminism. *Die Gleichheit* stressed, for example, that, unlike the bourgeois feminists, 'socialists understand the economic causes and necessities' of the 'woman question': 'in consequence of the class differences, the class situation, the realisation of the demands for women's rights will not at all bring about the social emancipation of the great mass of the female sex'.[39] For *Die Gleichheit*, class conflict took precedence over the demands of bourgeois feminism: 'Between workers and capitalists there can only be a reckoning between class and class', and 'The raising of the class situation of the proletariat, and also its ultimate liberation, takes place in conflict with the interests of the capitalists'.[40] Leading articles in *Die Gleichheit* cited Engels' *Origin of the Family* on the economic basis of prostitution, for example, cited *Das Kapital* on the economic causes of malnourishment among children and on child labour, and commemorated anniversaries such as the thirtieth anniversary of the founding of the First International.[41] *Die Gleichheit* explained to its readers the meaning of concepts like the dictatorship of the proletariat and the nature of exploitation of workers by the owners of the means of production, defined revolution as the outcome of the revolutionary transformation of the economic structure of society, and echoed Marx's writings in formulations like: 'The proletariat can only cease to exist when the social revolution has taken place which abolishes all classes'.[42]

The indirect qualitative influence of *Die Gleichheit*, as opposed to its more direct impact as measured through subscription figures, is hard to gauge. There is little disagreement, however, that the subscription figures, and readership, of the party's quality theoretical journal, Kautsky's *Die Neue Zeit*, and the revisionist *Sozialistische Monatshefte* (owned not by the party but privately under the direction of its editor Joseph Bloch) remained limited. *Die Neue Zeit*'s circulation was only a little over 10,000 at its peak before the First World War.[43]

---

38   Fricke 1976, pp. 429–33; for an analysis of the role of *Die Gleichheit* in fostering socialist women's militancy, see Maynes 1998.
39   'Zur Frauenfrage', *Die Gleichheit*, 5, 7 March 1892.
40   'Schwindelhalber', *Die Gleichheit*, 11, 1 June 1892.
41   'Auf der Armensünderbank', *Die Gleichheit*, 15, 27 July 1892; 'O Gott, daß Brot so theuer ist, Und so wohlfeil Fleisch und Blut', *Die Gleichheit*, 17, 24 August 1892; 'Lasset die Kindlein zu mir kommen!', *Die Gleichheit*, 13, 27 June 1894; 'Ein Geburtstag', *Die Gleichheit*, 20, 3 October 1894.
42   'Die Diktatur des Proletariats', *Die Gleichheit*, 5, 7 March 1894; 'Wer ist eine Proletarierin?', *Die Gleichheit*, 9, 3 May 1893; 'Die revolutionäre Sozialdemokratie', *Die Gleichheit*, 6, 22 March 1893.
43   Fricke 1976, p. 429. On Joseph Bloch and his influence on the revisionist wing of the party, see Fletcher 1984.

Arguably, the journal did have some broader diffusion: articles were occasionally reprinted or at least summarised and discussed in party newspapers. There were also proposals to use articles from the journal as the basis for discussions in party meetings.[44] This did sometimes occur, at least in the left-wing stronghold of Berlin's East End, where it is recorded that in February 1907, at the monthly local branch meetings, much of the meeting time was taken up with reading a *Neue Zeit* article by Kautsky, which analysed the January 1907 election result, taking issue with the revisionist views of Richard Calwer and Eduard Bernstein on the party's anti-imperialist platform, and it was noted that the Berlin comrades vehemently supported Kautsky's critique of revisionism.[45]

The party's illustrated humorous paper *Der Wahre Jakob*, on the other hand, enjoyed a genuine mass circulation, of some 371,000.[46] Hans-Josef Steinberg estimates that sales of 380,000 may have been equivalent to a readership of over 1.5 million.[47] Anecdotal evidence in the memoirs of Social Democratic workers also testifies to the popularity of *Der Wahre Jakob*. The metalworker Moritz Bromme, describing the reading habits of workers in the Gera machine and tool factory in which he worked, recalled that: 'The adult workers who were politically active took ... *Der Wahre Jakob*, *Der Süddeutsche Postillon*, and other party publications'.[48] Hamburg's political police also confidentially testified to the popularity of *Der Wahre Jakob*, as they recorded that workers would read articles aloud to each other and discuss them, as well as pieces from the Hamburg party paper the *Hamburger Echo*. Copies of the Social Democratic press were typically available for reading in pubs frequented by party members.[49] The emphasis of *Der Wahre Jakob* (and of its Munich-based counterpart, *Der Süddeutsche Postillon*, edited by Eduard Fuchs) was clearly on entertainment. It contained jokes, satirical verse, and cartoons which lampooned the Social Democrats' political opponents. A certain insouciance towards questions of socialist theory is indicated by *Der Wahre Jakob*'s response to the controversy over Marx's *Critique of the Gotha Programme*. A short poem addressed to 'Those Rejoicing over Marx's Critique' warned the party's enemies that if the socialists

---

44 E.g. LAB 030 Nr. 14148, Bl. 237–8, police report dated 12 October 1909, on a proposal of the party organisation in the Fourth Berlin electoral to distribute *Die Neue Zeit* gratis to local leaders for this purpose.

45 LAB A Pr. Br. Rep. 30, Nr. 14146, Bl. 254–5, police report of 14 February 1907. The article in question was Kautsky 1907.

46 Geary 2000, p. 391.

47 Steinberg 1979, p. 129; see also Hickethier 1979.

48 Bromme 1971 [1905], p. 286, see also pp. 261–2.

49 E.g. Staatsarchiv Hamburg (StAHH), 331–3 Politische Polizei, 5320 Vigilanzberichte Schutzmann Mebus, report dated 8 December 1908 (unfoliated).

had hitherto been hitting them with a jagged sword, they would soon be hitting them with a sharper one.⁵⁰ What counted, it seemed, was the vigour of the blows, rather than how sharp the theoretical blade was. However, the fun in *Der Wahre Jakob* was not ideologically neutral. The paper often carried commemorative articles on episodes from revolutionary and socialist history, and profiles of socialist leaders. National and international party congresses were observed. Friedrich Engels' death was observed by a special memorial issue of *Der Wahre Jakob*, with a substantial essay paying tribute to Engels by Eduard Bernstein.⁵¹ In addition, the paper regularly carried advertisements for socialist literature published by Dietz, including cheap editions of Marx and Engels, along with Bebel and others. The paper's cartoons can often be seen as carrying Marxian ideological messages. Along with allegorical representations of proletarian internationalism produced annually to mark May Day, there were also cartoons such as the one showing the proletariat as a chained Prometheus with the vulture Capitalism eating at his vitals, while the tiny figure of a bourgeois social reformer offered him a sticking plaster.⁵²

This was, of course, the heyday of the newspaper as the only real mass medium, with cinema still in its infancy before 1914. The Social Democratic Party was successful in this period at mobilising print culture in the service of an oppositional, socialist public sphere. In addition to the Berlin-based *Vorwärts* and other nationally distributed periodicals, the Social Democratic Party maintained an extensive network of newspapers all over Germany. By 1914, there were over 90 Social Democratic daily newspapers in Germany, with a total circulation approaching half a million, including such important city-based papers as the *Hamburger Echo* (circulation of 76,000 by 1913) and the *Leipziger Volkszeitung* (53,000 by 1913).⁵³ It would be reasonable to assume a multiplier in relation to the ratio of copies printed to readers, in view of what we know about how newspapers were available to be read in pubs frequented by party members, and also in view of the fact that copies delivered to workers' homes reached sometimes large households, which may have included lodgers. In 1900, a member of the party's press commission estimated that each copy of *Vorwärts* was read, on average, by three people.⁵⁴

---

50   J.St. [= Jakob Stern?], 'Den Bejublern der Marx'schen Programmkritik', *Der Wahre Jakob*, 121, 14 March 1891.
51   *Der Wahre Jakob*, 239, 21 September 1895.
52   *Der Wahre Jakob*, 136, 10 October 1891.
53   Fricke 1987, Bd. 1, pp. 540, 539. On the Social Democratic press, see also the works of Kurt Koszyk, including Koszyk 1953, 1966 and 1979.
54   *Vorwärts*, 237, 4 October 1900, clipping in LAB A Pr. Br. Rep. 30, Nr. 14150, Bl. 211.

In part, the spread of socialist ideas among workers in the late nineteenth century benefitted from technological advances in paper-making and printing (such as the rotary printing press) that enabled dramatically cheaper newspaper production: the shift to mechanical and chemical pulp for paper-making enabled the price of newsprint to fall to a third of its 1873 level by 1900, thus putting daily newspapers within reach of many workers.[55] If, as Benedict Anderson famously argued, the emergence of 'print capitalism' in early modern Europe facilitated the rise of the 'imagined community' of the nation,[56] the second wave of the industrial revolution, with the use of sophisticated machinery and innovations in the use of chemicals coinciding with a growing mass market for newsprint among a literate urban working class, led to print-capitalism 3.0,[57] which facilitated the rise of Marxian ideas of class consciousness and socialism in the period of the Second Internationalism. Later, in the Weimar Republic, the Social Democratic Party was to prove less well-equipped to meet the challenge of the cross-class appeal of the new mass media of film (which was increasingly controlled by large commercial interests) and public radio broadcasting (controlled by the state).

The third principal medium by which Marxian ideas and vocabulary could be disseminated among the rank-and-file membership of the Social Democratic Party was oral communication.[58] The party always placed a great deal of importance on what it called 'word of mouth' agitation. Effective speakers were in high demand across the country to speak in public meetings of local social democratic organisations, in addition to the adult education courses sponsored by the party. The topics for public meetings were, of course, frequently of a topical or practical nature, especially at election times, or even of a general educational character, but elucidation of the party programme also featured. In 1908, the party published a printed guide for its speakers, compiled by the Hessian revisionist Eduard David. Along with the ability to use language well, David's guide stressed the importance for Social Democratic agitators of reading. Along with a grounding in general knowledge, speakers also had to acquaint themselves with socialist theory. David's list of key texts for socialist speakers began with the Erfurt Programme and Kautsky's and Schoenlank's commentary on

---

55 Müller 2014, p. 192.
56 Anderson 1983.
57 We may consider the rise of the printing press and the rapid dissemination of its – increasingly vernacular – products in the early modern period, described by Anderson, as the first phase of print capitalism; the rise of daily newspapers with a bourgeois readership as the second phase; and the emergence of mass-produced cheap newsprint with a large, literate, urban working-class readership as a third phase.
58 On the significance of oral communication, see Loreck 1977, especially pp. 178–237.

it. He then referred readers to Marx's *Das Kapital* and Kautsky's condensed version of it (*Karl Marx' ökonomische Lehren*). Engels' work on *Socialism from Utopia to Science* was then recommended as an overview of socialist thought, although David suggested that the agitator-in-training could save Engels' *Anti-Dühring* until later. The *Communist Manifesto*, on the other hand, belonged among the works that 'every Social Democrat must read'.[59] Even the revisionist David gave primacy here to the writings of Marx and Engels.

In these days of dwindling attention spans and continual electronic distraction, there is something impressive about the crowds of workers gathered in beer halls or other meeting places on weekday evenings, usually after 9–10 hours at work in a six-day week, listening for two hours or so to addresses or lectures on often weighty topics. Sometimes there was no time for discussion (or even no inclination for it), but some meeting records show evidence of audience engagement with the topics. To take a few examples, more or less at random, out of many accounts of party meetings: in Berlin's Fifth electoral district, in February 1898, 'comrade Doctor' Julian Borchardt spoke on the question: 'Can practical parliamentary work go as far as voting for cannons?' Borchardt quoted Bebel's remark at the Erfurt party congress, that only a few of those present would experience the coming of the new age, before going on to talk about capitalism's tendency to undergo periodic crises, quoting passages from both Marx's *Capital* and Bebel's *Woman under Socialism*. In the ensuing 'extraordinarily lively discussion', a number of participants spoke out against the revisionist opinions recently expressed by Wolfgang Heine.[60] In the Fourth Berlin electoral district, in the working-class precincts of South-East Berlin, comrade Karl Wiesenthal gave a talk in July 1901 on 'Why must Social Democracy be victorious?' Wiesenthal gave a historical overview of the 'development of human society', closing with a discussion of both the necessity of a political struggle for socialism as well as a trade union struggle. A long discussion followed, 'which concerned particularly the Marxian crisis theory and Bernstein's views'. Wiesenthal spoke of his own journey from anarchism to Social Democracy as the product of his practical experiences in the metalworkers' union.[61] Also in Berlin's Fourth district, Eduard Bernstein spoke for two and a half hours in November 1902 on 'Changes in the Idea of Socialism', and was received with 'vigorous applause', but also with contradiction in the subsequent discussion, when a comrade referred to a recent article by Bernstein and argued that he was mistaken in ascribing a 'reduction of crises

---

59 David 1908, pp. 35–6.
60 LAB A Pr. Br. Rep. 30, Nr. 14150, Bl. 160, clipping from *Vorwärts*, 48, 26 February 1898.
61 LAB A Pr. Br. Rep. 30, Nr. 14145, Bl. 247, clipping from *Vorwärts*, 165, 18 July 1901.

to the existence of trusts and cartels'.[62] In 1906, the Fourth district held five simultaneous meetings on the same Tuesday evening in August, dedicated to the topic of 'The Class Struggle'. In one example of these meetings, in the Landsberger quarter in the East End, comrade Bernhard Düwell described the development of capitalism, citing the *Communist Manifesto*.[63] Staying in the Fourth electoral district, in March 1907, the editor comrade Block spoke to an audience of around 400, including about 60 women, in the Markgrafen halls in the Markgrafendamm, on the topic of 'What means of power does the proletariat possess?', arguing that as capital developed further, the proletariat also increased in size and potential strength.[64] The Berlin party organisation arranged a series of lectures on economics (naturally, from a Marxist perspective), featuring Rosa Luxemburg and other speakers, in 1910: it was reported that the large hall used for the lectures was filled with an audience of both sexes (and the lectures were also summarised in *Vorwärts* for a wider audience).[65]

More such examples could be cited. However sophisticated or otherwise the level of theoretical debate in such public meetings, such examples indicate that rank-and-file party members were exposed to concepts from Marxist theory, and some at least were often willing to join in the debate. In a similar vein, the adult education courses provided by the party included courses on the economic foundations of socialism (based on the Erfurt Programme), which was the most frequently held course in 1912/13, plus others on historical materialism, along with courses on general, practical or technical education.[66] Less formal avenues of oral communication, at the workplace and elsewhere, are also recorded (for example, in workers' autobiographies) as having an effect on workers' political views. Some workers, as recorded in the case of certain cigar workers, even read socialist literature aloud to their workmates at work.[67]

Despite Robert Michels' famous critique of the supposedly oligarchical tendencies of the party, the democratic structure of the party saw local party organisations holding meetings to send delegates to every year's party congress and to debate resolutions for the party congresses, and the party press would carry

---

62 LAB A Pr. Br. Rep. 30, Nr. 14146, Bl. 19, clipping from *Vorwärts*, 278, 28 November 1902.
63 LAB A Pr. Br. Rep. 30, Nr. 14146, Bl. 191, clipping from *Vorwärts*, 192, 19 August 1906.
64 LAB A Pr. Br. Rep. 30, Nr. 14146, Bl. 285–6, police report of 21 March 1907.
65 *Vorwärts*, 246, 20 October 1907, p. 2, Beilage: 'Die zweite Vortragsreihe über Nationalökonomie'.
66 *Protokoll*, Jena, 1913, pp. 39–43.
67 Lidtke 1985, p. 190; Otto Ernst, 'Akademie der Zigarrenmacher', in Rüden and Koszyk 1979, pp. 45–7.

reports on these meetings and the debates which took place at them. It is generally accepted that rank-and-file members of the party took a dim view of party intellectuals' theoretical disputes, and the tolerance for public displays of party disunity does seem to have been low.[68] On the other hand, it is worth noting that the proceedings of the annual party congress regularly sold 30–40,000 copies, and eventually even 50,000.[69]

The 1908 reform of the laws of association made women's participation in political organisations legal (although they were still to be denied the vote until the revolution of 1918–19). The Social Democratic Party debated the issue of women's role in the party organisation at the 1908 party congress in Nuremberg, which revealed a degree of mistrust among male delegates of the continuation of any separate women's organisation.[70] In speaking against any separate women's organisation, the trade unionist Adolf von Elm from the party's right wing referred slightly condescendingly to the 'moral obligation for the men, to educate the women to be comrades'.[71] The question of how best to promote education in socialist thought among women party members came to the fore with the 1908 organisational changes and the formal incorporation of women into the party. Despite von Elm's assumptions about the need for men to educate female comrades, female comrades in Berlin had already initiated special educational programmes for women in 1894, apparently with limited initial success, but these were revived by Ottilie Baader in 1904, who organised regular reading groups for small groups of women, aimed at women unionists, and particularly at those who might become activists, organisers, or delegates.[72] For the first few meetings of these groups, Ottilie Baader led the participants through the *Communist Manifesto*, with a part of the text being read aloud, and then discussed by the group.[73]

Subsequently, the party organisation in Greater Berlin took up the task of promoting women's reading and discussion groups (*Frauen-Leseabende*) as an official activity of the Berlin party district organisations.[74] Baader ran these reading groups again in late 1905, again going through the *Communist Manifesto*

---

68 See Evans 1989, pp. 246, 266–9.
69 Documented in the protocols themselves, in the reports on the previous year's activities.
70 See Quataert 1979, p. 146, and contrast the debates of the women's section of the Nuremberg party congress, *Protokoll*, Nuremberg, 1908, pp. 464–545 with the plenary debates, pp. 208, 243–9.
71 *Protokoll*, Nuremberg, 1908, p. 244.
72 Quataert 1979, pp. 193–4; LAB A Pr. Br. Rep. 30, Nr. 15852, Bl. 1.
73 LAB A Pr. Br. Rep. 30, Nr. 15852, Bl. 7.
74 Quataert 1979, pp. 194–200.

and answering questions about any passages the participants found difficult. Again, the groups remained relatively small, with sometimes fewer than ten women taking part.[75]

Initially, the women's reading and discussion groups in Berlin had a strong emphasis on Marxist theory. In late 1908, the party-sponsored women's reading and discussing groups were scheduled for the third Friday of every month, focussing on the theoretical part of the Erfurt Programme.[76] In May 1909, the women's reading and discussion evenings for the Third electoral district were conducted in the rooms of the trade union headquarters on the Engelufer by August Thalheimer, later one of the most important and original Marxist theorists of the German labour movement in the 1920s (and a leader of the anti-Stalinist Communist Party Opposition).[77] One such meeting was attended by 25 women (and four men). Thalheimer gave a lecture, and then asked his audience questions to make sure they had understood the key points. Then they read from Kautsky and Schönlank's *Grundsätze und Forderungen der Sozialdemokratie* as an exposition of the theoretical section of the Erfurt Programme.[78] A month later, Thalheimer asked one of the participants to read aloud from Engels' work *Die Entwicklung des Sozialismus von der Utopie zur Wissenschaft*, and then explained each section in turn after the reading. Interestingly, the group had grown to 38 women (and four men).[79] At a subsequent meeting, with the group continuing to work through Engels' exposition of socialist theory, one of the participants, a Frau Pohl (presumably the wife of the chairman of the local party organisation of the Third electoral district, August Pohl) complained that Thalheimer's lecture was too academic for the women in the group, and suggested that comrade Thalheimer should incorporate and discuss more practical examples. Thalheimer patiently explained that Engels' text was fundamental for understanding socialism, and that if the women comrades continued to participate actively in the discussion evenings and re-read the material at home and reflect on it, they would comprehend it.[80] The Engels readings continued, and Thalheimer kept most of his listeners (still 35 women and three men in late July 1909).[81] There was some concern in the Ber-

---

75 LAB A Pr. Br. Rep. 30, Nr. 15852, Bl. 12, police report of 15 November 1905.
76 LAB A Pr. Br. Rep. 30, Nr. 14148, Bl. 5, police report of 11 November 1908 (on the Fourth electoral district).
77 On Thalheimer, see Bergmann 2004.
78 LAB A Pr. Br. Rep. 30, Nr. 14144, Bl. 296, police report of 25 May 1909.
79 LAB A Pr. Br. Rep. 30, Nr. 14144, Bl. 301, police report of 18 June 1909.
80 LAB A Pr. Br. Rep. 30, Nr. 14144, Bl. 303, police report of 29 June 1909.
81 LAB A Pr. Br. Rep. 30, Nr. 14144, Bl. 312, police report of 27 July 1909.

lin party organisations about low attendance at the women's reading groups more generally, however, with complaints among district party leaders that 'not even party functionaries were attending with their wives'.[82] A review of the success of the women's reading and discussion evenings that took place in May 1910 found mixed results. The representative of the Fourth electoral district, Agnes Fahrenwald, supported continuing to discuss the party programme, 'which contains something for every aspect of life, from the cradle to the grave'. Other participants favoured increasing the emphasis on practical matters, however.[83] A mixture of theoretical, current political, and practical topics would have reflected the pattern of the usual party meetings' lectures. It remains noteworthy that there was a strong sense in the party organisations that women members needed to be brought up to date with Marxian theory.

In addition to various sources of quantitative evidence on workers' reading habits, outlined above, there is also the qualitative evidence offered by working-class autobiographies, which frequently testify to a strong autodidactic bent, with a strong desire for self-improvement through education. A good example of this mentality might be the woodworker Heinrich Georg Dikreiter, who in his memoir described his resolution, after his 'conversion' to Social Democracy, to become an agitator for the party, in a passage which mentions all three media of diffusion of Marxian ideas discussed above (newspapers, pamphlets and oral communication, through talking to comrades and attending meetings):

> I therefore went to every meeting, read my newspaper from the first to the last line, bought myself pamphlets on the fundamental questions of socialism. One of the first pamphlets which I bought was Engels' *Development of Socialism from Utopia to Science*. Since I didn't understand what I read at first, I read it through a second and a third time, copied out passages, entire pages, and learned what I had written by heart. I tried to draw comparisons, tried to work through a question in my mind through reflection on what I had read. I gradually learned to think logically and thus came to grasp socialism with my reason and not just with feelings. From semi-religious enthusiasm for socialism there developed clear thinking,

---

82 LAB A Pr. Br. Rep. 30, Nr. 14148, Bl. 127, confidential political police report of 14 April 1909. The marking of the report as 'confidential' suggests it derived from a covert police informer.

83 LAB A Pr. Br. Rep. 30, Nr. 15852, Bl. 48. Cf. Quataert's assessment of the mixed reception of the discussion evenings: Quataert 1979, pp. 194–200.

from a blind believer in the idea of a future state there grew the socialist fighting to raise the class position of the workers.[84]

The factory worker Otto Krille described spending all his spare time reading the Social Democratic *Sächsische Arbeiterzeitung* and current political pamphlets before his eldest brother took him to a meeting of the local Social Democratic association, which was the start of his 'conversion' to Social Democracy, a process which entailed attending numerous mass meetings of the party. Subsequently, Krille described his later discussions with an older worker, who not only read the daily party press but even *Die Neue Zeit*, who exercised an influence on his developing political consciousness.[85]

It could easily be objected that authors of autobiographies are inevitably unrepresentative.[86] On the other hand, the authors of these accounts were often party functionaries who put their reading to use in party meetings and speeches or educational courses given to the rank and file. It is reasonable to postulate a certain diffusion effect here. This was clearly the case in the example of one seamstress, herself the daughter of a worker in a sugar factory in Frankfurt an der Oder, born in 1847. Ottilie Baader became drawn to socialism during Bismarck's persecution of the party from 1878 on. She managed to acquire a copy of Marx's *Capital* and subsequently the first version of Bebel's book on women (printed in exile in Switzerland).[87] Baader later wrote:

> The two books I already mentioned, August Bebel's *Woman* and Karl Marx's *Capital*, aroused the greatest possible interest precisely in the period of the anti-Socialist law. Both works were immediately banned as dangerous to the state, but were nonetheless much and eagerly read and discussed. Since harsh punishment was threatened for disseminating these works, one had to be careful about how one secretly obtained them. [...] [After a copy of *Capital* was discreetly obtained] the reading began at home. Our father read it aloud, and we discussed it while I sewed. All in all we spent a year reading Marx's *Capital*. I then later read Bebel's *Woman* on my own, however.[88]

---

84   Dikreiter n.d. [1914], p. 183.
85   Krille 1975 [1914], pp. 93–7, 105–6 (also excerpted in Kelly 1987, pp. 274–7, 279–80).
86   See Kelly 1987, pp. 2–5; for a systematic analysis of working-class autobiographies, see Loreck 1977.
87   Baader 1979 [1921], p. 23.
88   Baader 1979 [1921], pp. 24–5. Baader erred in her belief that *Capital* had been banned, but it is not unlikely that many people assumed it would have been, and some pamphlets

This is, of course, the same Ottilie Baader who, 25 years later, led reading groups of women trade unionists in Berlin, taking them line by line through the *Communist Manifesto*.

Vernon Lidtke cites another working-class autobiographer, Otto Buchwitz, who once borrowed Marx's *Capital* from a workers' library in Dresden. Buchwitz wrote: 'back home I found out that in order to understand "anything", I first had to buy a dictionary of foreign terms. Only many years later was I able once again to begin to study this standard work with greater success'.[89] There is nothing surprising in Buchwitz's difficulties with *Capital*. What is noteworthy here is his conviction that it was worth the effort, and his persistence in the matter.

Buchwitz (and his fellow autobiographers with similar stories) may not have been typical in this last respect. But Marxian literature was sufficiently widely available to have a formative influence on the mental world of Social Democratic German workers, even if it was simplified and mixed in with other, more eclectic, influences. This influence was facilitated by the fact that for German workers before 1914 there seemed to be a striking consistency between a Marxian analysis of society and the reality of an Imperial German state in which class divisions were particularly salient (especially in states like Prussia and Saxony, which had unequal, property-based franchise laws), and in which economic distributive conflicts rapidly became highly politicised. Marxian theory also offered workers who were subject to considerable disadvantages in Imperial German society a positive perspective for the future. One of our most useful sources on the mentality of rank-and-file German Social Democrats in this period, the reports of the Hamburg political police on workers' pub conversations, analysed by Richard Evans and already discussed in previous chapters, indicates (according to Evans) that:

> The evolutionary version of Marxist theory propagated by Kautsky through the Party programme [...] seems to have filtered down to some extent to the rank and file. It can be seen, too, in their evident belief that the Party was being borne to ultimate victory on the wings of historical inevitability, expressed above all through its steady growth in electoral support.[90]

Occasionally the Hamburg policemen, acting as clandestine stenographers of workers' political conversations, captured discussions that showed that some

---

    based on *Capital*, for example, Johann Most's popularisation of the text under the title *Kapital und Arbeit*, were banned.
89   Lidtke 1985, p. 189.
90   Evans 1990, p. 144.

rank-and-file workers had indeed internalised the party's Marxian teachings, communicated through the newspapers and meetings. For example, in May 1902, in Diestel's basement pub in the Rostockerstrasse, Constable Hinz noted:

> 4 guests were present, who conducted the following conversation: Just as there as a definite conflict of interest between the buyer and seller of a commodity, with one wanting to buy as cheaply as possible and the other wanting to sell as expensively as possible, there is the same conflict between the capitalist and the worker, but with the difference that the capitalist is only after a bigger profit, but the worker on the other hand has to sell his labour power, that is, his whole life.

The group went on to discuss how strikes had usually ended unfavourably for the workers; however, this had 'improved greatly in recent times, as the workers had learned to act with their forces united'. They were confident that the power of the workers 'will become greater from year to year'.[91]

That the version of Marxian theory embraced even by the party's leaders and intellectuals had its limitations is well-established and a staple theme of the literature on German Social Democracy (and the Second International in general) in this period. However, some of the older literature on Marx reception in German Social Democracy arguably suffers from a tendency towards academic purism on the one hand, setting unrealistically high standards (asking, in effect, who read *Capital* from cover to cover, and developed an advanced level of understanding of the text). This level of criticism may be appropriate when analysing the writings of party leaders and theoreticians, but is less useful in approaching the broad reception of Marxian ideas among the party's rank and file. If one turns away from the sales figures of *Capital*, or the statistics on how often it was borrowed from workers' lending libraries, and considers the broader diffusion of Marxist ideas through newspapers, pamphlets, and oral communication, there is evidence of a much wider reception of Marxism than a more purist approach allows for. The period of the Second International in Germany was the period of that classic Bertolt Brecht figure, the 'worker who reads', and the combination of a thriving print culture making newspapers and other printed matter cheaply available and a literate population of urban workers, provided the preconditions for a broad reception of Marxian ideas.

---

91   StAHH 331–3, S5286, Vigilanzberichte Schutzmann Hinz, 31 October 1901–26 June, 26 July, 13 August–31 December 1902. Report of 16 May 1902.

CHAPTER 7

Workers and Cultural Activities: Culture, Sociability, Organisation

One of the most useful keys for understanding political life in Imperial Germany has been M. Rainer Lepsius's concept of the socio-political 'milieu'. In an essay first published in 1966, Lepsius argued that despite the shifting shapes of political party formations in Imperial Germany, they reflected four underlying social milieux, defined by strong class and religious cleavages in German society, that were remarkably stable and durable from the 1870s into the Weimar period. These milieux were: conservative, liberal, Catholic, and socialist.[1] In the case of the Catholic milieu, a 'particularly clear' example of this, Lepsius described the way in which the Catholic Centre party had been able to draw on a rich organisational culture created by Catholics since the 1850s, 'which had its foundation in a wealth of local church, charitable, and social organisations, often under the leadership of the clergy'. Over a generation, the Church had succeeded in creating 'a highly self-contained Catholic social milieu, regionally articulated and hierarchically organised', which proved successful in politically integrating German Catholics and which was especially resistant to political challenges in regions with a high degree of Catholic confessional homogeneity.[2] In a similar fashion, Lepsius suggested that the Social Democratic Party had its basis in its own specific subculture of workers' organisations (while he also argued that the party's focus on this subculture resulted in its eventual isolation).[3]

There is no doubt that Imperial Germany was characterised by a remarkably dense and diverse network of civil society organisations. It is equally true that these organisations reflected the highly segmented nature of late nineteenth-century German society. The German Social Democratic labour movement drew great strength from its connection with a milieu, its own subculture, and its own organisational networks. The party was strongest where a concentration of industry brought together workers who developed a sense of their com-

---

1 Lepsius 1993. Cf. Karl Rohe's division of German parties into three 'camps', rolling the Protestant liberals and Protestant conservatives into a single camp. Rohe 1992.
2 Lepsius 1993, p. 39.
3 Lepsius 1993, p. 45.

mon economic interests. In its strongholds, there were distinctly proletarian residential areas, in mining or industrial regions or in the large working-class suburbs of fast-growing cities like Hamburg or Berlin, with their rows of so-called 'Mietskasernen', 'rental barracks'. Workers, especially the men, sought sociability and escape from cramped living conditions in pubs, and in areas where the labour movement was strong the local pubs would typically display the Social Democratic newspapers and host local party meetings. As the network of Social Democratic cultural, leisure, and sporting organisations grew, organised workers could spend all their work within their own socialist social-moral milieu.

Some figures afford a sense of the density of the Social Democratic organisational networks that grew up by 1914. The party had a million members by 1914 (compared with 4.25 million voters in 1912). Close to 175,000 of these members were women (who had only been allowed to join political organisations since 1908, and who were still of course excluded from the vote). The membership of the Free Trade Unions, aligned with the Social Democratic Party and with overlapping membership, including among the leadership groups, albeit formally independent from the party, reached and exceeded 2.5 million by 1912. The party press boasted impressive subscription statistics: from 1911, the party's 'central organ' *Vorwärts*, which doubled as the Berlin party paper, fluctuated around 150–160,000 subscribers. Not far behind *Vorwärts* was the socialist women's paper, *Die Gleichheit* (125,000 subscribers by 1914). *Vorwärts* was outdone by the illustrated humorous-satirical weekly magazine, *Der Wahre Jakob*. Local papers in the party's big-city strongholds also showed impressive numbers considering they served members in a single city or region: e.g. a circulation of 76,000 for the *Hamburger Echo* (1913), and 53,000 subscribers for the *Leipziger Volkszeitung* (1914) (see Chapter 6 above). To cite only the main cultural, leisure and sporting organisations: the Deutscher Arbeiter-Sängerbund (the workers' singers' league) boasted over 100,000 active members by 1913 (over 92,000 men and over 15,000 women); the Freie Volksbühne (Free People's Stage) in Berlin had 18,000 members by 1914; the Arbeiter-Turnerbund (workers' gymnastics league) counted 186,000 members in over 2,400 separate associations in 1914; and the workers' cycling league, '*Solidarität*', sometimes nicknamed the 'red cavalry' for its courier services during election campaigns and other occasions for mobilisation, had 148,000 members by 1913. There were also smaller groups such as the first-aid organisation, the Workers' Samaritans; the Proletarian Free-Thinkers; the Workers' Abstinence League (never very numerous); Esperantists and Stenographers. There was also the large consumers' co-operative organisation aligned with the Social Democratic Party. The Zentralverband deutscher Konsumvereine claimed to represent over 1,000 associations with a total of over 1.7 million members by 1914.[4] It was thus more than likely that a typical Social Democratic Party member was organised in his or her trade union, subscribed to a party newspaper and possibly a magazine like *Der Wahre Jakob* or its Munich counterpart *Der Süddeutsche Postillon*, was a member of a consumers' co-operative, and quite possibly a sporting or cultural organisation as well. A male party member might well spend part of his free time in a pub attended by other party members (and quite possibly run by a publican who was a party member and organiser), in addition to attending the occasional week-night party meetings, and a big party festival on a weekend every couple of months.

The cultural organisations and activities of the Social Democrats were the focus of considerable historiographical attention from the late 1960s to the 1980s. One major area of research focus was the relationship between the established high culture of the German bourgeoisie and the emergent culture of the German working class, and the degree to which socialists drew on, or were influenced by, or criticised, the dominant cultural norms of the bourgeoisie.[5] An analysis of Social Democracy as a 'cultural movement' by Brigitte Emig in 1980 focussed on the extent to which the party's cultural activities transmitted bourgeois cultural values in their efforts to promote the self-improvement of the workers.[6] My own study of the Berlin Freie Volksbühne found that Social Democratic cultural organisations could be made to serve different rationales depending on which group was controlling them: as a vehicle for promoting avant-garde bourgeois literary culture when it was run by non-party intellectuals, as a venue for promoting socialist ideology through a strategy of selective and critical appropriation of the bourgeois literary heritage under Franz Mehring's direction, and as a means of promoting the positive integration of workers into bourgeois cultural life under a revisionist leadership after 1897.[7] Vernon L. Lidtke gave a detailed and convincing portrayal of Social Democratic cultural life as an authentic socio-cultural milieu alternative culture in Imperial Germany, one that was not necessarily fully theoretically articulated by the party, but one that was characterised by a consistent pattern of symbolic expression and by a common identifying 'language of social class' (with an emphasis on words such as *Arbeiter* –

---

4 In the place of numerous individual references for these figures, see the detailed handbook compiled by Dieter Fricke 1987.
5 For a key early work in this vein, see Fülberth 1972; see also Rüden 1973 and Trempenau 1979.
6 Emig 1980.
7 Bonnell 2005.

worker, of *Genosse* – comrade).⁸ Dick Geary has also written on the subject of German Social Democratic workers' associational life, stressing that it met the needs of its participants in a number of ways not reducible to the degree to which it assimilated bourgeois culture.⁹ Most recently, Sabine Hake has provided a challenging re-reading of German labour movement culture in a work entitled *The Proletarian Dream*, written from a cultural studies perspective incorporating approaches from the history of emotion. However, her focus is explicitly on cultural production and discourse, and disavows any attempt to see labour movement culture as a reflection of workers' material circumstances.¹⁰

Rather than rehearse the well-worn debates over the reception of bourgeois culture, or the theoretical shortcomings of attempts to fashion a new 'proletarian' culture within the Social Democratic Party's organisations, this chapter is an attempt to explore the various ways in which the party's associational life met the needs of its members, not just in terms of education and culture *per se*, but also through the ways in which it provided venues for working-class sociability and practical opportunities to gain experience at organisation. Given the wealth of both printed and archival material on the party's activities in Berlin, the main focus of this chapter will be on the Berlin party organisations, with some reference to the rest of the Reich.

It is worth recalling that the foundation of a separate working-class party (initially two parties) in Germany was at least in part a reaction against liberal tutelage over workers in workers' educational associations (some of which were also run by churches). Wilhelm Liebknecht's 1872 manifesto *Wissen ist Macht – Macht ist Wissen* is sometimes cited in an abbreviated form, i.e. as 'knowledge is power'. But the main thrust of Liebknecht's work was to reject the confinement of workers' organisation to educational associations and to press for more self-determining political organisations.¹¹ For all the emphasis on Social Democracy as a '*Kulturbewegung*', its organisational emancipation from liberal or bourgeois tutelage carried with it a determined emphasis on the 'primacy of politics'.¹² If the party used a plethora of cultural and leisure associations as camouflage during the period of the anti-socialist law, the principle of the primacy of the political struggle over educational or cultural activities was reasserted after 1890, with the adoption of the Erfurt Pro-

---

8   Lidtke 1985 (on the importance of language, see pp. 199–200). See also Groschopp 1985.
9   Geary 2000.
10 Hake 2017.
11 Liebknecht 1968.
12 Bonnell 2005, Ch. 2.

gramme. From time to time, party members continued to express reservations at the possibility that the party's cultural, educational, and sporting activities might be diverting time, energy and money from the more directly political struggle.[13]

This did not, however, prevent individual Social Democrats from continuing to seek further educational opportunities beyond the limited offerings of the state elementary school system, and from expressing an interest in getting a greater share of the cultural capital enjoyed by the German bourgeoisie. Thus, when members of the Freie Volksbühne had an opportunity to express their preferences for plays to be performed for the association, there was a request for 'something by Shakespeare' along with the then topical and controversial drama of the 1844 Silesian weavers' uprising, *Die Weber*, by Gerhart Hauptmann.[14] The workers' autobiographies discussed in Chapter 6, above, also testify to the desire for self-improvement and further education among their authors, but also among other organised workers with whom they came into contact. The steadily growing interest in the offerings of Berlin's Social Democratic Workers' Educational School (*Arbeiterbildungsschule*) also testifies to the desire of many organised workers (the school's chief constituency) for greater educational attainment (the number of those enrolled in the school increased from around 500 in the 1890s to over 2000 by 1907/08, with numbers fluctuating thereafter).[15] A workers' educational association *Vorwärts* was also founded in Munich, with similar objectives to the Berlin workers' school.[16] Following the 1906 Party Congress at Mannheim, the party created a Central Educational Commission to co-ordinate the party's educational activities.[17] By 1913, the Commission was able to report a broad palette of offerings across the country in the previous year, even if some party organisations still lacked their own local Educational Committees, with an emphasis on the delivery of lectures and educational courses (especially focussing on economics and 'scientific socialism'), for which it claimed over 44,000 participants nationally, as well as supporting artistic, literary, and musical events, and 'festivals with an artistic programme', such as March, May, Youth, Summer, Autumn, Winter, Founding and Trade Union Festivals, as well as Marx Festivals and even Rousseau Festivals. All in all, the attendance at such festivals was estimated at

---

13   E.g. LAB, A Pr. Br. Rep. 30, Nr. 14139, Bl. 25, police report of 13 August 1892.
14   Bonnell 2005, p. 161.
15   Fricke 1987, Bd. 1, pp. 677–8, figures p. 678; Lidtke 1985, pp. 162–5; Eckl, Iwan, and Weipert 1982.
16   Hausenstein 1909.
17   Lidtke 1985, pp. 166–9.

over 225,000. Some party branches even reported cinema performances under the auspices of their educational programme.[18]

Lidtke has drawn attention to a survey the recently constituted Central Educational Commission sent out to party and trade union organisations, as well as a list of women organisers supplied by Ottilie Baader, in February 1907.[19] The response rate of 404 out of 1123 perhaps reflected the unevenly developed state of educational organisation across the party, although the Commission considered that at least the most important places had responded, with large cities furnishing the most detailed responses, and there was at least some representation from all parts of the country.[20] Because the responses came from party organisations, they were not directly representative of rank-and-file opinion, but they constituted interesting feedback nonetheless. Interestingly, more trade union organisations reported engaging in educational work, including provision of libraries, single lectures, lecture series, etc., than party bodies (with a high percentage of women activists also engaged in educational work).[21] Organisations experienced difficulty with getting suitable venues – beer halls and similar venues often insisted on serving alcohol during lectures or courses, which was considered disruptive.[22] There was a demand for assistance from the central commission in the form of more speakers in the fields of economics, history, and socialism, a result that was quite gratifying to the Central Educational Commission as a reflection of participating organisations' priorities, as well as a request for more guidance in the setting-up of libraries.[23] Some feedback did provide some insight into the mood of the rank and file: it was reported that difficulties facing educational work included the fact that under the current economic conditions, workers faced long hours and low pay, were tired and sought relaxation rather than educational activities, and other kinds of associational life afforded more apolitical kinds of distraction. Some

---

18 *Protokoll über die Verhandlungen des Parteitages der Sozialdemokratischen Partei Deutschlands*. Abgehalten zu Jena vom 14. bis 20. September 1913, Berlin, 1913, pp. 37–9 (1912 had been the bicentenary of the birth of Rousseau); for examples of the Commission's work, including model book lists for workers' libraries and courses given by travelling instructors (*Wanderredner*), see the material in LAB a. Pr. Br. Rep. 30, Nr. 9267.

19 Lidtke 1985, pp. 168–9. The summary of the survey results and other papers of the Central Educational Commission are in the International Institute for Social History (= IISH), Amsterdam, Vollmar Nachlass, 240 (unfoliated).

20 'Das Ergebnis der Umfrage', IISH, Vollmar Nachlass, 240, p. 1. Some other responses arrived too late to be counted.

21 'Das Ergebnis der Umfrage', IISH, Vollmar Nachlass, 240, p. 3.

22 'Das Ergebnis der Umfrage', IISH, Vollmar Nachlass, 240, p. 7.

23 'Das Ergebnis der Umfrage', IISH, Vollmar Nachlass, 240, pp. 8, 11.

of the responses did testify to a 'Bildungshunger' (hunger for education) of the workers, but stressed the need for lectures to be accessible and relevant: a few individual responses that were cited included: 'Good educational and entertaining lectures are very popular among workers' (Marktredwitz); 'More could be done in the way of history, science, socialism and trade unionism, these lectures are always well attended' (Neugersdorff); 'There should be more lectures on science, because most people still believe that God created the world' (Oberehnheim); and from Hamburg: 'The education that is given about socialism mustn't come across as if it has just blown in from the outside'. Women comrades complained about a lack of support so far, as well as difficulties with the police and overcoming the indifference of other women.[24]

Surviving records of the meetings of the Central Educational Commission reveal some tensions between the left Marxist majority on the commission (including its chair Heinrich Schulz, Franz Mehring, and Clara Zetkin) and the revisionist or reformist right (Eduard David and Georg von Vollmar).[25] Of particular note is an intervention by the veteran party leader August Bebel (who was also a member of the commission) in the debates. In response to arguments by Eduard David against prioritising topics relevant for agitation (as advocated by Zetkin), and favouring a more eclectic approach to the arts and other areas of knowledge, Bebel stated: 'The debate reminds him of debates in the Leipzig Workers' Educational Association 46 years ago. We have to guard against a certain danger now as then, of fetishising education for its own sake [*Bildungssimpelei*]'.[26] The workers' hunger for education was a positive factor, but as in the 1860s and early 1870s, the primacy of the political struggle was necessary to avoid dissipating the energy of the workers' movement.

In addition to meeting workers' hunger for knowledge and cultural experiences, the party's organisational life also met the needs of providing regular occasions for sociability – between men, for men and women, and for families. In addition to the monthly party branch meetings usually held in pubs, where members were to pay their dues, or the larger meetings in halls with lectures of an agitational or educational kind, the local party organisations also had their annual round of festive occasions, as listed above by the Central Educational Commission: there were New Year's Festivals, Spring Festivals (which could coincide with an Easter holiday and/or the revolution-tinged March Festivals), May Day Festivals, Summer Festivals, usually in July, Lassalle Festivals

---

24   'Das Ergebnis der Umfrage', IISH, Vollmar Nachlass, 240, p. 10.
25   In IISH, Vollmar Nachlass, 3494 (unfoliated). Summarised in Lidtke 1985, pp. 168–9.
26   IISH, Vollmar Nachlass, 3494, Protokoll über die zweite Sitzung des Bildungsausschusses am 24. Juni 1907, p. 6.

in late August (although these were of decreasing importance after 1900, see Chapter 1), Autumn Festivals, Winter Festivals (sometimes coinciding with a Christmas holiday) and Founding-Day Festivals. There were also sometimes *Wald-Feste* – woods festivals, involving open-air excursions in the environs of the city. As Lidtke comments, 'Festivals were also family affairs', and as such they 'offered something for everyone' and increasingly offered a very varied programme of entertainments and activities.[27] If the male-centred (but not exclusively male) environment of the pub was the site of much of the regular activity of the Social Democratic Party, the weekend daytime festival (even if the venue was still a beer hall and its beer garden) was meant to be welcoming to both sexes. The value of combining agitation with opportunities for members to socialise with each other seems to have been appreciated by the leaders of party organisations, for example, the executive of Berlin's Wahlverein for the city's Sixth electoral district reported to a general meeting in 1907 that the association's Sunday meetings 'not only had an agitational value, but were also an occasion for sociability'.[28]

Daytime festivals (usually on Sundays, the only free day in the week for most workers) sometimes took the form of a 'matinee', starting around midday, and might be attended by more women and children than by men. Halls may or may not have been decorated 'in a Social Democratic manner', with red flags, busts of Marx and Lassalle, banners with socialist slogans, etc., depending in part on the arrangements with the hall's proprietors. Programmes for matinees tended to emphasise light entertainment: songs, operetta music, short comic plays or farces, gymnastic performances, comedy routines, and so on.[29] Sometimes, as the festivals grew larger and more sophisticated, they might even include a cinematographic show of some kind.[30] Often, the musical programmes did include the occasional socialist song among the light entertainment (especially when Social Democratic choirs took part), and often party festivals would

---

27   Lidtke 1985, pp. 78, 79. This chapter (Chapter 4) presents an excellent description of Social Democratic festival culture.

28   LAB A Pr. Br. Rep. 30, Nr. 14151, Bl. 13–14, police report of 13 February 1907.

29   E.g. LAB A Pr. Br. Rep. 30, Nr. 14139 (Berlin's First electoral district), Bl. 78, police report of 12 April 1898: '2,500 persons present, predominantly women and children'. References in this chapter to 'electoral districts' refer to Reichstag electorates.

30   E.g. LAB A Pr. Br. Rep. 30, Nr. 14140, Bl. 204–7 (summer festival of the Second electoral district in the Bocksbrauerei, Tempelhofer Berg, 11 September 1904); LAB A Pr. Br. Rep. 30, Nr. 14141, Bl. 76, *Volksfest* of the Second district, 8 September 1906. Short films included natural history topics such as 'How sardines are caught at sea', 'The wonderful chaotic world of bees', and 'A Sunday afternoon excursion to Moscow'; LAB A Pr. Br. Rep. 30, Nr. 14141, Bl. 214–15, *Volksfest* of 8 September 1907.

include a short address by a party leader.³¹ Heinrich Schulz, chairman of the Central Educational Commission and member of the party's Marxist Left wing, took the opportunity of his address at a Winter Festival in Berlin's Third electoral district on 26 December 1907 of pointing out the origins of Christmas as the Germanic winter solstice festival: 'Thus we also wish to celebrate Christmas, not for religious reasons and folding our hands in prayer, but by putting on artistic performances, for the purpose of education for socialist ideas'.³² However, given the legal prohibition against the participation of minors (and, before 1908, of women) in political activities, organisers of such festivities generally had to be somewhat circumspect about the overtly political character of the programming. At some festivals, party members took advantage of the gathering of like-minded comrades to collect money for elections or for other purposes, such as supporting the youth organisation, or assistance for striking workers. Sometimes Social Democratic pamphlets would also be offered for sale.³³ Selling party badges, pictures of party leaders, and other memorabilia also occurred at festivals, but could be hazardous – police once arrested dozens of such traders for selling goods without a trader's licence.³⁴

The party's festivals grew larger as membership growth accelerated after about 1905, and they also became less inhibited in their expression of political views. A summer festival in Berlin's Fourth electoral district in 1909 was attended by some 6,000 people, and numbers could reach 10,000 or more from that time on. In addition to the usual variety programme, visitors were treated to an 'exhibition' called 'Sights from the Three-Class Parliament'. As well as portraits of Chancellor Bülow and other establishment figures, which were subject to an ironic commentary from a 'guide' to the exhibition, exhibits included pictures of undercover police spies who had been unmasked by the party, the so-called '*Spitzelalbum*', or informers' album.³⁵

There would also often be dancing at the end of a day's festivities. This opportunity for socialising between men and women, in the evening, after the formal part of the programme, and after any children had been sent home, was clearly

---

31   E.g. at the 1906 autumn festival of the First electoral district, Karl Liebknecht gave an address. LAB A Pr. Br. Rep. 30, Nr. 14141, Bl. 158 (report of 16 October 1905).
32   LAB A Pr. Br. Rep. 30, Nr. 14144, Bl. 175.
33   LAB A Pr. Br. Rep. 30, Nr. 14144, Bl. 308, summer festival of Berlin's Third electoral district in the 'Neue Welt', Hasenheide, 24 July 1909; Nr. 14145, Bl. 56, celebration of Fourth Berlin electoral district, 16 December 1893.
34   LAB A Pr. Br. Rep. 30, Nr. 14145, Bl. 92: clipping from *Vorwärts*, 240, 13 October 1895; Nr. 14147, Bl. 200, 201: matinee of Fourth Berlin electoral district, 19 April 1908, and Bl. 207, concert on 8 June 1908.
35   LAB A Pr. Br. Rep. 30, Nr. 14148, Bl. 162, report of 4 July 1909.

popular. One party branch complained in its response to the Central Educational Commission's survey of 1907 that whenever tickets for an event went on sale, people would ask if there was to be dancing.[36] Sometimes it was noted that the gender balance of attendees changed in the course of the day, with more women and children during the daytime, but more equal numbers of men and women during the evening, for the dancing. Thus at a Summer Festival of the Second electoral district in the Berliner Bock-Brauerei in 1909, only about 10 men attended the start of the festival along with about 200 women, but after 7pm there were around 250–300 women and 250 men. 'Most of those present were married and brought their children with them'.[37] Sometimes men arriving late for the dancing would have to pay an extra 50 Pfennigs admission.[38] With dancing, the festivities could continue well into the morning, sometimes even to past 5am.[39] The ratio of women participating in these weekend festival activities was much higher than the ten per cent or so more typical of more formal party meetings, reaching parity with the men or better.

Among the cultural organisations of the Social Democratic Party, the Freie Volksbühne was notable for the fact that its membership also contained a rough parity of male and female members. Going to the theatre as a couple was made affordable by the relatively low subscription costs for the association compared with bourgeois theatres. The Sunday afternoon performances also made childcare arrangements easier for working parents than evening shows might have been, while some married party members joined separate sections to enable one partner to look after children while the other attended performaces.[40] The gender composition and membership growth of this association indicates that the theatrical organisation combined cultural activity with opportunities for sociability that were well received.

Children were catered for specifically by the inclusion of children's games on the programme, or such entertainments as puppet theatres (also facilitating the participation of their mothers, freeing them from childcare duties at home).[41] The Conservative press looked askance at the fact that children were being exposed to anti-monarchist and unpatriotic socialist influences in

---

36 IISH, Vollmar Nachlass, 240, p. 9.
37 LAB A Pr. Br. Rep. 30, Nr. 14142, Bl. 201.
38 LAB A Pr. Br. Rep. 30, Nr. 14141, Bl. 76.
39 LAB A Pr. Br. Rep. 30, Nr. 14143, Bl. 138, Foundation festival of Berlin's Third electoral district, 13 January 1900.
40 Selo 1930, p. 161.
41 E.g. LAB A Pr. Br. Rep. 30, Nr. 14142, Bl. 99–102, *Volksfest* of Second Berlin electoral district, 6 September 1908; Nr. 14145, Bl. 84–6: Woods festival of Fourth Berlin electoral district, 24 June 1895, Friedrichshagen.

these setting. One hostile description from the *Neue Preussische Zeitung* (better known as the *Kreuzzeitung* after the Iron Cross that adorned its masthead), described a game at an 1895 Berlin festival in which contestants could win a medallion 'with the picture of some Social Democratic prophet or idol on it' if they passed a 'lung-test' by blowing into a machine. According to the *Kreuzzeitung* journalist, a small boy cried out: 'I want a Kaiser, too!', only to be gruffly chided by his father (in working-class Berlin dialect): '*Kaiser jiebt es nich, höchstens Lassalle oder Singer!*' ('There aren't any Kaisers here, at most you get Lassalle or Singer!')[42] It was entirely characteristic of the coverage of Social Democracy by the Conservative *Kreuzzeitung* and the 'Free Conservative' newspaper *Post* that their hostility towards socialism was tinged with antisemitism – the paper singled out two Jewish Social Democrats as the rivals to the Kaiser, rather than, for example, Bebel or Wilhelm Liebknecht.

From about 1902, the practice began of presenting children who attended the larger Social Democratic festivals in Berlin with a free red lantern on a stick. The lanterns were decorated with a picture of Marx, Engels, Lassalle, Bebel or of other Social Democratic leaders, and inscriptions such as 'Liberty, Equality, Fraternity', or 'Workers of the World Unite', and all the children present had the chance to take part in a lantern parade at the end of the day.[43]

At a People's and Children's Festival in the Fourth electoral district of Berlin in summer 1909, most of the participants were women and children, and there were games for girls organised by the female members of the Social Democratic Gymnastics Association 'Fichte'. The garden was 'richly decorated with red flags in the Social Democratic manner', and the party slogans on display included 'Equal Duties, Equal Rights', suggesting an emphasis on equality for women, which the daughters of Social Democrats were to be instructed in from an early age.[44]

Special activities for children were sometimes organised outside of the big party festival days. One section of the Second Berlin electoral district put on an entertainment specifically for the children of the precinct: '*Nebelbilder*', or 'fog pictures' were projected onto a screen. The event did not escape police

---

42 LAB A Pr. Br. Rep. 30, Nr. 14145, Bl. 80: clipping from *Neue Preussische Zeitung*, 291, 24 June 1895: 'Sozialdemokratisches Sonntagsfest' (cited words underlined in green pencil by the police).

43 E.g. LAB A Pr. Br. Rep. 30, Nr. 14146, Bl. 6, 10–11: summer festival of the Fourth Berlin electoral district, 13 July 1902; LAB A Pr. Br. Rep. 30, Nr. 14146, Bl. 82: summer festival, 13 August 1905; Nr. 14147, Bl. 18: summer festival of Fourth electoral district, 28 July 1907, and Bl. 221–8 and 232–4, summer festival, 12 July 1908; Nr. 14149, Bl. 20, summer festival of Fourth electoral district, 3 July 1909.

44 LAB A Pr. Br. Rep. 30, Nr. 14148, Bl. 184–5, Festival of 26 July 1909.

surveillance: the police report counted 50 children (for whom admission was free), 13 women and 20 men (including known party members) in attendance. The police reported further, with their customary solemnity, that the show was not 'conducted in a Social Democratic sense', with pictures including motifs such as 'fox and goose, Little Red Riding Hood, Robinson [...] and other fairy stories'.[45] In Saxony, the authorities became concerned at reports of subversive conduct under the guise of festivals for children, given the prohibition on minors' involvement in political activities, and in 1894 the Saxon Interior Ministry instructed all regional administrators to refuse permission to any political events in the guise of children's festivals.[46] When Leipzig's Social Democrats then wanted to include a lantern procession for children (called a *Fackelpolonaise*) in a *Lassalle-Feier* in Stötteritz in Leipzig, in 1894, they were informed that they had to seek the permission of the local school inspectorate if school-age children were to take part, which was refused.[47]

Social Democratic festivals and cultural activities also provided party members with organisational experience, especially as festivals grew to encompass crowds of several thousand people, often taking place in a number of different venues simultaneously. A standard feature of these events was the presence of stewards (*Ordner*) or members of the festival's organising committee officiating, wearing red rosettes, carnations, or ribbons. For a day, the party members enjoyed a measure of authority in their own sphere, a foretaste of a democratic future state. Stewards would collect tickets, generally keep order, and would sometimes warn off uniformed members of the military, in the interests of the latter to preserve them from prosecution.[48] It was also recorded that at a summer festival of Berlin's Fourth electoral district in 1909 a steward informed the guests as to which waiters were 'not organised', presumably so that party members could boycott non-union labour and support unionised comrades instead.[49]

---

45 LAB A Pr. Br. Rep. 30, Nr. 14140, Bl. 25, report of 11 December 1905.
46 Sächsisches Hauptstaatsarchiv Dresden, 10736, Bl. 304–5, Ministerium des Innern, 10989/2, v. Metzsch, Ministerium des Innern an sämtliche Kreishauptmannschaften, 12 July 1894.
47 Announcement in *Der Wähler* (Leipzig), 198, 28 August 1894, in Sächsisches Staatsarchiv Leipzig, 20028 Amtshauptmannschaft Leipzig, 2718, and in the same file Bl. 12, Richard Lipinski to Bezirksschulinspektion Leipzig II, 30 August 1894, and Bl. 44–5, Lipinski to Kreishauptmannschaft Leipzig, 18 September 1894.
48 LAB A Pr. Br. Rep. 30, Nr. 14139 (Berlin's First electoral district), Bl. 78, police report of 12 April 1898.
49 LAB A Pr. Br. Rep. 30, Nr. 14149, Bl. 162, summer festival of Fourth Berlin electoral district, 3 July 1909.

Such organisational experience was not confined to one-day festivals. Larger Social Democratic cultural organisations like the Freie Volksbühne also sought to implement a degree of internal democracy in their statutes, and as the organisations expanded, they created a cadre of functionaries who took on roles such as *Ordner* (stewards) on an ongoing basis, and who had clearly defined responsibilities and at least some voice in the running of the organisation.[50] While the development of cadres of functionaries in such organisations can be viewed critically as conducive to bureaucratisation (as in Robert Michels' view of the Social Democratic Party's evolution), it also gave workers experience of exercising responsibility in a larger collective undertaking, built their capacity, and gave them experience of internal democratic structures. These were intangible but not negligible benefits given the authoritarian nature of the Imperial German state within which these organisations operated.

As far as the content of Social Democratic festivals was concerned: if one constraint on the programme was the need to entertain a diverse audience, often including whole families, another constraint was official censorship, which was especially watchful when women and minors were present. A number of festival presentations in the early to mid-1890s fell foul of the authorities in Berlin: a series of '*tableaux vivants*' on the theme of the French Revolution (by the playwright known as 'C.M. Scävola') was banned in January 1893 when it was planned for inclusion in a festival of the Berlin *Arbeiter-Bildungsschule*.[51] A couple of years later, a 'political-satirical puppet show' that was to feature in a summer festival of the same school was heavily censored before permission was given to perform it.[52] The Freie Volksbühne struggled with the police censorship of theatre, despite its attempt to evade censorship by claiming to be a private association. The difficulties with censorship were a prime motive for Franz Mehring's decision in 1895 to wind up the association, although it was subsequently re-opened in 1897 under a different leadership.[53]

Over time, however, Social Democratic festivals were able to smuggle more and more political and satirical material into their variety programmes, especially following the partial liberalisation of the laws of association in 1908. One of the most notable exponents of topical satire in a variety entertain-

---

50   Chung 1989, pp. 115, 132–44.
51   *Vorwärts*, 19, 22 January 1893, p. 1, Beilage.
52   *Vorwärts*, 183, 8 August 1895, p. 2, Beilage; *Vorwärts*, 213, 12 September 1895. For another case involving censorship of puppet theatres, see *Vorwärts*, 107, 10 May 1902.
53   Bonnell 2005, pp. 172–4.

ment format was the troupe of Boleslaw Strzelewicz.[54] The Berlin political police noted the Strzelewicz Company's appearance (in the form of a trio of performers, two men and a woman) at a festival of the Fourth electoral district in December 1893. The theme of the performance was a critical view of militarism, which 'was received by the comrades with great applause'.[55] The Strzelewicz Company (previously also known as 'Gesellschaft Vorwärts') seems to have enjoyed a higher profile after 1906, however. The Company featured in a matinee of the Fourth Berlin electoral district in April 1906, at which the programme included numerous satirical items, with titles like 'All wheels will stand still', a poem (referring to the well-known strikers' motto: 'All wheels will stand still, if it is your powerful will'), and 'Pictures from the Well-Ordered State', which included the scenes: 'in the factory', 'in court', and 'And more and more soldiers'. The police noted that there were also some improvisations after some of the items on the programme, which included attacks on the Reich Chancellor and the Minister for Agriculture. The police summed up the programme as 'very much taking liberties in regards to politics, and some items received very strong applause'.[56] A simultaneous matinee of the Fourth district, held on the same day but in a different venue, also included some political satire, with poetic recitations on topics such as 'The Berlin Police Swamp', satirising recently uncovered police spies, and other poems treating Prussia's Three-Class Franchise and the topic of modern war.[57] At a Foundation Festival held by the Fourth district in 1908, the Strzelewicz Company again 'performed pieces which took great liberties'. One member of the company played the role of a carpenter who featured in the Social Democratic illustrated magazine *Der Wahre Jakob*, passing comments on current political events, concluding by calling on the women present to join the party organisation (which had just been legalised by the reform to the laws of association).[58] In March 1910, members of the party in the Fourth electoral district 'followed with quite particular interest' performances by Strzelewicz's Company of sketches on 'The Black-Blue Schnaps-Bloc' (attacking the coalition of conservatives and Centre party responsible for indirect tax increases), 'German "Cultural" Types', and

---

54 On Strzelewicz and his troupe, see Knilli and Münchow 1970, pp. 319–38 (including some original Strzelewicz texts); Rüden 1973, pp. 100–6. See also the selection of materal in Strzelewicz n.d. (a numbered series of booklets).
55 LAB A Pr. Br. Rep. 30, Nr. 14145, Bl. 56, police report of 17 December 1893.
56 LAB A Pr. Br. Rep. 30, Nr. 14146, Bl. 129, report on matinee of the Fourth Berlin electoral district, 15 April 1906.
57 Ibid, Bl. 130–1.
58 LAB A Pr. Br. Rep. 30, Nr. 14148, Bl. 7–8, festival of 15 November 1908.

'That's How it's Done', on the practices of the police.⁵⁹ The company engaged in direct agitation along with their entertainment again in the same Berlin electoral district in 1910, at the party organisation's Christmas matinee, where they recited verses satirising the most recent political events, and also conducted propaganda for the campaign to leave the state church, as well as recruiting for the party.⁶⁰ If the Strzelewicz Company liked to push the boundaries of what the police would allow them to get away with, they did not always do so with impunity. At another event in 1910, when the Company sang their political parody version of the Christmas carol 'Silent Night' (*Stille Nacht*), which turned it into an attack on poverty and the exploitation of workers, the police stepped in and arrested Strzelewicz on the stage.⁶¹ There was no doubting the popularity of the Strzelewicz Company among the Social Democratic rank and file. They toured widely around the country, and even in the sleepy and conservative province of Oldenburg the local party organisation reported that the Strzelewicz troupe were the only cultural activity that always enjoyed a full house there.⁶²

The Strzelewicz Company were not the only performers of satirical recitations or songs at Social Democratic festivals. In April 1907, the Easter matinee of the Sixth Berlin electoral district, held in the Kronen-Brauerei in Moabit, were entertained by an unnamed singing duo, whose song 'African Heroes', which constituted a 'sharp attack on our colonies', was received with 'great applause'.⁶³ At the same time, the 'Berliner Ulk-Trio' entertained other members of the Sixth district at a venue in the Badstrasse, Wedding, also in the working-class northern suburbs of Berlin.⁶⁴ The humorous Ulk-Trio (*Ulk* meaning a joke, prank, or lark), reciting verses and singing in a similar vein to the Strzelewicz Company, became a regular feature of Berlin party festivals, including the overtly political May Day festivals.⁶⁵ Police noted that the recitations and songs of the Ulk-Trio

---

59   LAB A Pr. Br. Rep. 30, Nr. 14148, Bl. 324, 327, matinee of 27 March 1910.
60   LAB A Pr. Br. Rep. 30, Nr. 14149, Bl. 183, matinee of 26 December 1910.
61   According to an account cited in Rüden 1973, pp. 103–4. Strzelewicz was also sentenced to a month in prison in 1904, for insulting religion, and to a further two months in 1910 for blasphemy, in each case on the basis of one his self-published texts. *Vorwärts*, 222, 21 September 1904, p. 4, Beilage, and 6, 8 January 1910. A planned Strzelewicz performance in the trade union hall in Breslau was banned ostensibly on the grounds of licensing regulations. *Vorwärts*, 95, 24 April 1912.
62   Rüden 1973, p. 104; IISH, Vollmar Nachlass, 'Das Ergebnis der Umfrage', p. 9.
63   LAB A Pr. Br. Rep. 30, Nr. 14151, Bl. 59, matinee of 1 April 1907. On Social Democratic responses to the war in South-West Africa, see Bonnell 2018.
64   LAB A Pr. Br. Rep. 30, Nr. 14151, Bl. 71–2, matinee of 1 April 1907.
65   E.g. LAB A Pr. Br. Rep. 30, Nr. 14151, Bl. 147–9, summer festival of the Sixth Berlin electoral district, 14 July 1907, along with the Workers' Bicyclists' League *Solidarität*; the Free Gym-

uniformly 'gave expression to Social Democratic views', sometimes touching on current political events.[66] In 1910, the current political allusions included satirical comments on Chancellor Bethmann Hollweg's unsuccessful proposal to reform the Prussian franchise, the Prussian Junkers, the Berlin Police President, and the notorious comment by a German Conservative leader that at any time a lieutenant and 10 men should be able to close down the German Reichstag.[67] The political songs of the Ulk-Trio sometimes took up the theme of how long-suffering the German 'Michel' – the proverbially mild-mannered German Everyman, typically portrayed wearing a nightcap – was in the face of the behaviour of Germany's government.[68] The German 'Michel' was also the subject of a short play at another festival at which other artists performed in 1908: the German Michel was presented as a peasant, whose role it was to pay taxes, serve as a soldier, but otherwise keep his mouth shut and not grumble.[69]

Other satirists also featured in Social Democratic festivals, along with short plays or skits with a political point. In April 1907, a matinee in Berlin's Sixth electoral district featured the 'soubrette' Lilly Schumann and the 'humorist' B. Bogdanowitz. The political police were prompted by this appearance to look into Bogdanowitz's background and discovered that he was a 'convinced Social Democrat'.[70] Schumann sang a piece dedicated to the party newspaper *Vorwärts*, making negative comments about pro-government newspapers and presenting *Vorwärts* as the only paper that stood up for the interests of the proletariat. The matinee programme also included a short one-act play called 'The Strike Leader', featuring the characters of the honest unionist Franz Stand and a secret policeman called Schnüffel (Snoop). The action of the play was described as follows: 'stalwart worker resists the demands of the capitalist magnate and kicks out a secret policeman sent to spy on him'. At the end of the day, proceedings closed with the 'Workers' *Marseillaise*'.[71] Skits at the expense of the

---

nasts, and the Workers' Singers' League; LAB A Pr. Br. Rep. 30, Nr. 14148, Bl. 256, report on foundation festival of the Fourth Berlin electoral district, 14 November 1909; LAB A Pr. Br. Rep. 30, Nr. 14153, Bl. 99–102, May Day celebration in the Sixth electoral district.

66 LAB A Pr. Br. Rep. 30, Nr. 14152, Bl. 3, Christmas matinee of the Sixth Berlin electoral district, 26 December 1907; LAB A Pr. Br. Rep. 30, Nr. 14152, Bl. 73, matinee in Sixth electoral district, 20 April 1908.
67 LAB A Pr. Br. Rep. 30, Nr. 14148, Bl. 305, concert in Fourth electoral district, 20 February 1910; LAB A Pr. Br. Rep. 30, Nr. 14148, Bl. 320–3, matinee on 27 March 1910.
68 LAB A Pr. Br. Rep. 30, Nr. 14152, Bl. 96, concert on 8 June 1908 in Badstrasse, Wedding.
69 LAB A Pr. Br. Rep. 30, Nr. 14152, Bl. 84–6, matinee in Sixth electoral district, 20 April 1908.
70 LAB A Pr. Br. Rep. 30, Nr. 14151, Bl. 105–8, 115–17.
71 LAB A Pr. Br. Rep. 30, Nr. 14151, Bl. 105–8.

political police were popular. In a festival in Moabit in 1909, a one-act farce called 'Fallen for it, or: The Police Informer Tricked' by H. Lewandowsky was performed, with characters including the sturdy worker Fritz Kraft (= strength) and a police agent called Hieronymous Strohkopf (= head of straw).[72]

Another humorous act, 'Die lustigen Brüder' ('The Merry Brothers') contributed their politically satirical songs and skits to a matinee in Moabit's Kronen-Brauerei in April 1908, which also featured a short play based on the lives of workers, including a labour dispute between an honest worker (called Treu = faithful, loyal) and a businessman. The songs again also included the 'Workers' Marseillaise'.[73] Lilly Schumann and the *lustige Brüder* both featured in a concert held for the comrades of the Sixth electoral district in the same venue, the Kronen-Brauerei, in June 1908. Some verses alluding 'in a derogatory fashion' to the recent scandal around Prince Philipp Eulenburg (a close confidant of the Kaiser who became embroiled in court cases over allegations of homosexuality) were added to the programme, and were 'received with great enthusiasm on the part of the comrades'.[74] There were also some digs at the monarchy in the 'Artistic Evening' put on by a section of the party organisation in the Sixth electoral district in the *'Germania-Säle'* in the Chausseestrasse in September 1908, the humorous recital by Max Laurence querying the expenses of Kaiser Wilhelm II's amateur archaeological project on the island of Corfu as well as making fun of the education of the Prince August Wilhelm (both satirical pieces on the monarchy were received with conspicuous enthusiasm by the listeners, according to the police report).[75]

Attacks on German colonial policy featured in another satirical presentation, by the humorist Paul Krajewski at Easter 1909. Playing a missionary in South-West Africa, he brandished a cardboard box resembling a Bible with a golden cross on the cover, then removed from his 'Bible' a whip and a revolver – the means by which he planned 'to save the souls of the Negroes'. This anti-colonial (and anti-clerical) skit was 'particularly loudly applauded'.[76] Another somewhat drastic satire on the German army's repression of rebellious African subjects was written by the humorist H. Lewandowsky, who performed in Berlin Social Democratic festivals. His sketch 'African Idyll, or How Wars Begin' told

---

72   LAB A Pr. Br. Rep. 30, Nr. 14153, Bl. 82–4, matinee of 12 April 1909.
73   LAB A Pr. Br. Rep. 30, Nr. 14151, Bl. 67, matinee of 20 April 1908.
74   LAB A Pr. Br. Rep. 30, Nr. 14152, Bl. 93, 95, concert of 8 June 1908. On the Eulenburg affair, and the role of the Social Democratic press in reporting on it, see Kohlrauch 2005, pp. 186–243; Hall 1977, pp. 164–7.
75   LAB A Pr. Br. Rep. 30, Nr. 14152, Bl. 163–5, report on 'Kunstabend', 12 September 1908.
76   LAB A Pr. Br. Rep. 30, Nr. 14152, Bl. 70, matinee in Sixth electoral district, 12 April 1909.

the tale of a Lieutenant von Schnodderich, whose advances are rejected by an African woman, after which he orders his troops to conduct a massacre.[77]

Another comedian, Max Schneltzer, performed for the comrades in Wedding at Christmas 1908, reciting a number of political verses, which targeted 'the present government, the Reichstag, the Prussian Landtag, the Reich Chancellor and the current social order', at the same time as he presented the Social Democratic Party as the 'only true representatives of the welfare of the people and of justice', calling on his listeners to join the 'iron organisation for freedom and justice', as the 'red brothers were under attack'.[78] Sometimes humorists could test the limits of the permissible in terms of morality as well as politics: a police report found the humorist Willy Meibryck's verse 'couplets' to be 'questionable in relation to politics as well as to morality'.[79] The latter type of verses could arouse the ire of Social Democratic Party organisers as well as of the police. Some leaders of the party organisation in Berlin's Sixth district around this time complained that some humorous recitations in the variety programme of recent festivals had contained 'smutty' verses, which were not appropriate for a people's festival (frequently attended by families), and it was resolved that the owners of venues should be advised accordingly (suggesting that at some venues, artists were engaged by the venue owners rather than by the party organisation). Interestingly the same meeting of district party leaders expressed interest in 'tableaux vivants', provided the police did not ban them on grounds of incitement to class hatred, indicating that there was still a strong sense of the bounds that could be imposed by political censorship despite the number of satirical declamations and recitations that were put on.[80]

If most of the music performed at Social Democratic workers' festivals was intended to entertain, music was also frequently used to express political identity and promote a feeling of solidarity among the audience, as the references to the playing of the 'Workers' *Marseillaise*' may have already indicated. The several Social Democratic singing clubs and choirs usually included rousing tunes from the labour movement's own repertoire among their other songs. For example, the socialist singing club '*Nordwacht*' performed at a number of Social Democratic festivals, and would finish with the 'Workers' *Marseillaise*'.[81] The

---

77 LAB A Pr. Br. Rep. 30, Nr. 14153, Bl. 89–90, police report of 13 April 1909.
78 LAB A Pr. Br. Rep. 30, Nr. 14152, Bl. 242.
79 LAB A Pr. Br. Rep. 30, Nr. 14151, Bl. 37–8, foundation festival of Sixth electoral district, 16 March 1907.
80 LAB A Pr. Br. Rep. 30, Nr. 14151, Bl. 89, police report of 19 April 1907.
81 E.g. LAB A Pr. Br. Rep. 30, Nr. 14152, Bl. 73–4, matinee of 20 April 1908 in Sixth electoral district.

'Nordwacht' also sang songs such as 'Die Freiheit habe ich mir erkoren' ('The freedom I have chosen'), 'Es beginnt die Frühlingszeit' ('Springtime is beginning'), and 'Der Wandersbursch' ['The travelling journeyman'], all of which could be understood to carry socialist connotations.[82] A 'Symphony Concert' for the Social Democratic Party members of the Fourth Berlin electoral district, attended by some 1,200 people, included the overture 'Robespierre' by Henry Litolff. This piece incorporated a rendition of the *Marseillaise*, which 'received thunderous applause'. The concert also included readings by a *Rezitator* called Stripp, which, according to the police report, 'had a revolutionary character and were therefore received with thunderous applause' as well.[83] The *Marseillaise*, and its version with a German text, was enduringly popular among Social Democrats, being regularly included in concerts and festival programmes. Members of the party organisation for the Sixth electoral district saw in the New Year of 1908 singing the 'Workers' *Marseillaise*' at their New Year's Eve celebration, which also included other socialist songs from the singing club 'Freiheit Nord' (Freedom North), humorous recitals, also of a political complexion, and dancing.[84] Song sheets for sale at these festivals included the 'Workers' *Marseillaise*', 'Prussian Christmas Carol', 'The Song of Labour', 'The Proletarians' Son', 'What is a Socialist?', Max Kegel's 'March of the Socialists', and others.[85]

By 1913, the District Educational Commission of the Greater Berlin Social Democratic Party organisations felt the need to issue printed guidelines for educational work, including a set of model festival programmes. The Commission complained that the planning of festivals in the recent past had been too haphazard, lacking a clear cultural or educational goal. Festivals had tried to do too much at once: 'an artistic evening was supposed to provide the participants with both entertainment and instruction, there was to be dancing, and finally, a surplus was also to be realised'. Of course, the Educational Commission conceded,

> the *need for entertainment and the need for education* of party members had to be accommodated by the educational committees and the party

---

82   LAB A Pr. Br. Rep. 30, Nr. 14152, Bl. 6, matinee of 26 December 1907 in Sixth electoral district.
83   LAB A Pr. Br. Rep. 30, Nr. 14146, Bl. 280–2, concert of 17 March 1907.
84   LAB A Pr. Br. Rep. 30, Nr. 14152, Bl. 13; see also LAB A Pr. Br. Rep. 30, Nr. 14152, Bl. 59–60, for a performance of Jakob Audorf's version of the *Marseillaise* at the foundation festival of the Sixth electoral district, 14 March 1908; LAB A Pr. Br. Rep. 30, Nr. 14148, Bl. 151, concert in Fourth electoral district, in Viktoriagarten, Treptow, 31 May 1909, finishing with the *Arbeitermarseillaise*.
85   LAB A Pr. Br. Rep. 30, Nr. 14152, Bl. 80–3, report on matinee of 20 April 1908, in Badstrasse, Wedding.

executive bodies as far as possible. The proletarian above all others has the right to a few hours of cheerful sociability. [...] Organised workers, however, who are led by an earnest conviction in all their life and thought, have to apply another measure to their pleasures and entertainments than the dull-minded mass lacking any convictions.[86]

The Educational Commission also criticised the common practice of taking children to 'artistic evenings', even though it acknowledged that parents were often doing it to avoid leaving them unsupervised at home. Instead, the Commission advocated the planning of more carefully designed events specifically for children.[87] Reading hundreds of reports of Social Democratic festivities, it is possible to see how the Educational Commission arrived at its conclusions. Much of the cultural fodder on offer at festivals differed little from the commercial mass culture which socialist intellectuals regarded with intense suspicion as products of capitalist profit-seeking. In seeking the broadest possible audience for its products, the culture industry did not cultivate class-based collective identities, rather the contrary. Many of the entertainments on offer at festivals were run-of-the-mill vaudeville fare, like the notoriously corny English bourgeois farce *Charley's Aunt*.[88]

The eminent American historian of German Social Democracy, Vernon Lidtke, gave a rather more balanced verdict on Social Democratic festival culture than the earnest cultural pedagogues of the Greater Berlin District Educational Commission. Lidtke saw that festival planners 'recognised a need to set aside time that could be devoted exclusively to socialising and amusement for amusement's sake' at the same time as concerts and processions also attended to the work of communicating and symbolising socialist ideology. Lidtke argued that: 'Despite the increasing importance of performance and sociability, labour movement festivals never lost their political implications'.[89] One could add to Lidtke's analysis the extent to which, as festivals grew to 10,000 participants or more, while cultural and sporting organisations also grew to embrace many thousands of members, more and more rank-and-file party members were gaining valuable organisational experience, learning to exercise responsibility and the little authority bestowed by a red rosette or ribbon, and generally learned more about how to function as part of a large organisation and move-

---

86   Bezirksbildungsausschuss Gross-Berlin 1913, pp. 33–4. Model festival programmes are given, pp. 55–72.
87   Bezirksbildungsausschuss Gross-Berlin 1913, p. 35.
88   LAB A Pr. Br. Rep. 30, Nr. 14152, Bl. 225–7, Christmas matinee in Sixth electoral district, 1908.
89   Lidtke 1985, p. 100.

ment. Even in the large festivals in hired commercial premises in Berlin with untidy and crowded entertainment programmes, political messages were still conveyed to the audience, perhaps even increasingly so as performers kept testing the limits of police repression. At the same time, the experience of being in a space temporarily administered by party stewards, marked off from the bourgeois world outside by red flags and other party symbols, conveyed a foretaste of a socialist society, a feeling reinforced by the collective experience of singing familiar songs like the 'Workers' *Marseillaise*'. Lidtke sums it up well:

> festivals brought together diverse strands into living units that could be experienced by participants as coherent wholes. In a day's activities festivals brought together in one concentrated event many, of not all, of the ingredients of the socio-cultural world of the socialist labor movement. They contributed to the substance and especially to the image of the Social Democratic labor movement as a solid phalanx of enthusiastic followers with a well-integrated set of political principles and cultural values.[90]

Robert Michels saw the proliferation of associations under the umbrella of the Social Democratic labour movement as proof that 'the German worker had contracted the same disease that is endemic among our philistine petite bourgeoisie', namely '*Vereinsmeierei*', the obsession with clubs and associations:

> In the big cities, partly even in smaller towns, there is a veritable plethora of workers' gymnastic associations, workers' singing clubs, workers' theatre associations, even workers' smoking clubs, workers' bowling clubs, worker-regatta clubs, athletics associations, all activities that do not lose any of their innate petit bourgeois spirit from the fact that they sail under a Social Democratic flag. A Skat club is a Skat club, even if it calls itself 'Skat Club Freedom'![91]

The Berlin political police could not be as confident of this last statement as Michels was. In October 1898, a member of the political police monitoring Social Democratic activities in the city's Fourth electoral district reported having received 'confidential intelligence' (a formulation which invariably meant a tip-off from an informant or police spy) that in a certain pub, run by a Comrade

---

90   Lidtke 1985, p. 101.
91   Michels 1906, pp. 538–9. *Skat* is a popular German three-handed card game.

Erbe, the local organisers (*Vertrauensmänner*) and district group leaders from the South-East side of the district gathered every Thursday evening under the guise of a 'Skat Club *Tourney*' to talk over political matters and 'promote the closer cooperation of the leading party comrades of the 4th district (South-East)'.[92] The constable kept Erbe's pub and its suspicious Skat games under surveillance for a couple of months, without being able to come up with any more concrete, incriminating intelligence.[93]

Unfortunately, our sources here end up being inconclusive: was the Skat club in fact just a Skat club, as the constable eventually came to think? Did it serve a political purpose for the cadres in the South-East side party organisation in Berlin's Fourth electoral district? Or was it a double-bluff, a prank played on the police spies, whose presence was always suspected in socialist circles in the Reich capital, in order to confuse and distract them? This may seem far-fetched, but it would not have been the only time a Skat club was used as a ruse to deceive the police – in 1908, the political police discovered that a supposedly private Skat club in a pub in Berlin's Sixth electoral district was being used as a trick to get around police restrictions on the pub's opening hours, so that the comrades could continue their meetings after official closing time.[94] Sadly, it is now impossible for us to tell.

---

92   LAB, A Pr. Br. Rep. 30, Nr. 14145, Bl. 166: police report of 10 October 1898.
93   LAB, A Pr. Br. Rep. 30, Nr. 14145, Bl. 167–9.
94   LAB, A Pr. Br. Rep. 30, Nr. 14152, Bl. 31: police report of 13 February 1908.

CHAPTER 8

Socialism and Republicanism in Imperial Germany

In November 1918, German Social Democrats were suddenly confronted with the need to establish a new republican state order in Germany following the collapse of the Empire. In light of the difficulties Social Democrats experienced in founding a stable and viable republic in 1918–19, the question of their prior understanding of republicanism – including the importance attached to the issue within the party – merits closer attention. Theoretically, the Social Democratic Party in Imperial Germany was opposed in principle to the monarchical state. This opposition was manifested in a number of ways, such as refusing to take part in demonstrations of loyalty to the crown, in the Reichstag, for example, a policy that precluded Social Democrats from taking up a Vice-President's (i.e. Deputy Speaker's) position in the parliament when the party's numbers would have justified it. The demand that the German empire be transformed into a democratic republic, however, was generally muted in the party's public agitation. Robert Michels, during the time in which he identified with the left of the party, criticised it for placing too little emphasis on agitation for a republic: this he saw as 'a mistake, that may be half attributed to a certain degree of complacency in the party, but [...] equally to our monarchical institutions [themselves] with their rubbery law paragraphs on *lèse-majesté*'.[1] Perhaps it was a demonstration of the effectiveness of the latter that Michels published his own most trenchant critiques of the reign of Kaiser Wilhelm II in the relative safety of Italy, in Italian.[2] It is clear that the Social Democratic Party was, to some extent, constrained by the prevailing laws from making open attacks on the monarchy. Other reasons for this restraint could hypothetically include the possibility of residual monarchical sentiments among German workers, and the state of development of socialist state theory during the period of the Second International.

In early 1910, mass demonstrations in a number of German states demanded a reform of electoral systems. The campaign was particularly vigorous in Prussia, where the Social Democratic Party demanded the abolition of the highly discriminatory three-class franchise for the Prussian Landtag (state parliament). Rosa Luxemburg, writing in the Breslau Social Democratic paper *Die*

---

1   Robert Michels, 'Monarchie oder Republik?', *Frankfurter Volksstimme*, 213, 1904, reprinted in Michels 2008, pp. 103–6, here p. 103.
2   Michels 1908.

Volkswacht in March 1910, argued that it was necessary to go beyond the campaign for 'universal, equal, direct suffrage for all adults, without distinction of sex'. In order to step up the agitation, it was necessary to raise the demand for a republic, which she claimed constituted 'the first point in our programme'. 'Up to now the republican slogan has played a slight role in our agitation', Luxemburg stated, which was justified in so far as the working class needed to realise that 'the best bourgeois republic is no less a class state and bulwark of capitalist exploitation than a contemporary monarchy'.[3] In the prevailing political circumstances, however, Luxemburg suggested:

> Through the emphasis on the republican character of Social Democracy, we gain above all one more opportunity to illustrate our opposition in principle as a class party of the proletariat to the united camp of bourgeois democrats in a tangible, popular manner. The appalling decline of bourgeois liberalism in Germany is after all expressed particularly drastically, *inter alia*, in the Byzantinism in the face of the monarchy, in which the liberal bourgeoisie outdoes even the conservative Junkers.[4]

Luxemburg subsequently attempted to publish her demand for openly republican agitation, along with her views on the debate over the political mass strike, in the central theoretical journal of the party *Die Neue Zeit*, only to have the passages dealing with the republic knocked back by its editor, Karl Kautsky. Kautsky objected that the party programme did not actually mention the word republic, and that Luxemburg should not take it upon herself to open up such a major subject for agitation on her own initiative. Furthermore, Kautsky wrote, '[t]his new agitation is ... such that it is not suitable for public discussion'.[5]

Kautsky was technically correct in asserting, *contra* Luxemburg, that the party programme did not explicitly mention the party's republican objective. The first point of the party's 1891 Erfurt Programme contained a set of demands which would have amounted to a significantly more democratic political system: universal adult suffrage (above the age of 20), including female suffrage,

---

3   Luxemburg, 'Zeit der Aussaat', originally in *Volkswacht* (Breslau), 71, 25 March 1910, in Luxemburg 1981, Vol. 2, pp. 301, 302.
4   Luxemburg 1981, Vol. 2, p. 302.
5   Cited in Luxemburg, 'Die Theorie und die Praxis', in Luxemburg 1981, Vol. 2, p. 380. Surprisingly, Gary P. Steenson's (1991, pp. 169–74) treatment of the Kautsky-Luxemburg split discusses the differences between the two over the 'mass strike' question, but omits any mention of the issue of agitation for a republic. On Luxemburg's agitation, see Laschitza 1969 and Laschitza 1996, pp. 331–76.

with secret ballot (the German Reich had manhood suffrage only, and only from the age of 25); proportional representation, prior to the introduction of which electoral boundaries should be regularly adjusted according to population changes (something which failed to occur in Imperial Germany, despite decades of dramatic population shifts); and remuneration for parliamentarians (which was finally introduced in 1906). Other points included elements providing for 'legislation by the people', 'self-determination and self-administration of the people' at all levels of government (i.e. elements of direct democracy alongside a reformed system of representative government), and the disestablishment of religion. The Programme was, however, silent on the issue of the monarchy.[6]

Kautsky was also able to point to the fact that the previous Party programme, the Gotha Programme of 1875, had also avoided mentioning the word 'republic', and cited Marx and Engels as both having recognised the need for restraint on this point, despite their criticisms of the Gotha Programme in particular.[7] In his critique of the Gotha Programme, Marx had – grudgingly – acknowledged that it was prudent, 'since circumstances require caution', not to include explicitly the demand for a democratic republic in the Programme, characterising the existing Prussian-German state as 'a bureaucratically cobbled-together military despotism, guarded by the police, disguised with parliamentary forms and at the same time already influenced by the bourgeoisie [*ein mit parlamentarischen Formen verbrämter und zugleich schon von der Bourgeoisie beeinflußter, bürokratisch gezimmerter, polizeilich gehüteter Militärdespotismus*]'.[8] Similarly, while Friedrich Engels considered it essential that the Social Democratic Party, while drafting the 1891 Erfurt Programme, should be clearly aware that its goals could only be realised in a democratic republic (and a unitary republic, necessitating the abolition of the petty states), he recognised that legal barriers prevented 'an openly republican Party programme' from being published in Germany: 'Not much out of all these things will be allowed into the programme', Engels concluded.[9]

As early as 1869, the so-called 'Eisenacher' Social Democratic Workers' Party had decided against adopting an explicitly republican programme, although, in contrast to the largely Prussian-based 'Lassallean' Social Democrats who were more inclined to seek some accommodation with the existing state in

---

6 Text in Kautsky 1980 [1922], pp. 255f.
7 Kautsky, cited in Luxemburg 1981, Vol. 2, p. 380.
8 Marx, 'Kritik des Gothaer Programms', in MEW, Vol. 19, p. 29.
9 Engels, 'Zur Kritik des sozialdemokratischen Programmentwurfs 1891', in MEW, Vol. 22, pp. 235, 236.

the hope of influencing an evolution in the direction of a 'social monarchy',[10] the 'Eisenacher' socialists favoured a republic and were particularly hostile to the prospect of a Germany dominated by the Prussian monarchy. A motion put to the Eisenach social democratic workers' congress did call for the programme to include the words 'republican state', and one delegate (Hermann Greulich, significantly from Switzerland) welcomed the programme as 'republican through and through' because of its provision for a democratic and confederally decentralised party structure.[11] The motion was defeated, however, mainly because the word 'republic' was seen as a potential obstacle to the founding of Social Democratic associations (in effect, party branches) in the territory of the Prussian-dominated North German Confederation. In addition, a motion to call the party Social Republican, instead of Social Democratic, was also rejected, partly because the word 'democratic' was seen to be more comprehensive, potentially implying republicanism in any case.[12] Wilhelm Liebknecht declared that he was himself a 'republican', and believed that everyone present was also one, and he was convinced that 'the social democratic state can only be a republic, that the republic is the state of the future'. Under the circumstances prevailing in North Germany, however, the party had to consider the fact that 'not a single association would receive permission to constitute itself with a statute in which the 'republic' was stated as a goal'.[13] The first article of the 1869 Eisenach Programme in its finally adopted form called for the establishment of a 'free people's state [*freier Volksataat*]', a formulation understandably condemned by Marx as vacuous, even if he did concede the practical difficulties in the way of spelling out the goal of a republic.[14]

That the vague formula '*freier Volksstaat*' – which was echoed by the name of the party newspaper of the Eisenacher Social Democrats, *Der Volksstaat* – was code for a democratic republic was more or less conceded at the Leipzig trial for high treason of August Bebel, Wilhelm Liebknecht and Adolf Hepner in 1872. The indictment repeatedly emphasised the republican aims of the accused, as well as their commitment to a revolutionary overthrow of the existing state.[15] While Bebel and Liebknecht confessed that they personally understood '*freier*

---

10 However, see Lehnert 2014, who stresses the democratic and social revolutionary elements in Lassalle's thought, viewing the rhetorical gestures of accommodation with the existing state as essentially tactical.
11 *Protokoll über die Verhandlungen des Allgemeinen Deutschen sozialdemokratischen Arbeiterkongresses zu Eisenach* am 7., 8. und 9. August 1869, Leipzig, 1869, pp. 21, 27.
12 *Protokoll* Eisenach 1869, pp. 31, 28.
13 *Protokoll* Eisenach 1869, p. 31.
14 Marx, in MEW, Vol. 19, pp. 27 f.
15 Leidigkeit 1960, pp. 32, 34 ff., 38.

Volksstaat' to mean a republic, without this necessarily being the official position of the party, they insisted that the advocacy of a republic was not illegal in itself, provided such advocacy was conducted by legal means. In the same vein, they argued that the socialist party could view itself as working for a revolutionary transformation of society, without the word 'revolution' necessarily meaning a resort to violence or illegality.[16] The court remained unimpressed by this line of argument, sentencing both Bebel and Liebknecht to two years' fortress imprisonment (while Hepner was acquitted).

After the legal persecution experienced by the Social Democrats throughout the 1870s and 1880s, especially the 12 years during which the Social Democratic Party was banned (1878–90), it is understandable that some caution prevailed in the phrasing of the 1891 Party Programme, as noted above. Nonetheless, it was clear to both supporters and opponents of the Social Democratic Party that it was not a supporter of monarchism in general or of the Hohenzollern dynasty in particular. This was perhaps most evident in the Reichstag, where the Social Democratic deputies demonstratively boycotted the parliament's formal manifestations of allegiance to the crown.[17] In the Saxon state parliament (the Landtag), in the late 1870s, Social Democrats chose to comply *pro forma* with the requirement for newly elected deputies to swear an oath of allegiance to the King of Saxony, rather than forgo their hard-won right to represent their constituents, but this outward show of compliance clearly fooled, or satisfied, no-one.[18] In 1895, the 14 Saxon Social Democratic Landtag deputies chose the simple expedient of absenting themselves briefly from the chamber rather than swear the oath to the King, and were able to return and resume their seats afterwards.[19]

Conversely, the official patronage bestowed on anti-socialist organisations such as the Christliche Zeitschriftenverein (Christian Periodicals Association) and the Reichsverband gegen die Sozialdemokratie (Reich Anti-Socialist Association), coupled with the manifold examples of discriminatory behaviour against Social Democrats on the part of the authorities, made it sufficiently clear that the Prussian and imperial authorities did not consider membership of the Social Democratic Party compatible with loyalty to the throne.[20] After

---

16   Leidigkeit 1960, pp. 24f., 59f. (statements by Liebknecht); pp. 60, 65f., 71f. (statements by Bebel).
17   Matthias and Pikart 1966, pp. cxliv–cil.
18   Retallack 2017, pp. 192–3.
19   Retallack 2017, pp. 282–3. The following year, a new three-class franchise in Saxony sharply reduced the number of Social Democrats in the Landtag.
20   See especially Saul 1972 and Hall 1976.

speeches in which Kaiser Wilhelm II had complained about the 'treasonous mob', 'rabble unworthy of being called German', and 'unpatriotic enemies of the God-given order of things' who were allegedly behind the Social Democratic Party, the socialist historian and journalist Franz Mehring wrote in *Die Neue Zeit*:

> The Kaiser seems to place great value on demonstrating to everybody how unbridgeable the gulf is which separates him from the largest party of the German people, and it goes without saying that we can neither prevent him from drawing such a conclusion nor do we have any desire to do so.[21]

Gilbert Badia has summed up the situation as follows: 'To be a Social Democrat was to be a supporter of a republic. That was – tacitly – understood'. But, on the other hand, 'the transformation of the form of government was neither a topic of agitation nor an immediate demand'.[22] By 1909, however, Ludwig Quessel, on the right wing of the party, pointed out the absence of a clear, definitive position on the republic in the party's programme and literature, in order to argue that Social Democrats did not necessarily have to be partisans of a republic.[23] In 1912, Quessel (who by this time was an outspoken advocate of a more pro-imperialist orientation on the part of Social Democrats) argued that there was no significant difference between a constitutional monarchy and a republican presidential system, optimistically predicting that Germany would follow the English evolution to constitutional monarchy. In the same article, Quessel also observed that when abroad he often encountered surprise expressed at the fact that even those Social Democrats who publicly professed to be republicans never proposed any practical measures for moving towards a republic, apparently lacking the courage of their convictions.[24]

Even after the end of Bismarck's anti-Socialist law in 1890, and Bismarck's own departure from the Chancellorship, the precarious legal situation in which the Social Democratic Party operated still militated against anything resembling an explicit campaign for a republican form of government. The activities of the Social Democratic Party were subject to numerous restrictions and means of harassment and repression from the authorities. All meetings of workers' organisations had to be announced to the authorities in advance and were subject to police surveillance, which could ban or close a meeting at the

---

21 Mehring 1895, p. 769.
22 Badia 1975, p. 161.
23 Quessel 1909.
24 Quessel 1912.

slightest provocation. Demonstrations involving the display of red flags, or red ribbons on wreaths at the funerals of Social Democrats could lead to police intervention. In the state of Saxony, the display of red flags or cockades came under the legal ban (dating from 1849) on the display of republican symbols, as a result of which the Social Democratic Party resorted to expedients such as decorating their meeting halls with mixed red and white bunting.[25] The courts tended to support the police in any cases of arbitrary action against the Social Democratic Party. Throughout the 1890s, the party newspaper *Vorwärts* carried a monthly register of party members' convictions, prison sentences and fines, with Social Democratic newspaper editors being especially at risk. Klaus Saul writes, without exaggeration: 'In the 1890s there was scarcely a trade union or party editor who did not spend several months in gaol for libel and slander [*Beleidigung*] against the Kaiser, the sovereign of the particular state, state officials or employers'.[26]

One law which lent itself to particularly arbitrary application against Social Democrats and which directly limited any possibility of criticism of the monarchy, was the law concerning *lèse-majesté* (Article 95 of the penal code, or *Strafgesetzbuch*), which provided for an unlimited period of imprisonment of *not less than* two months for 'anyone whose spoken or written words could be construed as intending an insult to the Kaiser's majesty'.[27] That this law was anything but a dead letter is illustrated by figures showing that the average annual number of convictions under Article 95 for the period 1889–95 was 551, peaking at 622 in 1894. In the years 1889–93, a total of 1,239 years imprisonment was meted out by German courts, averaging 175 days per convicted person.[28] *Vorwärts* pointed out, with bitter irony, that such numbers ought to be an embarrassment for 'friends of the prevailing order', as the frequency of *lèse-majesté* cases tended to contradict the official belief in the deeply mon-

---

25   This ban was somewhat modified in 1910 to allow red badges or rosettes on clothing, but carrying red flags or wearing red scarves was still banned. Sächsisches Staatsarchiv Chemnitz (= SStAC), Amtshauptmannschaft Zwickau, 1578, Bl. 107–9. The modification followed repeated conflict with police over wreaths with red ribbons at the burial of Social Democrats.
26   Saul 1972, p. 310. This article is a useful reference for the measures taken against Social Democrats in general. See also Saul 1974.
27   Hall 1973–74, p. 101. See also Hartmann 2006 (which includes texts of the relevant law from the North German Confederation and the revised 1876 version, pp. 299–301).
28   Hall 1973–74, p. 102; cf. also the analysis of statistics from official sources and *Vorwärts* in Hartmann 2006, pp. 114–18. In view of these figures, Mark Hewitson's comment in a widely-used textbook that the law against *lèse-majesté* was 'occasionally invoked' is surprising, although perhaps symptomatic of the relative neglect of the labour movement in some recent historiography. Hewitson 2008, p. 48.

archist sentiments of the German people.²⁹ Perhaps the most celebrated case of *lèse-majesté* involved the young historian (and later noted pacifist activist) Ludwig Quidde, whose essay on Caligula in the journal *Die Gesellschaft* was suspected of being a veiled lampoon on Kaiser Wilhelm II.³⁰ The case against Quidde collapsed, however, the authorities being unwilling to pursue the parallels between the Kaiser and Caligula too closely, although Quidde was a marked man thereafter as far as the police and courts were concerned.³¹ This *cause célèbre* notwithstanding, Article 95 was overwhelmingly used against Social Democrats. Even trivial remarks which did not actually mention the Kaiser directly could result in stiff penalties. The law on *lèse-majesté*, Kurt Eisner claimed, was simply a disguised anti-socialist law – comment which was followed by a nine-month prison term for Eisner.³² Social Democratic editors continued to be sentenced to imprisonment and fines under Article 95 in the years leading up to the outbreak of the First World War.³³ To cite a couple of notable and characteristic cases: the editor of the *Hamburger Echo*, Gustav Wabersky, was convicted some 27 times within ten years (between March 1897 and October 1906), mostly for either *lèse-majesté* or for other instances of *Beleidigung* (slander, or insult). These convictions cost him two years of his life, adding up his custodial sentences, as well as almost 3,000 marks in fines.³⁴ Hall also cites the case of Hugo Haase, the Social Democratic lawyer and Reichstag deputy, who had to defend the editors of the *Königsberger Volkszeitung* on no fewer than 64 occasions within 17 years – mostly unsuccessfully, generally for some kind of *Beleidigung*.³⁵ It is not surprising that in the 1890s it was sometimes suggested that the hazardous position of legally responsible editor of a Social Democratic newspaper be rotated amongst younger, unmarried comrades, without families to support, who could afford to spend a few months in gaol.

Given that the German Reich contained 22 monarchical states, each with its own crowned head (plus three republican states: Bremen, Hamburg, Lübeck, and the *Reichsland* Alsace-Lorraine), the opportunities to insult monarchs were correspondingly multiplied, and it was also possible to be charged

---

29 *Vorwärts*, 29 October 1898, cited in Hartmann 2006, p. 113.
30 Quidde 1894, pp. 413–30. The essay was also published separately as a pamphlet. While Quidde took cover behind a plethora of learned footnotes to the ancient sources on Caligula, the parallels were irresistible to a contemporary readership.
31 Balfour 1975, p. 180; Hall 1973–74, pp. 104f.
32 Hall 1973–74, p. 106; cf. Eisner 1979, pp. 13f.
33 Hall 1973–74, p. 111.
34 Hall 1973–74, p. 102.
35 Hall 1977, p. 71.

with insulting monarchs of other German states than the one in which the offence was committed.³⁶

It was in the nature of the law of *lèse-majesté* that there was no clear distinction between a libel on the person of the Kaiser himself, and the institution of the monarchy in Germany – a problem compounded by the Kaiser's own apparent inability in his public utterances to see such a distinction. It is clear that under these conditions any explicit agitation for the abolition of the monarchy in Germany would have been a particularly risky undertaking. This was recognised by Karl Kautsky, who wrote a letter to Franz Mehring in 1909 in which he stressed the need for Social Democrats to avoid any monarchical demonstrations in parliaments:

> One might well say that the existing legal system makes it impossible to conduct republican propaganda. It is all the more necessary, then, to avoid anything which might be interpreted as surrendering our republican convictions.³⁷

For this reason, Kautsky, having opposed Luxemburg's republican agitation in 1910, censured the Social Democratic Landtag deputies of Württemberg for their participation in the usual demonstrations of loyalty at the opening of the Landtag by the King of Württemberg after the 1912 *Land* election. Kautsky emphasised the moral influence of such traditions and symbols which counted against a young oppositional party such as Social Democracy, unless it showed that it had the power to defy them. To claim republican convictions while still participating in demonstrations of loyalty to the monarchy represented 'a victory for the bearer of the power of the bourgeois state over the classes of the population who are rising up in struggle against this state power'.³⁸

It is worth noting that in Rosa Luxemburg's own agitation in 1910 in which she raised the issue of the republic, she appears to have done so in a relatively circumspect manner despite her otherwise strikingly radical language. In her speech to a meeting in Frankfurt am Main in April 1910 on the campaign for suffrage reform in Prussia, subsequently printed as a pamphlet, Luxemburg held German bourgeois liberals responsible for the persistence of such oppressive and anachronistic institutions as the Prussian three-class franchise. In 1848,

---

36   See, for example, Hessisches Staatsarchiv Darmstadt, Generalstaatsanwalt, Nr. 231, Strafsachen wegen Beleidigung des Landesherrn, von Landesfürsten und von Regierungen.
37   Karl Kautsky to Franz Mehring, 21 January 1909, cited in Laschitza 1969, p. 162.
38   Kautsky 1913, p. 607.

Luxemburg argued, the liberals should have used the early successes of the revolution to chase the Prussian King (Friedrich Wilhelm IV), who had betrayed his promise of giving the people a liberal constitution, from his throne, along with the rulers of the other German states, and proclaim a republic, bringing about German unification on a liberal, democratic basis.[39] Despite her argument, in the strongest terms, that a German republic should have been created in 1848, and her sharp attacks on the Prussian three-class franchise in the present in the same speech, she did not explicitly call for the replacement of the regime of the current Kaiser and King of Prussia by the installation of a republican form of government In a speech in Bremen in the same month, as part of the same campaign against the Prussian three-class franchise, Luxemburg had used the same allusion to the failure of the liberals to create a republic in Germany in 1848, while also criticising the institution of the Prussian monarchy and the imperial throne for supporting the power of the Junker aristocracy in Prussia – points which were noted by the police officer conducting the surveillance of the meeting.[40] While this speech was perhaps even bolder in its language than the Frankfurt speech (at least than the published version of the latter), the conclusion that the existing monarchy should be replaced by a republic was not explicitly stated, even if – according to Luxemburg – this should have been done in 1848. The rhetoric in these speeches possibly represents a probing of the limits of legally permissible public discourse on the monarchy. It is clear from the above evidence that public discussion on constitutional alternatives in Imperial Germany was severely inhibited by legal constraints, especially the arbitrarily implemented law on *lèse-majesté*.

There is also the possibility that the republic was not advocated more strongly out of consideration for the continuing strength of popular patriotism and attachment to the monarchy. This might be suggested by, for example, the work of Werner Blessing on the cult of monarchy and the workers' movement in Imperial Germany.[41] Blessing describes how traditions of popular loyalty to the Bavarian monarchy, maintained by an array of baroque rituals which penetrated the life of small communities, came to be overlaid by the cult of the German Kaiser, with its association with national power in more modern

---

39   Luxemburg, 'Der preußische Wahlrechtskampf', in Luxemburg 1981, Vol. 2, pp. 316–18.
40   Documentation in Nishikawa 1990, pp. 517, 524. Luxemburg also made a jocular comment on Bremen's republican tradition as a Hanseatic town, adding that this tradition was incapable of being taken seriously in the past and did not prevent the application of Prussian police methods in Bremen in the present. Nishikawa 1990, pp. 515 f.
41   Blessing 1978.

forms. He notes, however, that 'the relationship between the two cults [was] fraught with conflict'.[42] Indeed, the potential conflicts between the principle of legitimacy, to which the Hohenzollerns could adhere as the ruling house of Prussia, and the manner in which the Hohenzollerns had become the imperial and national ruling dynasty by trampling on the prerogatives of some other German princes, as well as the contradiction between the plebiscitary forms with which the German empire sought popular legitimation and the reality of the blocked process of parliamentarisation, meant that the legitimacy of the Reich's constitution was permanently open to question.[43]

In the South and South-West German states – Bavaria, Baden, and Württemberg, attachment to the traditional ruling house could also be a way of expressing dissatisfaction with Prussian domination of the Reich, especially as these states had a longer tradition of constitutional government than Prussia, and a more liberal political climate. In the 1860s, the nascent (non-Lassallean) labour movement in Southern Germany, along with middle class democrats, had joined particularists in opposing a *Kleindeutschland* under Prussian domination (as discussed in Chapter 2). Social Democrats such as August Bebel, whose views were influenced by the recollection of that period, occasionally contrasted the South German monarchs with the Prussian royal house, to the advantage of the former, because of the stronger constitutional and parliamentary traditions in the South.[44] These were also alluded to by the Württemberg Social Democrat, Wilhelm Keil, in his reply to Kautsky's criticisms of the conduct of the Württemberg socialist Landtag deputies, mentioned above. Besides, Keil added, after stating that he and his fellow Social Democratic deputies were, of course, republicans, the present King of Württemberg had never publicly attacked Social Democracy nor had he provided 'any particular cause for anti-monarchical demonstrations'.[45]

The Badenese Social Democrats Ludwig Frank and Wilhelm Kolb, both on the right wing of the party and both members of the Baden Landtag (Frank was also a Reichstag deputy), caused a similar controversy when they took part in the funeral procession and ceremony for Grand Duke Friedrich of Baden in October 1907, despite the abstention of the Social Democratic caucus in the Landtag from a condolence motion. This apparent demonstration of fealty to the deceased Grand Duke caused a storm of disapproval in the Social Democratic Press, with *Vorwärts* finding the conduct of Frank and Kolb simply

---

42   Blessing 1978, p. 368.
43   See Domann 1974, pp. 45–50.
44   For examples, Domann 1974, pp. 60, 129.
45   Keil 1913, pp. 682, 683.

'incomprehensible'.⁴⁶ The attempt of the Baden party newspaper, the Mannheim *Volksstimme*, to defend the gesture as an expression of human tact and decency across the political divide was rejected by *Vorwärts* as unconvincing: there was hardly a suggestion that Frank and Kolb had any kind of personal relationship to the Grand Duke, so their demonstration had to be considered as pertaining to the institution of the monarchy *per se*.⁴⁷ (The fact that Karl Liebknecht was at the same time standing in a political trial for 'high treason' in Berlin set the behaviour of Frank and Kolb in Baden in particularly stark relief.) In following days, numerous party papers echoed *Vorwärts'* condemnation of Frank and Kolb (with the exception of the Württemberg paper *Schwäbische Tagwacht*, which cautiously reserved its judgement, the *Karlsruher Volksfreund*, edited by Kolb himself, the Frankfurt *Volksstimme* and the *Mainzer Volkszeitung*, both belonging to the party's revisionist camp).⁴⁸ A meeting of the Baden party leadership subsequently passed a resolution that accepted that Frank and Kolb had acted in good faith, but affirmed that the party would not participate in any monarchical demonstrations in future.⁴⁹ The party leader August Bebel himself weighed into the controversy after Kolb and Frank quoted him out of context as stating that the party opposed the institution of monarchy and not the person of the monarch. Like other critics of Kolb's and Frank's action, Bebel pointed out that there could hardly be a question of personal relations or reciprocity between a Social Democratic politician and a monarch – a monarch would hardly attend the funeral of a Social Democratic leader, and Bebel added that the late Grand Duke's support for anti-socialist legislation was well-known. The worse breach of tact and decency was Kolb's and Frank's offence against the democratic sentiments and principles of their party comrades.⁵⁰ Bebel did not forget Kolb's and Frank's breach of socialist principle, bringing it up again during the debate over the Baden Social Democrats' controversial vote for the state government budget in 1910 at the Magdeburg Party Congress of that year.⁵¹

---

46   *Vorwärts*, 236, 9 October 1907, 1. Beilage.
47   *Vorwärts*, 237, 10 October 1907.
48   Excerpts in *Vorwärts*, 239, 12 October 1907, p. 1. Beilage. See also *Vorwärts*, 240, 13 October 1907, p. 1, Beilage: 'Aus der Partei', for Kolb's self-justification printed in the *Karlsruher Volksfreund*, which combined the appeal to 'human tact and decency' with political and tactical considerations in view of possible coalition negotiations in Baden, which *Vorwärts* found equally unconvincing; *Vorwärts*, 241, 15 October 1907, p. 1, Beilage: 'Nochmals die Demonstration Frank-Kolb'; *Vorwärts*, 243, 17 October 1907: 'Aus der Partei'.
49   *Vorwärts*, 247, 22 October 1907, p. 1, Beilage: 'Aus der Partei'.
50   *Vorwärts*, 242, 16 October 1907, p. 1, Beilage: 'Zur Kolb-Frank-Affäre'.
51   *Protokoll über die Verhandlungen des Parteitages der Sozialdemokratischen Partei Deutschlands*. Abgehalten in Magdeburg vom 18. bis 24. September 1910, Berlin, p. 250.

The same Bebel had used the occasion of a Reichstag debate on the Reich budget in 1894 to put the Social Democrats' republican principles unambiguously on the public record:

> we have never made a secret of our antimonarchical ideas, which are the same thing as republican sentiments, just as little as we have hidden our Social Democratic, that is socialist, ideas.[52]

The significance of regional differences in political culture is illustrated by a newspaper report of a Social Democratic meeting in Würzburg in January 1906, one of many hundreds called around the Reich to mark the anniversary of 'Bloody Sunday' in St. Petersburg and the outbreak of the 1905 Russian Revolution. The speaker, city councillor Konrad Eberhard, condemned the absolute rule of the Tsar, whom he characterised for good measure as a weakling and a perjurer. The speaker went on to stress the peaceful nature of the Social Democrats' demonstrations in support of the Russian Revolution, something that would only be endangered if there were provocative behaviour on the side of the authorities. Eberhard compared the Bavarian Prince Ludwig favourably with the Kaiser and the Prussian Crown Prince, calling the Bavarian a 'model prince', and complaining that the Prussians had presumed to give the Bavarians directions on how to respond to the Social Democrats' demonstrations that month, resulting in a disproportionately high police presence. A 'comrade from Dresden', present at the gathering by chance, complained vigorously about the police, called for greater efforts to spread enlightenment among the masses, and criticised the fact that South German comrades avoided confronting the power of the priests. Comrade Eberhard replied that the Würzburg police weren't as bad as the police elsewhere, were poorly paid and had to work long hours. Another comrade retorted to the Dresdener that 'religion was the private and conscientious matter of each individual comrade'.[53] The visitor from the capital of 'Red Saxony', where bloody clashes had taken place between protesting Social Democrats and police only the previous month,[54] may have wondered if he had arrived on a different planet in Würzburg, where the monarch, the police, and the priests were benign, or at least mostly harmless.

---

52   Bebel in Reichstag, 14 March 1894, in Bebel 1995–97, Vol. 3, p. 434.
53   Bayerisches Hauptstaatsarchiv München, MJu, Nr. 17455 (unfoliated), clipping from *Neue Bayerische Landeszeitung*, 18, 23 January 1906.
54   Retallack 2017, pp. 396–9; for an overview of the development of Social Democracy in Würzburg, see Schönhoven 1978.

In general, however, Blessing finds that, by the end of the nineteenth century, 'where workers were guided in their attitudes and behaviour by the social democratic movement, trade unions and their subsidiary organisations ... they detached themselves from the monarchy and its cult', even if labour movement ritual borrowed some formal aspects from official political symbolism.[55]

Alex Hall has considered the possible effect of the huge amount of official monarchist propaganda on the Social Democrats' working-class supporters, suggesting: 'Undoubtedly, the ordinary working-man was often caught up in the elaborate pageantry of state ceremonial and the excitement of a visit from the *"Reisekaiser"* [the "travelling emperor": a reference to Wilhelm II's penchant for both ceremonious journeys around his realm and royal tourism abroad]', and noting that any possible evidence of working-class support for the Kaiser was eagerly registered by the political police.[56] Hall also finds, however, that Social Democrats were much more likely to express republican sentiments than allegiance to the Kaiser, a generalisation which, if not universally valid, included even such right-leaning Social Democrats as Karl Frohme of Hamburg.[57]

There is some evidence of working-class monarchism in the Ruhr mining region, where the Social Democratic Party and its allies in the Free Trade Unions had to compete with confessionally based trade unions for the support of workers. In the 1889 Ruhr miners' strike, 'strike meetings often ended with a cheer for the Kaiser', and the miners sent a delegation to present a petition to the Kaiser in person, hoping for his intervention in their interest.[58] Even ten years later, the Kaiser was apparently well received on a visit to Dortmund and assured by local authorities 'that the many social democratic voters have long been not true socialists but citizens loyal to their Empire and King'.[59] Helga Grebing has suggested, however, a number of reasons why the 1889 petition to the Kaiser should not be viewed simply as evidence of a conservative, monarchist outlook on the part of the miners: it was a bid for public recognition of the collective representation of miners' interests; it sought to bring public opinion onto the side of the miners, putting the mine-owners under pressure; and it showed the readiness of miners' representatives to display a united front, unlike the employers in the dispute. Similarly, the framing of the

---

55 Blessing 1978, pp. 369–71.
56 Hall 1977, p. 156. On the importance of pageantry and political symbolism in nineteenth- and early twentieth-century Germany, see especially Mosse 1991 [1975].
57 Hall 1977, p. 156.
58 Hickey 1985, p. 208; see also Saul 1981, especially 214–25; Grebing 1985, pp. 9–33.
59 Hickey 1985, p. 280n102.

petition in traditional, conservative terms can be seen as tactically motivated in this context.⁶⁰ In any case, any hopes that were vested in the young Kaiser at his accession, when he advocated less repressive policies in the social sphere than had been the rule during Bismarck's chancellorship, were disappointed in the long run, as the hostility of the Wilhelmine state towards the labour movement became more clearly marked, with machine guns being deployed against mining strikes at Mansfeld in 1909 and in the Ruhr in 1912.⁶¹

Richard Evans' research into political police surveillance reports of working-class pubs in Hamburg – a Social Democratic stronghold as well as a Hanseatic city with its own republican tradition which was a matter of pride for many Hamburg workers⁶² – reveals 'complex' attitudes towards the Kaiser and the monarchy.⁶³ Workers frequently expressed criticisms of Kaiser Wilhelm II (although they tended to be cautiously expressed except when the speaker was drunk – the existence of police surveillance was not a secret), but Evans also argues that the cult of monarchy which was being actively propagated 'does seem to have left its mark on the Social Democratic rank and file'. This was far from unconditional, however, with workers refusing to embrace 'the anti-democratic and imperialist aspect of the monarchical cult', preferring to view the German Empire as developing into a true constitutional monarchy.⁶⁴ One consistent feature of the conversations reproduced by Evans, however, is that workers perceived a deep antagonism existing between the Social Democratic Party and the monarchy, and vice versa. One worker, for example, praised the party's Hamburg newspaper, the *Hamburger Echo* on the grounds that 'at least it doesn't crawl up the royals' a[rses]', going on to assert that he found the existence of monarchs unnecessary: 'the people could govern themselves without princes'.⁶⁵ This last sentiment seems to have been common among workers who identified themselves with Social Democracy – it is sometimes, but not

---

60   Grebing 1985, p. 28. For the background of the tradition of miners' complaints and petitions to authorities, see Tenfelde and Trischler 1986.
61   Saul 1981.
62   See *Hamburger Echo*, 140, 19 June 1895, Beilage: 'Republikaner und Monarchen'.
63   Evans 1989, pp. 322–40; Evans 1990, pp. 159–63. The significance of republican constitutions in Hanseatic towns such as Hamburg and Bremen within the Reich was limited by the preponderance of Prussia within the Reich's supposedly federal constitution (not to mention the plutocratic tendencies of these city-states). Nonetheless, Social Democrats did call for a similar republican status for the Reichsland Alsace-Lorraine, partly because a Reichsland directly under the rule of the Kaiser would strengthen Prussia's position in the Bundesrat (Upper House of parliament). See Emmel 1911.
64   Evans 1990, pp. 162, 163; Evans 1989, pp. 322ff.
65   Evans 1989, p. 330 (a tactful ellipsis in the police report).

always, possible to distinguish between 'organised' and 'unorganised' workers in the surveillance reports of Hamburg's political police. A common theme was the outrage on the part of workers at the extravagance and expenses of maintaining the Kaiser's opulent way of life, and that of Germany's other princely houses, and acknowledgement that the Social Democratic Party was the only party to consistently vote against increases in the royals' 'civil list'. The Kaiser's wealth was contrasted with the straitened conditions of the working class, confronted with rising food prices, and with the poverty of the unemployed.[66] Other workers displayed an allergic reaction to precisely the media-driven cult of the monarchy to which Evans refers. One worker complained, for example, that the volume of newspaper reports of Prince Heinrich's 1902 voyage to America was 'enough to make you sick', and expressed scepticism as to whether the voyage would be at all economically beneficial for Germany.[67] When another worker (possibly not a Social Democrat) expressed the view that countries headed by a monarch enjoyed better 'order' than republics, another worker was quick to contradict him:

> Whatever disadvantages a republic may have compared with a monarchical state, in a republic the people's views are put into effect, whereas in a monarchical state, the Junkers rule. Where this control by the Junkers leads, we see it every day.
>
> If Germany was a republic, the workers and the middling sort would be considerably better off, and also we wouldn't have to pay such high taxes, as a President can't spend as much money as a Kaiser.[68]

Workers were also well aware of the Kaiser's penchant for inflammatory rhetoric, directed especially against the Social Democratic Party and its 'disloyal' supporters.[69] Where workers identified as Social Democrats, there was less ambivalence towards the Kaiser, and more overt hostility, than Evans' cautious formulation suggests. This is perhaps particularly the case in police reports from later in the Kaiser's reign.

---

66   E.g. Staatsarchiv Hamburg (= StAHH), 331–3 (Politische Polizei), S5315, Vigilanzberichte Schutzmann Neumann, report of 17 June 1910; StAHH, 331–3, S5316, Vigilanzberichte Schutzmann/ Wachtmeister Meyer, report of 13 June 1910; StAHH 331–3, 5320 Vigilanzberichte Schutzmann Mebus, report of 28 December 1908.
67   StAHH, 331–3, S5286, Vigilanzberichte Schutzmann Hinz, report of 5 March 1902.
68   Ibid., report of 12 April 1902.
69   E.g. StAHH, 331–3, 5204, Vigilanzberichte Schutzmann Jochum, report of 30 January 1895; StAHH, 132-I: 3403, Senatskommission für die Reichs- u. auswärtigen Angelegenheiten, Bl. 22a (report of a meeting of waterside workers held on 1 March 1908).

A significant example of the resistance to the officially promoted cult of the monarchy among Berlin's Social Democrats was furnished by the ceremonial inauguration of the grandiose monument to Kaiser Wilhelm I erected on the *Schlossfreiheit*, the place in front of Berlin's royal palace, in 1897, on the occasion of the centenary of the birth of the Reich's founding emperor. *Vorwärts* responded to the event with a front-page compilation of quotations from Wihelm I which highlighted the late Kaiser's reactionary attitudes.[70] *Vorwärts* also drily pointed out that efforts to promote the use of the epithet 'Wilhelm the Great' for the late Kaiser were failing to gain traction.[71] Most notably, *Vorwärts* reported that despite the call from Berlin's city government for residents to greet the official Kaiser centenary festivities by lighting up their homes, the overwhelming majority of dwellings in the working-class suburbs remained obdurately dark, with the exception of a few shops, restaurants, or perhaps the homes of minor government officials. A *Vorwärts* reporter toured the city's northern and eastern precincts to furnish his readers with a detailed account of how many residences in these areas boycotted the celebration.[72] Some Berlin comrades marked the day by visiting the graves of the revolutionaries of March 1848.[73] Despite such efforts to promote popular monarchical sentiment, German workers were not deterred from voting for the Social Democratic Party by the knowledge that Kaiser Wilhelm II violently disapproved of the party. Nor was much working-class loyalty to the throne in evidence by November 1918, when the army informed Wilhelm that his safety (from his 'own' people) could no longer be guaranteed and the Hohenzollern dynasty, along with the other German royal houses, fell with little regret expressed by workers at their departure.

There remains the question of whether German Social Democrats considered the question of the desirability of a republican constitution for Germany sufficiently important for it to be made a focus of agitation. This, in turn, raises the question of the adequacy of Marxian socialist theory on the state in the period of the Second International. For many socialists, the essential issue was the class conflict between proletariat and bourgeoisie – and the essence of this conflict, being rooted in the capitalist mode of production, would not be altered by a change in the form of the constitution while the bourgeoisie remained dominant. Friedrich Engels, writing to the French socialist Paul Lafar-

---

70   *Vorwärts*, 68, 21 March 1897: 'Zur Charakteristik Wilhelm's I'.
71   *Vorwärts*, 69, 23 March 1897: 'Wilhelm der Große'.
72   *Vorwärts*, 69, 23 March 1897: 'Die Zentenarfeier in den Arbeitervierteln'.
73   *Vorwärts*, 69, 23 March 1897, Beilage: 'Lokales'. I owe the reference to this incident to Rausch 2006, pp. 379–91, where a more detailed account can be found.

gue in 1894, had conceded that France had an advantage in already possessing a republican constitution, 'the ready-made state form for the future rule of the proletariat'. 'As for the rest of us', Engels went on,

> we still have to lose 24 hours [!] in order to create it. However, the republic like any other form of government is determined by its content: as long as it is the means of rule by the bourgeoisie, it is just as hostile to us as any monarchy.[74]

August Bebel, in debate with French socialists at the Socialist International conference at Amsterdam in 1904, followed Engels' relativisation of the distinction between monarchy and republic, in defending the tactics of the German Social Democrats against criticism from Jean Jaurès.[75]

The sceptical attitude of German Social Democratic leaders and theoreticians towards formal constitutional questions was not only a legacy of Marxian economism, however. Peter Domann has also pointed to the influence of Ferdinand Lassalle's writings from the period of the 1860s constitutional conflict in Prussia.[76] In 1862/63, Lassalle displayed a clear recognition of the nature of Bismarckian *Realpolitik*, equating the 'constitution' of a country with 'the actual power relations' existing in the country, which in Prussia included the King's command over the army, the capitalists' ability to dispose of their wealth, and such manifestations of institutionalised inequality as the Prussian three-class electoral system. In contrast to the organised political power of the government, Lassalle saw the Prussian bourgeoisie as too unorganised to convert the pretence of constitutionalism in Prussia to a more genuine form of constitutional government.[77] The Lassallean realist legacy of interpreting constitutional questions as essentially questions of power was in a sense the logical product of the outcome of the Prussian constitutional crisis as resolved by Bismarck in defiance of parliamentarism, and of the failure of German middle-class liberals to uphold constitutional principle in the face of this challenge.

Franz Mehring, the leading Social Democratic journalist and historian, who was later one of Luxemburg's close allies on the radical left of the Social Democratic Party, was influenced both by Marxian reasoning and Lassalle's

---

74 Engels to Lafargue, 6 March 1894, in MEW, Vol. 39, pp. 215f. This excerpt from Engels' letter was also selected for publication in *Die Neue Zeit*, Engels 1901, pp. 425–6; cf. Domann 1974, p. 200 (where the letter is incorrectly dated).
75 Domann 1974, pp. 200f.; Maehl 1980, pp. 390–2.
76 Domann 1974, pp. 7ff.
77 Lassalle, 'Ueber Verfassungswesen', in Lassalle 1891–93, Vol. I, pp. 465–535.

realism, and emphasised the primacy of class struggle over abstract constitutional issues. In mid-1910 he wrote:

> [w]hile we conduct the struggle against the domination by a class, we also conduct the struggle against the monarchy, but whoever carries on the struggle against the monarchy, is not necessarily thereby carrying out the struggle against class society. For this simple and clear reason it is a tactical error to make the monarchy the slogan of the class struggle, and it was precisely for this reason that Marx so roundly mocked [Karl] Heinzen [an 1848 democrat] and his comrades.[78]

This argument of Mehring's provoked another article by Luxemburg, entitled 'Der Kampf gegen Reliquien' [The Struggle against Relics], which was again turned down by *Die Neue Zeit*. Luxemburg insisted that the recent increases in the Prussian civil list would have made a suitable occasion for pro-republican agitation.[79] But even Luxemburg was not especially concerned about the constitutional form of a possible republic, but was more interested in the efficacy of republicanism for agitational purposes. The 'republic' was a slogan, rather than a goal, a means to the ultimately more important end of raising the radical consciousness of the workers, rather than a desired form of government. As such, it was, for Luxemburg, one agitational weapon among others, in an arsenal which also included Prussian franchise reform and the mass strike debate.

For both Luxemburg and Kautsky, however, a republic could not in itself be the final goal of the socialist movement. The '*Zukunftsstaat*', the socialist state of the future, could not, on the other hand, be precisely described. As Kautsky wrote in his commentary to the party's Erfurt Programme: 'to put up a plan of how the "future state" should be set up has not only become pointless, it is also not in the least compatible with the present scientific point of view'.[80]

To provide a blueprint of the socialist society of the future would be a utopian fantasy (*à la* Fourier), and would therefore represent a departure from the tenets of 'scientific socialism'. On the other hand, a 'bourgeois republic' would not suffice, as it would fail to transcend capitalism and class society. Thus the version of 'historical materialism' prevalent during the time of the Second International engendered a degree of abstinence in the field of state

---

78 Mehring, 'Der Kampf gegen die Monarchie', in Mehring 1960 ff., Vol. 15, p. 501 (originally in *NZ*, 28, no. 2, 1909/10, pp. 609–12).
79 Luxemburg, 'Der Kampf gegen Reliquien' (originally published in the *Leipziger Volkszeitung*, 182, 9 August 1910), in Luxemburg 1981, Vol. 2, pp. 421–6.
80 Kautsky 1980, p. 133.

and constitutional theory. This abstinence was not complete, however. In 1898, the Dietz Verlag, Stuttgart, the home of *Die Neue Zeit* and of much Social Democratic Party literature, published a book called *Ein Blick in den Zukunftsstaat* – a look at the future state, with a preface by Karl Kautsky. The author, a statistician called Karl Ballod, who, to protect his career, published the book pseudonymously, sought to demonstrate the economic feasibility of socialism. The book thus dealt more with economic than with constitutional questions. Kautsky distanced himself from some of Ballod's propositions, notably his assumption that a socialist state, to be self-sufficient, needed colonies.[81] Kautsky himself wrote a booklet on *Parliamentarism and Democracy* in 1893, in which he defended the role of representative parliamentary institutions, provided they were based on a genuinely democratic suffrage, against Swiss-style concepts of direct democracy.[82] And in 1909, Georg Gradnauer, former editor of the *Sächsische Arbeiter-Zeitung* (1897–1905), in which capacity he had many brushes with the Saxon justice system, and then an editor of *Vorwärts* (1906–18), and a member of the Reichstag (1898–1907, 1912–18), published a study of constitutions and constitutional struggles in Germany.[83] Gradnauer tackled the then recent controversy over the concept of the Kaiser's 'personal rule', providing a sharp criticism of the constitutional provisions that made such an experiment in neo-autocracy possible.[84] Against these monarchical excesses, Gradnauer postulated as a norm of modern states that these should evolve from the rule of one or of a few to 'the self-government of the people'.[85] In this process, Gradnauer considered Germany's brand of constitutional monarchy to be a transitional phenomenon, arguing for a more truly parliamentary system, with more democratic electoral laws.[86] While Gradnauer focussed on specific parliamentary and electoral reforms, his longer-term vision was at least implicitly republican: in the course of peoples achieving self-determination, they 'strive for democracy, in which every citizen is subject to the whole, and at the same time has a share in the supreme power in the same measure under the law as every other citizen'.[87] In 1909, Karl Kautsky published his pamphlet *Der Weg zur Macht* (The Path to Power), which reaffirmed the revolutionary goals of the party and openly canvassed the prospects of the working class taking power in Germany,

---

81 Ballod 1898, with preface by Karl Kautsky. My thanks to Sébastien Budgen for bringing this text to my attention.
82 Kautsky 1922 [1893].
83 Gradnauer 1909 (published in the party's Buchhandlung Vorwärts).
84 Gradnauer 1909, pp. 134–8.
85 Gradnauer 1909, p. 132.
86 Gradnauer 1909, pp. 138, 140–2.
87 Gradnauer 1909, p. 155.

only to have to agree to modifications in the second edition when the party executive feared that the radical republican nature of the publication might lead to prosecutions for high treason.[88] Kautsky's reservations towards Luxemburg's advocacy in 1910 of openly republican agitation may need to be viewed against the background of his own experience of the treatment of *Der Weg zur Macht* the previous year.

Despite the party executive's trimming in the matter of Kautsky's *Weg zur Macht*, it should not be supposed that Social Democratic agitation did not try to test the limits of what could be said about the monarchy. The extravagance of lavish expenditure on the monarchy was a common theme of agitation, which dovetailed with Social Democratic critiques of the Reich's fiscal priorities and anti-worker taxation policies. For example, in a public meeting in Berlin attacking the 1909 Reich finance reform, comrade Martha Hoppe considered it a mockery of ordinary people that the Kaiser was said to be spending nine million marks on a new yacht.[89] Social Democratic speakers could also use historical and foreign examples to make their point, for example, through references to the French Revolution. At a meeting in the Hamburg suburb of Wandsbek in 1891, the speaker, comrade Cohn, spoke on the subject of the French Revolution, describing Louis XVI as a 'glutton, a wastrel, and an exploiter of his people'.[90] The French Revolution was a subject of very considerable interest in the publications and cultural activities of German Social Democracy.[91]

The most concerted push back against the 'personal rule' of Wilhelm II occurred in 1908, when Social Democrats took advantage of the public commotion over the Kaiser's notoriously indiscreet interview published in the British *Daily Telegraph*. The affair exposed the risks involved in the Kaiser's inept forays into personal diplomacy as well as revealing a measure of dysfunction in his government and his relationship with Chancellor Bülow.[92] The Social Democratic Party organised a series of mass meetings on the topic of the *Daily Telegraph* affair and the 'personal rule' of the Kaiser, both in the Reich cap-

---

88 Kautsky 1909; see the commentary and documentation in Georg Fülberth's edition, Frankfurt/M., 1972; Ratz 1967. On Kautsky's republican views, see Lewis 2015.
89 LAB, A Pr. Br. Rep. 30, Nr. 14144, Bl. 319–20, report of 18 August 1909. In a similar vein, LAB, A Pr. Br. Rep. 30, Nr. 14144, Bl. 252–3; LAB, A Pr. Br. Rep. 30, Nr. 14148, Bl. 114–15.
90 StAHH, 422–15 Ea1 Wandsbek Polizeibehörde (unfoliated), report of 20 July 1891. (The policeman taking notes at the meeting repeatedly wrote the date of the Revolution as '1798').
91 Ducange 2012.
92 For an authoritative account of the affair, see Röhl 2014, pp. 662–95. On the topic of royal scandals and their media resonance in this period more generally, see Kohlrauch 2005 (on the *Daily Telegraph* affair, pp. 243–63).

ital and around the country. In Berlin, the party announced 13 simultaneous meetings in the city proper (not counting the suburbs outside the formal limits of the municipality) on 10 November 1908, the purpose of which was to 'give our Reichstag and Landtag deputies the opportunity to give an account of the results of the system of absolute rule'.[93] While speeches by revisionists like Gustav Noske and Eduard David were listened to 'calmly' by those present, police noted that Fritz Zubeil's speech, in the Urania in Wrangelstrasse, 'was full of hateful attacks on H[is] M[ajesty]', and was received with 'great enthusiasm' by the audience.[94] Following the meetings, some participants formed into street processions calling for an end to Bülow's government.[95] Similar protests took place all over the Reich, and hundreds of thousands of copies of a flyer criticising the 'Personal Rule' were distributed (and occasionally confiscated, as in Prussian Stargard).[96] In Strasbourg, the *Freie Presse* decided that it was an auspicious occasion to reprint an excerpt from Heinrich Heine's great satirical poem *Deutschland, ein Wintermärchen*, ending its selection with the lines:

> Betrachte ich die Sache ganz genau,
> So brauchen wir gar keinen Kaiser.

> If I consider the matter precisely,
> We don't need a Kaiser at all.[97]

In Hamburg, the political police sought to investigate the views of the workers in response to the Social Democratic agitation over the *Daily Telegraph* affair.[98] The police found workers highly receptive to anti-monarchical Social Democratic propaganda.[99] One recurring theme in workers' responses to the incident was that the Kaiser had undermined Germany's credibility internationally and

---

93 LAB, A Pr. Br. Rep. 30, Nr. 12428, betreffend Kundgebungen zur Politik des Kaisers. The meetings were attended by around 11,000 people, according to police figures (Bl. 11–13). See also LAB, A Pr. Br. Rep. 30, Nr. 14152, Bl. 205, 209–12.
94 LAB, A Pr. Br. Rep. 30, Nr. 12428, Bl. 11–13.
95 LAB, A Pr. Br. Rep. 30, Nr. 12428, Bl. 15–18; LAB, A Pr. Br. Rep. 30, Nr. 14152, Bl. 276 (referring to 300,000 copies of the *Daily Telegraph* interview flyer distributed in Berlin's Sixth electoral district alone).
96 See ibid.; for Stargard, Bl. 150.
97 *Freie Presse*, Strasbourg, 261, 7 November 1908, clipping in LAB, A Pr. Br. Rep. 30, Nr. 14152, Bl. 66.
98 StAHH, 331–3, S6581, Vigilanzberichte: Daily Telegraph-Interview.
99 StAHH, 331–3, 5320, Vigilanzberichte Schutzmann Mebus, reports of 14 November, 8 December 1908.

had also exposed the hypocrisy of Germany's ruling elite in professing peace-loving intentions while engaging in a naval arms race and continuing to press for greater militarisation of German society – 'all the cries for peace are nothing but a fraud'.[100] After a few weeks of the controversy, and a round of Social Democratic Party meetings on the topic in Hamburg, one worker believed that the 'Kaiser has made himself so hated in recent times' that he would hesitate to attend a public occasion in Hamburg, in case someone might throw a bomb at him.[101] One worker, perhaps unconsciously echoing Heinrich Heine, exclaimed: 'what do we need a Kaiser for?'[102] When Portugal became a republic in 1910, this was noticed by some Social Democrats, for whom it underlined how obsolete Prussian and Reich constitutional arrangements were.[103]

In Imperial Germany, a democratic republic could not be considered a practicable immediate demand of the Social Democratic Party, but nor was it the final goal. The final goal sketched out in August Bebel's *Woman Under Socialism*, the most popular socialist theoretical work in Germany, was a socialist society in which the abolition of private property of the means of production and of class divisions would necessarily be followed by the dissolution of the state.[104] Those right-leaning Social Democrats – like Ludwig Quessel – who argued for a concentration on immediate practical goals sought an accommodation with the monarchy (and in Quessel's case, with militarism and colonialism as well), while the left radicals' aims went beyond a 'bourgeois republic'.

The failure to theorise what a social democratic republic might involve in the medium term was one of the several handicaps with which Social Democrats had to cope when Friedrich Ebert took over the receivership of the bankrupt Empire at the end of 1918. This was not simply the product of the economistic ways of thinking prevalent in Second International Marxism, but was also a product of the political perspectives generated by the conflict with the German Second Empire, with its peculiar variety of parliamentary monarchy. Working-class monarchical sentiment would seem to have been a less significant reason for Social Democracy's reticence on this issue than the combination of these other factors. The Weimar Republic that followed it was not, as is often claimed,

---

100 StAHH, 331–3, 5320, report of 4 November 1908, similarly 12 and 25 November 1908.
101 StAHH, 331–3, 5320, report of 28 November 1908.
102 StAHH, 331–3, 5320, report of 8 December 1908.
103 SStAC, Amtshauptmannschaft Zwickau, 1592, Bl. 13–14, report of a meeting in Wilkau, 16 October 1910.
104 Bebel 1980b, pp. 395–7. Theoretical ambivalence towards parliamentary institutions did not, however, prevent the Social Democratic Reichstag *Fraktion* (parliamentary caucus) from consistently insisting upon, and attempting to enlarge the scope of, the parliamentary accountability. See Domann 1974; cf. also Pracht 1990, especially chapter 6.

a 'republic without republicans' – the elections for the National Assembly in January 1919 showed an initial overwhelming majority of support for the parties that supported the republic – but the republicans had had insufficient opportunity to educate themselves and other Germans about what a republic meant.

Conclusion

The German Social Democratic Party was by far the largest and most well-organised socialist party in the Second International. It would go beyond the scope of this book to provide a detailed comparative analysis of the German party *vis-à-vis* other socialist and workers' parties.[1] It is, however, possible to identify a number of factors that favoured the growth of Social Democracy in Imperial Germany as a working-class-based mass party with an explicitly socialist programme.

Firstly, the period leading up to the First World War saw the rise of the classic industrial working class, with over 11 million Germans (42 per cent of the population) working in the industrial or manual labouring sector, along with nearly 3.5 million (26.8 per cent) in commerce and transportation, a dramatic increase in the number of workers working in large firms of 1,000 or more, and a rise in the proportion of women in paid employment.[2] The social base of the labour movement was large and continuing to grow. Workers experiencing the unequal power relations, exploitation of their labour power, and growing economic inequalities of capitalism were receptive to socialist ideology, and their experience of the need to organise collectively to improve their material position promoted labour movement values along with growth in trade union organisations.

Secondly, in a country that was marked by a high degree of social, regional, and confessional segmentation, Imperial Germany saw the growth of distinct socio-cultural milieux. In cities such as Berlin, Hamburg, and Leipzig, and industrial and mining regions such as the Ruhr and the textile-producing regions of Saxony, the labour movement was able to take strong root in areas where the working class made up a dominant majority of the population (numerically, if not in terms of political power). With its rich network of trade unions, consumer associations, and numerous recreational and cultural associations, as well as its political organisation, the Social Democrats were able effectively to mobilise these milieux. In strongly Catholic regions, the Social Democrats had to compete for working-class support with the Catholic organisational and associational milieu, but the Catholic Christian trade unions reached 350,000 by 1912 compared with the Social Democrat-aligned Free Trade Unions' 2.5 million.

Thirdly, the fact that by the late nineteenth century there was near-universal literacy among urban workers in Germany (in contrast to Southern Europe and

---

1 A useful place to start on this is Geary 1992. See also Eley 2002.
2 Detailed figures in Hohorst, Kocka, and Ritter 1975, pp. 57–93.

much of the Russian Empire), and the rise of cheap paper and printing technology, facilitated the transmission of a version of Marxist socialist ideology to a wide mass readership. Even if workers did not follow abstract theoretical debates, cheap pamphlets, newspapers, and illustrated papers like *Der Wahre Jakob* or the *Süddeutscher Postillon*, as well as the oral communication networks within the party organisations, enabled the dissemination of core concepts of class struggle and the need for united collective organisation to democratise the Imperial German state as well as to change the existing economic system. The capacity of the phase of 'print capitalism' that prevailed in the late nineteenth century to promote collective identities other than nationalism should not be underestimated.

Fourthly, the continuous confrontation with, and exclusion from, the authoritarian Imperial German state shaped the Social Democratic labour movement. With the early emergence of an autonomous socialist party, breaking with middle-class liberalism in the early 1860s, Social Democracy quickly became the target of repressive actions by the state, culminating in Bismarck's effort to outlaw socialism altogether from 1878 to 1890. The repressive conduct of state authorities, discrimination against socialists, and the continuing exclusion of organised workers from state-sector employment, all contributed to the belief of the party's rank and file that the Imperial German state was, as Marxian theory outlined, a tool of ruling-class domination, thwarting the aspirations of working people. While manhood suffrage enabled mass political mobilisation in Imperial Germany after 1871, powerful constitutional checks on democratisation at the state level and in Germany's upper houses of parliaments kept the representatives of the working class away from the exercise of real political power in the state. The result was what could be characterised as a pressure-cooker environment in German political culture – mass mobilisation from the Left, encountering waves of mobilisation from a gradually modernising German Right (involving imperialist, nationalist, and antisemitic pressure groups), but at the same time limited opportunity for opposition parties to gain a meaningful share of state power. This Janus-faced nature of the Imperial German state was in itself conducive to the radicalisation of opposition parties. Workers' experience of the state in their own lives – military service characterised by loss of personal freedom and often physical abuse, police harassment of workers' associations, and the intervention of police and the military in large-scale industrial conflicts – all added to the sense of alienation from the Imperial German regime.

Fifthly, the Social Democratic Party was successful at simultaneously addressing workers' everyday concerns and offering a prospect of transformational change that would bring about a better future for workers. If theoreticians disagreed about the relative weight given to the 'final goal', or to the reforms that could be achieved along the way to that goal, rank-and-file Social Democrats do not seem to have perceived a conflict between seeking to improve their material lot in the present and aspiring to a future in which the working class would replace the current ruling classes. In framing issues such as the price of bread, meat, or beer in ways that showed how workers were materially disadvantaged by the existing power structures of the German Empire, and arguing for the need for concerted political action to change these structures, the Social Democratic Party created what we might now call a coherent and convincing 'narrative', which was internalised by many rank-and-file members.

Drawing on socialist theory, but also on the lived experience of workers subject to capitalist labour relations and an authoritarian state, Social Democrats were able to connect with the values and aspirations of a broad mass membership and to construct a party that was able to mount a growing electoral challenge to the ruling elite of Imperial Germany. By 1912, the party had 34 per cent of the national vote. Despite unreformed electoral boundaries, this equated to 110 Reichstag seats out of 397, making the Social Democrats the largest group in parliament. By 1914, the party counted over a million members, 175,000 of whom were women in a country in which women had only been allowed to organise politically (at least in most of the country) since 1908. Historical counterfactuals are always pointless, but it is tempting to speculate on what a peacetime 1917 election in Imperial Germany might have brought. Would the working-class support of the party have peaked after 1912, or would the continuing momentum of the labour movement have posed the threat of an ungovernable Reichstag? The coming of the 'Great War' in 1914 destroyed the cherished unity of the labour movement for the rest of the twentieth century, along with much else, and paved the way for even more virulent strains of counter-revolution than those manifested in the pre-war German Reich.

Bibliography

Archival Sources

International Institute for Social History, Amsterdam
Wolfgang Heine Nachlass:
No. 26–123: Vereine und Versammlungswesen
Georg v. Vollmar Nachlass:
No. 420, 1916, 3494, 3495, 3496

Stiftung Archiv der Parteien und Massenorganisationen der DDR im Bundesarchiv Berlin
NY4002/63 (Rosa Luxemburg)

Geheimes Staatsarchiv, Berlin-Dahlem
VI, HA, Nachlass Schmoller

Landesarchiv Berlin
Pr. Br. Rep 30 Berlin C (Polizei-Präsidium):
8809, 8987–91, 9061, 9267, 12428, 13427, 14086, 14139–53, 14169, 14739, 14740, 15432, 15805, 15806, 15852, 15985

Staatsarchiv Bremen
Bestand 4, 14, 1 Politische Polizei
XII. A.3.a.1.–2., A3.a.4, A.3.b.1.–11
Bestand 2–Q.9., 520
Senatsregistratur, S.30.2, 3, 6, 22, 26

Sächsisches Staatsarchiv Chemnitz
Amtshauptmannschaft Zwickau 1568, 1578, 1590–2

Hessisches Staatsarchiv Darmstadt
G15 Alsfeld Q11
G15 Erbach Q1, Q3, Q4, Q5, Q8
G15 Friedberg G35, Q53, Q54, Q55, Q56, Q57, Q72
G15 Dieburg R21
G15 Lauterbach, Nr. 2252
G24 Generalstaatsanwalt, Nr. 230, 231

Sächsisches Hauptstaatsarchiv Dresden
10717 Ministerium der Ausw. Angelegenheiten, Nr. 4781, 4782
10736 Ministerium des Innern, Nr. 10989–91, 10998a, 11280
10747 Kreishauptmannschaft Dresden, Nr. 1072
10789 Polizepräsidium, Nr. 13, 14
11250 Sächs. Militärbevollmächtigter in Berlin, Nr. 3–5, 46, 94, 110, 115, 116, 121, 123–5, 129

Nordrhein-Westfälisches Landesarchiv, Düsseldorf
Reg. Düsseldorf 1029, 9030-2, 9062-6, 15904-6, 15984, 15994, 42803, 42804, 42814

Bundesarchiv-Militärarchv, Freiburg im Breisgau
PH 1/22, 23
RM 3/10025–10027
RM 31/ 660, 2291
RM 38/158

Staatsarchiv Hamburg
111–1: 8534
132-I: 3403
331–3 (Politische Polizei):
V328 Bd. 10, V330 Bd. 14, V334a Bd. 28, 2838, 3235, 3300, 4459, 4462, 5204, 5247, 5255, 5286, 5288, 5291, 5297–9, 5302, 5304, 5313–16, 5318–20, 5325, 5415, 6581, 7949–2 UA1 and UA2, S23511, S23512
411–2: II K 1454, II L 6035, II N 823
422–15: Ea1, Ea5, Bd. 1–2

Sächsisches Staatsarchiv Leipzig
20028 Amtshauptmannschaft Leipzig 2584, 2662, 2675–82, 2718, 2719
20030 Amtshauptmannschaft Rochlitz 143
20031 Polizeipräsidium 3182, 4051, 5450

Stadtarchiv Leipzig
Polizeiamt 2, 4, 15, 19

Hessisches Staatsarchiv Marburg
165, 706/4

Bayerisches Hauptstaatsarchiv München
Landtag 2395
M.Inn 38969, 46071, 46114, 66310–12
MJu 13240, 17364, 17388, 17455, 17469

BIBLIOGRAPHY

Bayerisches Hauptstaatsarchiv München – Abteilung IV Kriegsarchiv
E. Zivil und Staatssachen 437, 438

Staatsarchiv München
Polizei-Direktion München 5086–9, 5101–3, 5106, 5107, 5131

Stadtarchiv München
Polizeidirektion 225, 231, 365

Państwowe Archiwum w Poznaniu
Landrats-Amt Graetz 112, 113
Landrats-Amt Posen-Ost 120, 133, 135–7, 1425 (= former 112a)
Landrats-Amt Posen-West 151, 154, 155, 157
Polizei-Präsidium Posen 2667, 2668, 2670, 2675–7, 2687

Hessisches HauptStaatsarchiv Wiesbaden
Abt. 405 Kgl. Preuß. Reg. Wiesbaden, Nr. 2765
Abt. 407 Polizeipräsidium Frankfurt am Main, Nr. 162, Bde. 2 and 8, 164, 166, 515, 701, 702
Abt. 420 Kreis Usingen, Nr. 269
Abt. 422 Kgl. Landrats-Amt Wiesbaden, Nr. 41
Abt. 461 Staatsanwaltschaft Landgericht Frankfurt am Main, Nr. 53, 55, 63, Bde. 1–3, 67, 75, 298/298a

Państwowe Archiwum we Wrocławiu
Oberpräsidium zu Breslau 302, 351, 353, 354, 363
Magistrat Glatz 515, 516, 518, 4775, 4808

Printed Primary Sources

Party Congress Protocols
Protokolle der sozialdemokratischen Arbeiterpartei (1869–1887) (reprint in 2 vols.), Glashütten im Taunus/ Bonn Bad Godesberg, 1976.
Protokoll der Verhandlungen der sozialdemokratischen Partei Deutschlands. Abgehalten … Halle, 1890 – Jena 1913.

Newspapers and Periodicals
Agitator
Demokratisches Wochenblatt

Die Gleichheit
Hamburger Echo
Leipziger Volkszeitung
Die Neue Zeit
Neuer Social-Demokrat
Der Sozialdemokrat
Sozialistische Monatshefte
Der Volksstaat
Volksstimme (Frankfurt/M.)
Vorwärts, 1876–78
Vorwärts. Berliner Volksblatt, 1891–1914*Der Wahre Jakob*

(Other newspapers have been consulted as required on specific matters)

Contemporary Books and Articles, Edited Primary Sources

Atzrott, Otto 1971 [1886], *Sozialdemokratische Druckschriften und Vereine verboten auf Grund des Reichsgesetzes gegen die gemeingefährlichen Bestrebungen der Sozialdemokratie vom 21. Oktober 1878*, Berlin: Carl Heymanns Verlag (reprint: Glashütten/Ts.).

Baader, Ottilie 1979 [1921], *Ein Steiniger Weg. Lebenserinnerungen einer Sozialistin*, Berlin and Bonn: J.H.W. Dietz Nachf.

Ballod, Karl (under pseudonym of 'Atlanticus') 1898, *Ein Blick in den Zukunftsstaat. Produktion und Konsum im Sozialstaat*, with preface by Karl Kautsky, Stuttgart: J.H.W. Dietz Nachf.

Bebel, August 1980a, *Aus meinem Leben*, Berlin: Dietz Verlag.

Bebel, August 1980b, *Die Frau und der Sozialismus*, Berlin and Bonn (reprint of 1929 jubilee edition): J.H.W. Dietz Nachf.

Bebel, August 1995–97, *Ausgewählte Reden und Schriften*, ed. R. Dlubek et al., Munich, New Providence, London, Paris: K.G. Saur, 10 vols. in 14 (vols. 1–2 originally Berlin: Dietz Verlag, 1970, 1978).

Belli, Joseph 1978 [1912], *Die rote Feldpost unterm Sozialistengesetz*, ed. Hans J. Schütz, Berlin and Bonn: J.H.W. Dietz Nachf.

Bernstein, Eduard 1894/95, 'Zur dritten Auflage von Fr. Engels' "Herrn Eugen Dühring's Umwälzung der Wissenschaft"', *Die Neue Zeit*, 13, no. 1: 101–11, 142–7, 172–6.

Bernstein, Eduard 1978 [1928], *Sozialdemokratische Lehrjahre*, Berlin and Bonn: J.H.W. Dietz Nachf.

Bezirksbildungsausschuss Gross-Berlin (ed.) 1913, *Leitfaden für die Bildungsarbeit in Groß-Berlin* (Vol. 1), Berlin.

Blumenberg, Werner (ed.) 1965, *August Bebels Briefwechsel mit Friedrich Engels*, The Hague: Mouton & Co.

Brod, J. 1911/12, 'Die Betriebsunfälle als soziale Massenerscheinung', *Die Neue Zeit*, 30, no. 2: 124–9.

Bromme, Moritz Th.W. 1971 [1905], *Lebensgeschichte eines modernen Fabrikarbeiters* (introduction by Bernd Neumann), Frankfurt/M: Athenäum Verlag.

David, Eduard 1908, *Referenten-Führer. Eine Anleitung zum Erwerb des für die sozialdemokratische Agitationstätigkeit nötigen Wissens und Könnens*. Berlin: Buchhandlung Vorwärts.

Deutsche Wehrordnung vom 22. November 1888 1904, updated edition, Berlin: Ernst Siegfried Mittler und Sohn.

Dikreiter, Heinrich Georg n.d. [1914], *Vom Waisenhaus zur Fabrik. Geschichte einer Proletarierjugend*, Berlin: Buchhandlung Vorwärts.

Dlubek, Rolf et al. (eds) 1964, *Die Internationale in Deutschland (1864–1872)*, Berlin: Dietz Verlag.

Dowe, Dieter and Klotzbach, Kurt (eds) 1973, *Programmatische Dokumente der deutschen Sozialdemokratie*, Berlin/Bonn-Bad Godesberg: J.H.W. Dietz Nachf.

Durkheim, Emile 2002 [1897], *Suicide: A Study in Sociology*, translated by John A. Spaulding and George Simpson, London and New York: Routledge.

Emmel, J.L. 1911, 'Verfassungsreform für das Reichsland Elsaß-Lothringen', *Die Neue Zeit*, 29, no. 1 (1910–11): 670–4.

Engels, Friedrich 1901, 'Briefe von F. Engels über die französische Arbeiterpartei' (with preface by Clara Zetkin), *Die Neue Zeit*, 19, no. 1 (1900–01): 420–7.

Evans, Richard J. (ed.) 1989, *Kneipengespräche im Kaiserreich. Stimmungsberichte der Hamburger Politischen Polizei 1892–1914*, Reinbek bei Hamburg: Rowohlt.

Fricke, Dieter and Knaack, Rudolf (eds) 1984, *Dokumente aus geheimen Archiven. Übersichten der Berliner politischen Polizei über die allgemeine Lage der sozialdemokratischen und anarchistischen Bewegung 1878–1913, B.1. 1878–1889*, Weimar: Hermann Böhlaus Nachf.

Göhre, Paul 1891, *Drei Monate Fabrikarbeiter und Handwerksbursche. Eine praktische Studie*, Leipzig: Fr. Wilh. Grunow.

Gradnauer, Georg 1909, *Verfassungswesen und Verfassungskämpfe in Deutschland*, Berlin: Buchhandlung Vorwärts.

Hasenclever, Wilhelm n.d. [1877/1987], *Erlebtes. Erinnerungen 1857–1871*, Leipzig, reprint: Arnsberg.

Heid, Ludger, K.-D. Vinschen, and Elisabeth Heid (eds) 1989, *Wilhelm Hasenclever. Reden und Schriften*, Bonn: J.H.W. Dietz Nachf.

Hervé, Florence (ed.) 2008, *Clara Zetkin oder: Dort kämpfen, wo das Leben ist*, Berlin: Karl Dietz Verlag.

Die indirekten Steuern und Zölle. Wer sie zahlt und wem sie nützen 1911, Berlin: Buchhandlung Vorwärts (= Sozialdemokratische Flugschriften VIII).

Institute of Marxism-Leninism of the CC, CPSU (ed.) n.d., *The General Council of the First International 1868–1870. Minutes*, Moscow: Progress Publishers.

Kautsky, Karl 1907, 'Der 25. Januar', *Die Neue Zeit*, 25, no. 1 (1906–07): 588–96.
Kautsky, Karl 1909, *Der Weg zur Macht*, 2nd revised edn., Berlin: Buchhandlung Vorwärts.
Kautsky, Karl 1913, 'Aus dem württembergischen Hexenkessel', *Die Neue Zeit*, 31, no. 1 (1912–13): 602–7.
Kautsky, Karl 1922 [1893], *Parlamentarismus und Demokratie*, Stuttgart: J.H.W. Dietz Nachf.
Kautsky, Karl 1980, *Das Erfurter Programm* (reprint of 1922 edn.), Berlin/Bonn: J.H.W. Dietz Nachf.
Kautsky, Karl 1960, *Erinnerungen und Erörterungen*, edited by Benedikt Kautsky, 's Gravenhage: Mouton & Co.
Kautsky, Karl and Schoenlank, Bruno 1910, *Grundsätze und Forderungen der Sozialdemokratie. Erläuterungen zum Erfurter Programm*, Berlin: Buchhandlung Vorwärts.
Keil, Wilhelm 1913, 'Eine Kette von Verstößen', *Die Neue Zeit*, 31, no. 1 (1912–13): 680–8.
Keil, Wilhelm 1947, *Erlebnisse eines Sozialdemokraten*, 2 vols., Stuttgart: Deutsche Verlags-Anstalt.
Kelly, Alfred (ed.) 1987, *The German Worker: Working-Class Autobiographies from the Age of Industrialization*, Berkeley, Los Angeles and London: University of California Press.
Krille, Otto 1975 [1914], *Unter dem Joch. Geschichte einer Jugend*, edited by Ursula Münchow, Berlin: Akademie-Verlag.
Kummer, Fritz 1911, 'Der industrielle Großbetrieb', *Die Neue Zeit*, 29, no. 2 (1910–11): 26–8.
Lassalle, Ferdinand 1891–93, *Reden und Schriften*, edited by Eduard Bernstein, 3 vols., Berlin: Vorwärts.
Laufenberg, Heinrich 1911, *Geschichte der Arbeiterbewegung in Hamburg, Altona und Umgegend*, Bd. 1, Hamburg: Auer & Co.
Lebensmittelwucher und Warenteuerung 1910, Berlin: Buchhandlung Vorwärts (= Sozialdemokratische Flugschriften VI).
Leidigkeit, Karl-Heinz (ed.) 1960, *Der Leipziger Hochverratsprozess vom Jahre 1872*, Berlin: Rütten & Loenig.
Lenin, V.I. 1985 [1916], *Imperialism, the Highest Stage of Capitalism*, in *Collected Works*, Vol. 22, Moscow: Progress Publishers.
Levenstein, Adolf 1909, *Aus der Tiefe. Beiträge zur Seelen-Analyse moderner Arbeiter*, Berlin: Morgen-Verlag.
Levi, Paul 1914, *Luxemburg-Prozeß und Soldatenmißhandlungen*, Frankfurt/M: Union-Druckerei.
Liebknecht, Karl 1958ff., *Gesammelte Reden und Schriften*, 9 vols., Berlin, Dietz Verlag.
Liebknecht, Wilhelm 1968, *Wissen ist Macht – Macht ist Wissen und andere bildungspolitisch-pädagogische Äußerungen*, edited by Hans Brumme, Berlin: Volks und Wissen.

Luxemburg, Rosa 1970 ff., 2014, 2017, *Gesammelte Werke*, edited by G. Radczun et al., 7 vols. in 9, Berlin: Dietz Verlag (Vols. 6 and 7: Karl Dietz Verlag).

Luxemburg, Rosa 1981–84, 1993, *Gesammelte Briefe*, edited by Annelies Laschitza, Günter Radczun, et al., 6 vols., Berlin: Dietz Verlag.

Marx, Karl and Engels, Friedrich 1956 ff., *Werke*, edited by Institut für Marxismus-Leninismus beim ZK der SED, 39 vols. plus supplementary vols., Berlin: Dietz Verlag.

Matthias, Erich and Pikart, Eberhard (eds) 1966, *Die Reichstagsfraktion der deutschen Sozialdemokratie 1898 bis 1918. Erster Teil* (= Quellen zur Geschichte des Parlamentarismus und der politischen Parteien. Erste Reihe, Band 34), Düsseldorf: Droste.

Mayer, Gustav 1970 [1909], *Johann Baptist von Schweitzer und die Sozialdemokratie*, Jena; reprint Glashütten/ Ts.: Detlev Auvermann.

Mehring, Franz [signed with cipher] 1895, 'Kleine Zankäpfel', *Die Neue Zeit*, 13, no. 2 (1894–95): 769–73.

Mehring, Franz 1960 ff., *Gesammelte Schriften*, edited by Thomas Höhle et al., 15 vols., Berlin: Dietz Verlag.

Mehring, Franz 1980, *Geschichte der deutschen Sozialdemokratie*, Vol. 2 (= *Gesammelte Schriften* 2).

Michels, Robert 1908, 'Guglielmo II e il popolo Tedesco', *Rivista Popolare di Politica, Lettere e Scienze Sociali*, anno XIV, no. 24 (31 December): 659–62.

Michels, Robert 1906, 'Die deutsche Sozialdemokratie', *Archiv für Sozialwissenschaft und Sozialpolitik*, 23: 471–556.

Michels, Robert 1911, *Zur Soziologie des Parteiwesens in der modernen Demokratie*, Leipzig: Werner Klinkhardt.

Michels, Robert 1962, *Political Parties*, translated by Eden and Cedar Paul, New York: Free Press.

Michels, Robert 2008, *Soziale Bewegungen zwischen Dynamik und Erstarrung*, edited by Timm Genett, Berlin: Akademie-Verlag.

Moltke, Count H. Von 1892, *Gesammelte Schriften und Denkwürdigkeiten*, Vol. VII (Reden), Berlin: Ernst Siegfried Mittler und Sohn.

Murr, Karl Borromäus and Resch, Stephan (eds) 2012, *Lassalles 'südliche Avantgarde'. Protokollbuch des Allgemeinen Deutschen Arbeitervereins der Gemeinde Augsburg (1864–1867)* (= *Archiv für Sozialgeschichte* Beiheft 28), Bonn: J.H.W. Dietz Nachf.

Na'aman, Shlomo with Harstick, H.-P. (ed.) 1974, *Die Konstituierung der deutschen Arbeiterbewegung 1862/63*, Assen: Van Gorcum.

Osterroth, Nikolaus 1980 [1920], *Vom Beter zum Kämpfer*, Berlin, Bonn: J.H.W. Dietz Nachf.

Pommer, Hans 1914, *Zwanzig Jahre als Infanterieoffizier in den Reichslanden*, Frankfurt/M.: Neuer Frankfurter Verlag.

Popp, Adelheid 1978 [1915], *Jugend einer Arbeiterin*, edited by Hans J. Schütz, Berlin and Bonn: J.H.W. Dietz Nachf.

Protokolle der Sitzungen des Parteiausschusses der SPD 1912 bis 1921 1980, 2 vols. Nachdrucke, edited by Dieter Dowe, Berlin and Bonn: J.H.W. Dietz Nachf.

Quessel, Ludwig 1909, 'Sind wir Republikaner?', *SM*, 13 (new series): 1254–62.

Quessel, Ludwig 1912, 'Sozialdemokratie und Monarchie', *SM*, 16: 271–5.

Quidde, Ludwig 1894, 'Caligula. Eine Studie über römischen Cäsarenwahnsinn', *Die Gesellschaft*, 10, no. i (April): 413–30.

Rademann, Otto n.d. [ca. 1889], *Wie nährt sich der Arbeiter?*, Frankfurt a.M.: Gebrüder Knauer.

Ratz, Ursula 1967, 'Briefe zum Erscheinen von Karl Kautskys "Weg zur Macht"', *International Review of Social History*, 12: 432–77.

Rehbein, Franz 1985, *Das Leben eines Landarbeiters*, edited by Urs J. Diederichs and Holger Rüdel, Hamburg: Christians.

Rosa Luxemburg im Kampf gegen den deutschen Militarismus 1960, edited by Institut für Marxismus-Leninismus beim ZK der SED, Berlin: Dietz Verlag.

Rüden, Peter von and Koszyk, Kurt (eds) 1979, *Dokumente und Materialien zur Kulturgeschichte der deutschen Arbeiterbewegung*, Frankfurt/M.: Büvhergilde Gutenberg.

Scheidemann, Philip 1929, *Memoirs of a Social Democrat*, translated by J.E. Michell, London: Hodder and Stoughton.

[Schippel, Max] ms 1891/92, 'Die neuen Handelsverträge', *Die Neue Zeit*, 10, no. 1: 399–405.

Siebertz, Paul 1901, *Brodwucher? Eine populäre Zurückweisung sozialdemokratischer Hetzreden zur Getreidezoll-Frage*, Kempten: Jos. Kösel.

Die Sozialdemokratie im Deutschen Reichstag. Tätigkeitsberichte und Wahlaufrufe aus den Jahren 1871 bis 1893 1909, Berlin: Buchhandlung Vorwärts.

Sozialdemokratischer Parteivorstand (ed.) 1910, *Die Finanzreform von 1909 und die Parteien des Reichstages*, Berlin: Buchhandlung Vorwärts.

Sozialdemokratischer Parteivorstand (ed.) 1898, *Handbuch für Sozialdemokratische Wähler. Der Reichstag 1893–1898*, Berlin: Buchhandlung Vorwärts.

Sozialdemokratischer Parteivorstand (ed.) 1903, *Handbuch für Sozialdemokratische Wähler. Der Reichstag 1898–1903*, Berlin: Buchhandlung Vorwärts.

Sozialdemokratischer Parteivorstand (ed.) 1907, *Handbuch für sozialdemokratische Wähler anläßlich der Reichstagsauflösung 1906*, Berlin: Buchhandlung Vorwärts.

Sozialdemokratischer Parteivorstand (ed.) 1911, *Handbuch für sozialdemokratische Wähler. Der Reichstag 1907–1911*, Berlin: Buchhandlung Vorwärts.

Strzelewicz, B[oleslaw] n.d., *Sammlung von Liedern, Kouplets, Duetten, Soloscenen*, Pankow-Berlin: Verlag von B. Strzelewicz.

Vahlteich, Julius 1978 [1904], *Ferdinand Lassalle und die Anfänge der deutschen Arbeiterbewegung*, Munich, reprint: Berlin and Bonn: J.H.W. Dietz Nachf.

Weber, Max 1967, *From Max Weber: Essays in Sociology*, edited by W.W. Gerth and C. Wright Mills, London: Routledge and Kegan.

Weber, Max 1968, *On Charisma and Institution Building*, edited by S.N. Eisenstadt, Chicago: University of Chicago Press.
Winnig, August 1910, *Preussischer Kommiss. Soldatengeschichten*, Berlin: Buchhandlung Vorwärts.
Winnig, August 1932, *Der weite Weg*, Hamburg: Hanseatische Verlagsanstalt.
Wissell, Rudolf 1983, *Aus meinen Lebensjahren* (= IWK-Beiheft 7, edited by Ernst Schraepler), Berlin: Colloquium Verlag.
Woldt, Richard 1913 [1910], *Der industrielle Grossbetrieb*, Stuttgart: J.H.W. Dietz Nachf.
Woldt, Richard 1911, *Das großindustrielle Beamtentum*, Stuttgart: J.H.W. Dietz Nachf.

Secondary Literature

Abendroth, Wolfgang 1974, *Aufstieg und Krise der deutschen Sozialdemokratie*, Mainz: Stimme-Verlag.
Achten, Udo 1979, *Illustrierte Geschichte des 1. Mai*, Oberhausen: Asso Verlag.
Anderson, Benedict 1983, *Imagined Communities*, London: Verso.
Badia, Gilbert 1975, *Rosa Luxemburg. Journaliste, Polémiste, Révolutionnaire*, Paris: Editions sociales.
Balfour, Michael 1975, *The Kaiser and His Times*, Harmondsworth: Penguin.
Barkin, Kenneth D. 1970, *The Controversy over German Industrialization 1890–1902*, Chicago: University of Chicago Press.
Bendix, Reinhard 1962, *Max Weber: An Intellectual Portrait*, New York: Doubleday.
Berger, Stefan 2000, *Social Democracy and the Working Class in Nineteenth and Twentieth Century Germany*, Harlow: Longman.
Bergmann, Theodor 2004, *Die Thalheimers. Geschichte einer Familie undogmatischer Marxisten*, Hamburg: VSA Verlag.
Blessing, Werner K. 1978, 'The Cult of Monarchy, Political Loyalty and the Workers' Movement in Imperial Germany', *Journal of Contemporary History*, 13: 357–75.
Boch, Rudolf 1985, *Handwerker-Sozialisten gegen Fabrikgesellschaft: Lokale Fachvereine, Massengewerkschaft und industrielle Rationalisierung in Solingen 1870 bis 1914*, Göttingen: Vandenhoeck & Ruprecht.
Boll, Friedhelm 1980, *Frieden ohne Revolution? Friedensstrategien der deutschen Sozialdemokratie vom Erfurter Programm 1891 bis zur Revolution 1918*, Bonn: Verlag Neue Gesellschaft.
Bonnell, Andrew G. 1993, 'Enlightenment, the Other(s) of Reason, and German Social Democracy', in *Reason and Its Other: Rationality in Modern German Philosophy and Culture*, edited by Dieter Freundlieb and Wayne Hudson, Oxford: Berg, pp. 249–50.
Bonnell, Andrew G. 2001, '"Cheap and Nasty": German Goods, Socialism, and the 1876 Philadelphia World Fair', *International Review of Social History* (= IRSH), 46.

Bonnell, Andrew G. 2005, *The People's Stage in Imperial Germany: Social Democracy and Culture, 1890–1914*, London: IB Tauris.

Bonnell, Andrew G. 2013, 'Transnational Socialists? German Social Democrats in Australia before 1914', *Itinerario*, 37, no. 1: 101–13.

Bonnell, Andrew G. 2014, 'Explaining Suicide in the Imperial German Army', *German Studies Review*, 37, no. 2: 275–95.

Bonnell, Andrew G. 2018, 'Social Democrats and Germany's War in South-West Africa: The View of the Socialist Press', in *Savage Worlds: German Encounters Abroad, 1798–1914*, edited by Matthew P. Fitzpatrick and Peter Monteath, Manchester: Manchester University Press, pp. 206–29.

Bouvier, Beatrix 1982, *Französische Revolution und deutsche Arbeiterbewegung*, Bonn: Verlag Neue Gesellschaft.

Bouvier, Beatrix 1988, 'Die Märzfeiern der sozialdemokratischen Arbeiter: Gedenktage des Proletariats – Gedenktage der Revolution', in *Öffentliche Festkultur. Politische Feste in Deutschland von der Aufklärung bis zum Ersten Weltkrieg*, edited by Dieter Düding, Peter Friedemann, and Paul Münch, Reinbek bei Hamburg: Rowohlt, pp. 334–51.

Bouvier, Beatrix 1998, 'Zur Tradition von 1848 im Sozialismus', in *Europa 1848. Revolution und Reform*, edited by Dieter Dowe, Heinz-Gerhard Haupt, and Dieter Langewiesche, Bonn: J.H.W. Dietz Nachf, pp. 1169–200.

Bouvier, Beatrix 2012, 'Die französische Revolution und die Grundwerte der Sozialdemokratie', in *Deutsche Sozialdemokratie in Bewegung 1848–1863–2013*, edited by Anja Kruke and Meik Woyke, Bonn: J.H.W. Dietz Nachf., pp. 28–35.

Brandt, Peter and Lehnert, Detlef (eds) 2014, *Ferdinand Lassalle und das Staatsverständnis der Sozialdemokratie*, Baden-Baden: Nomos.

Brauer, Juliane 2012, '"Ein begeisterndes und begeistertes Gedicht": "Bundeslied" und "Arbeiter-Marseillaise"', in *Deutsche Sozialdemokratie in Bewegung*, edited by Anja Kruke and Meik Woyke, Bonn: J.H.W. Dietz Nachf., pp. 54–8.

Brose, Eric Dorn 1985, *Christian Labor and the Politics of Frustration in Imperial Germany*, Washington, DC: Catholic University of America Press.

Brose, Eric Dorn 2001, *The Kaiser's Army: The Politics of Military Technology in Germany during the Machine Age, 1870–1918*, Oxford: Oxford University Press.

Burhop, Carsten 2011, *Wirtschaftsgeschichte des Kaiserreichs 1871–1918*, Göttingen: Vandenhoeck & Ruprecht.

Calmann, Hanns M. 1922, *Die Finanzpolitik der deutschen Sozialdemokratie*, Munich: Rösl & Cie.

Chung, Hyun-Back 1989, *Die Kunst dem Volke oder dem Proletariat? Die Geschichte der Freien Volksbühnenbewegung in Berlin 1890–1914*, Frankfurt/M.: Peter Lang.

Conze, Werner and Groh, Dieter 1966, *Die Arbeiterbewegung in der nationalen Bewegung*, Stuttgart: Ernst Klett.

Crothers, George Dunlap 1968 [1941], *The German Elections of 1907*, New York: AMS Press.
Deist, Wilhelm 1974, 'Armee und Arbeiterschaft 1905–1918', *Francia. Forschungen zur Westeuropäischen Geschichte*, 2.
Domann, Peter 1974, *Sozialdemokratie und Kaisertum unter Wilhelm II*, Wiesbaden: Steiner.
Dominick, Raymond H. 1982, *Wilhelm Liebknecht and the Founding of the German Social Democratic Party*, Chapel Hill, NC: University of North Carolina Press.
Dowe, Dieter 1989, 'Einige Bemerkungen zur Berufsstruktur des Lassalleschen Allgemeinen Deutschen Arbeitervereins Ende der 1860er Jahre', in *'Der kühnen Bahn nur folgen wir ...'. Ursprünge, Erfolge und Grenzen der Arbeiterbewegung in Deutschland*, Bd. 1, edited by Arno Herzig and Günter Trautmann, Hamburg: Reidar Verlag, pp. 135–47.
Ducange, Jean-Numa 2012, *La Révolution française et la social-démocratie. Transmissions et usages politiques de l'histoire en Allemagne et Autriche 1889–1934*, Rennes: Presses Universitaires de Rennes.
Eckert, Georg 1965, *100 Jahre Braunschweiger Sozialdemokratie, 1. Teil. Von den Anfängen bis zum Jahre 1890*, Bonn: J.H.W. Dietz Nachf.
Eckl, Hans-Jürgen, Karin Iwan, and Wolfgang Weipert 1982, 'Die Arbeiterbildungsschule in Berlin (1891–1914)', in *Arbeiterbildung nach dem Fall des Sozialistengesetzes (1890–1914)*, edited by Josef Olbrich, Braunschweig: Westermann, pp. 137–63.
Eisenberg, Christiane 1989, 'Basisdemokratie und Funktionarherrschaft. Zur Kritik von Robert Michels' Organisationsanalyse der deutschen Arbeiterbewegung', *Mitteilungsblatt des Instituts zur Erforschung der europäischen Arbeiterbewegung*, 9: 8–30.
Eisner, Freya 1979, *Kurt Eisner. Die Politik des libertären Sozialismus*, Frankfurt/M.: Suhrkamp.
Eley, Geoff 1986, 'Joining Two Histories: The SPD and the German Working Class, 1860–1914', *Radical History Review*, 28–30 (1984): 13–44, reprinted in *From Unification to Nazism: Reinterpreting the German Past*, Boston: Allen & Unwin, pp. 171–99.
Eley, Geoff 2002, *Forging Democracy: The History of the Left in Europe, 1850–2000*, Oxford: Oxford University Press.
Emig, Brigitte 1980, *Die Veredelung des Arbeiters. Sozialdemokratie als Kulturbewegung*, Frankfurt/M., New York: Campus.
Evans, Richard J. 1979, *Sozialdemokratie und Frauenemanzipation im deutschen Kaiserreich*, Berlin/Bonn: J.H.W. Dietz Nachf.
Evans, Richard J. 1990, *Proletarians and Politics: Socialism, Protest and the Working Class in Germany before the First World War*, New York: St Martin's Press.
Fletcher, Roger 1984, *Revisionism and Empire: Socialist Imperialism in Germany, 1897–1914*, London: George Allen & Unwin.
Förster, Stig 1985, *Der doppelte Militarismus. Die deutsche Heeresrüstungspolitik zwischen Status-Quo-Sicherung und Aggression 1890–1913*, Stuttgart: F. Steiner.

Frevert, Ute 2001, *Die kasernierte Nation. Militärdienst und Zivilgesellschaft in Deutschland*, Munich: C.H. Beck.

Fricke, Dieter 1964, *Die deutsche Arbeiterbewegung 1869–1890: Ihre Organisation und Tätigkeit*, Leipzig: Verlag Enzyklopädie.

Fricke, Dieter 1976, *Die deutsche Arbeiterbewegung 1869 bis 1914. Ein Handbuch über ihre Organisation und Tätigkeit im Klassenkampf*, Berlin: Dietz Verlag.

Fricke, Dieter 1987, *Handbuch zur Geschichte der deutschen Arbeiterbewegung 1869 bis 1917*, 2 vols., Berlin: Dietz Verlag.

Friederici, Hans-Jürgen 1985, *Ferdinand Lassalle. Eine politische Biographie*, Berlin: Dietz Verlag.

Fülberth, Georg 1972, *Proletarische Partei und bürgerliche Literatur*, Neuwied and Berlin: Luchterhand.

Fullerton, Ronald A. 1976–77, 'Creating a Mass Book Market in Germany: The Story of the "Colporteur Novel", 1870–1890', *Journal of Social History*, 10: 265–83.

Fullerton, Ronald A. 1978–79, 'Toward a Commercial Popular Culture in Germany: The Development of Pamphlet Fiction, 1871–1914', *Journal of Social History*, 12: 489–511.

Gabriel, Elun 2014, *Assassins and Conspirators: Anarchism, Socialism, and Political Culture in Imperial Germany*, DeKalb, IL: Northern Illinois University Press.

Geary, Dick 1981, *European Labour Protest 1848–1939*, London: Methuen.

Geary, Dick (ed.) 1992, *Labour and Socialist Movements in Europe before 1914*, Munich: Berg.

Geary, Dick 2000, 'Beer and Skittles? Workers and Culture in Early Twentieth-Century Germany', *Australian Journal of Politics & History*, 46, no. 3: 388–402.

Gerschenkron, Alexander 1989 [1943], *Bread and Democracy in Germany* (with a foreword by Charles S. Maier), Ithaca, NY: Cornell University Press.

Gerwarth, Robert 2005, *The Bismarck Myth: Weimar Germany and the Legacy of the Iron Chancellor*, Oxford: Oxford University Press.

Graf, Angela 1998, *J.H.W. Dietz 1843–1922. Verleger der Sozialdemokratie*, Bonn: J.H.W. Dietz Nachf.

Graf, Angela, Horst Heidemann, and Rüdiger Zimmermann 2006, *Empor zum Licht! 125 Jahre Verlag J.H.W. Dietz*, Bonn: J.H.W. Dietz Nachf.

Grebing, Helga 1966, *Geschichte der deutschen Arbeiterbewegung*, Munich: Nymphenburger.

Grebing, Helga 1985, *Arbeiterbewegung: Sozialer Protest und kollektive Interessenvertretung bis 1914*, Munich: dtv.

Grebing, Helga 2007, *Geschichte der deutschen Arbeiterbewegung. Von der Revolution 1848 bis ins 21. Jahrhundert*, Berlin: vorwärts buch.

Griessinger, Andreas 1981, *Das symbolische Kapital der Ehre. Streikbewegungen und kollektives Bewußtsein deutscher Handwerksgesellen im 18. Jahrhundert*, Frankfurt/M.: Ullstein.

Groh, Dieter 1973, *Negative Integration und revolutionärer Attentismus. Die deutsche Sozialdemokratie am Vorabend des Ersten Weltkrieges*, Frankfurt/M., Berlin, Vienna: Propyläen.

Groh, Dieter and Brandt, Peter 1992, *'Vaterlandslose Gesellen': Sozialdemokratie und Nation 1860–1990*, Munich: C.H. Beck.

Groschopp, Horst 1985, *Zwischen Bierabend und Bildungsverein. Zur Kulturarbeit in der deutschen Arbeiterbewegung vor 1914*, Berlin: Dietz Verlag.

Grote, Heiner 1968, *Sozialdemokratie und Religion 1863–1875*, Tübingen: J.C.B. Mohr.

Grüttner, Michael 1982, 'Working-class Crime and the Labour Movement: Pilfering in the Hamburg Docks, 1888–1923', in *The German Working Class, 1888–1933*, edited by Richard J. Evans, London and Totowa, NJ: Croom Helm, pp. 54–79.

Grüttner, Michael 1984, *Arbeitswelt an der Wasserkante. Sozialgeschichte der Hamburger Hafenarbeiter 1886–1914*, Göttingen: Vandenhoeck & Ruprecht.

Guttsman, W.L. 1981, *The German Social Democratic Party, 1875–1933*, London: Allen & Unwin.

Hake, Sabine 2017, *The Proletarian Dream: Socialism, Culture, and Emotion in Germany, 1863–1933*, Berlin/Boston: De Gruyter.

Hall, Alex 1973–74, 'The Kaiser, the Wilhelmine State and Lèse-Majesté', *German Life and Letters*, 27: 101–15.

Hall, Alex 1976, 'The War of Words: Anti-Socialist Offensives and Counter-propaganda in Wilhelmine Germany, 1890–1914', *Journal of Contemporary History*, 11: 11–42.

Hall, Alex 1977, *Scandal, Sensation and Social Democracy: The SPD Press and Wilhelmine Germany 1890–1914*, Cambridge: Cambridge University Press.

Hartmann, Andrea 2006, *Majestätsbeleidigung und Verunglimpfung des Staatsoberhauptes (§§ 94ff. RStGB, 90 StGB). Reformdiskussion und Gesetzgebung seit dem 19. Jahrhundert*, Berlin: BWV.

Hausen, Karin 2010, 'Work in Gender, Gender in Work: The German Case in Comparative Perspective', in *Work in a Modern Society: The German Historical Experience in Comparative Perspective*, edited by Jürgen Kocka, Oxford: Berghahn.

Hausenstein, Wilhelm 1909, 'Arbeiterbildungswesen in Bayern', *Sozialistische Monatshefte*, 13 (new series): 1058–60.

Heid, Ludger 1989, '"... gehört notorisch zu den hervorragendsten Leitern der sozialdemokratischen Partei". Wilhelm Hasenclever in der deutschen Arbeiterbewegung', in *Wilhelm Hasenclever. Reden und Schriften*, edited by Ludger Heid, K.-D. Vinschen, and Elisabeth Heid, Bonn: J.H.W. Dietz Nachf.

Herzig, Arno 1988, 'Die Lassalle-Feiern in der politischen Festkultur der frühen deutschen Arbeiterbewegung', in *Öffentliche Festkultur*, edited by Dieter Düding et al., pp. 321–33.

Hewitson, Mark 2008, 'Wilhelmine Germany', in *Imperial Germany 1871–1918*, edited by James Retallack, Oxford: Oxford University Press.

Hickethier, Knut 1979, 'Karikatur, Allegorie und Bilderfolge. Zur Bildpublizistik im Dienste der Arbeiterbewegung', in *Beiträge zur Kulturgeschichte der deutschen Arbeiterbewegung 1848–1918*, edited by Peter von Rüden et al., Frankfurt/M., Vienna, Zurich: Büchergilde Gutenberg, pp. 79–165.

Hickey, S.H.F. 1985, *Workers in Imperial Germany: The Miners of the Ruhr*, Oxford: Oxford University Press.

Hirsch, Helmut and Pelger, Hans 1982, 'Ein unveröffentlichter Brief von Karl Marx an Sophie von Hatzfeldt – Zum Streit mit Karl Blind nach Ferdinand Lassalles Tod', *IRSH*, 26: 208–38.

Hobsbawm, Eric 1984, 'Mass Producing Traditions: Europe 1870–1914', in *The Invention of Tradition*, edited by Eric Hobsbawm and Terence Ranger, Cambridge: Cambridge University Press, pp. 263–307.

Höhn, Reinhard 1961–69, *Sozialismus und Heer*, 3 vols., Bad Harzburg: Verlag für Wissenschaft, Wirtschaft und Technik.

Hohorst, Gerd, Jürgen Kocka, and Gerhard A. Ritter 1975, *Sozialgeschichtliches Arbeitsbuch. Bd. 3: Materialien zur Statistik des Kaiserreichs 1870–1914*, Munich: C.H. Beck.

Homburg, Heidrun 1991, *Rationalisierung und Industriearbeit. Das Beispiel des Siemens-Konzerns Berlin 1900–1939*, Berlin: Haude & Spener.

Hübner, Manfred 1988, *Zwischen Alkohol und Abstinenz. Trinksitten und Alkoholfrage im deutschen Proletariat bis 1914*, Berlin: Dietz Verlag.

Hughes, Michael 1988, *Nationalism and Society: Germany 1800–1945*, London: E. Arnold.

Johansen, Anja 2004, 'Policing and Repression: Military Involvement in the Policing of French and German Industrial Areas, 1889–1914', *European History Quarterly*, 34, no. 1: 69–98.

Jorke, Wolf-Ulrich 1973, *Rezeptions- und Wirkungsgeschichte von Lassalles politischer Theorie in der deutschen Arbeiterbewegung: Von der Aufhebung des Sozialistengesetzes bis zum Ausgang der Weimarer Republik*, doctoral dissertation, Ruhr-Universität Bochum.

Journal of Modern European History 2009, 7, no. 2, Health and Safety at Work: A Transnational History.

Kanigel, Robert 1999, *The One Best Way*, New York: Penguin.

Kirn, Daniel 2009, *Soldatenleben in Württemberg 1871–1914. Zur Sozialgeschichte des deutschen Militärs*, Paderborn: Schöningh.

Kitchen, Martin 1968, *The German Officer Corps 1890–1914*, Oxford: Oxford University Press.

Kling-Mathey, Christiane 1989, *Gräfin Hatzfeldt 1805 bis 1881. Eine Biographie*, Bonn: J.H.W. Dietz Nachf.

Knilli, Friedrich and Münchow, Ursula 1970, *Frühes Deutsches Arbeitertheater 1847–1918: Eine Dokumentation*, Munich: Hanser.

Kocka, Jürgen 1983, *Lohnarbeit und Klassenbildung – Arbeiter und Arbeiterbewegung in Deutschland 1800–1875*, Berlin and Bonn: J.H.W. Dietz Nachf.

Kocka, Jürgen with Schmidt, Jürgen 2015, *Arbeiterleben und Arbeiterkultur. Die Entstehung einer sozialen Klasse*, Bonn: J.H.W. Dietz Nachf.

Kohlrauch, Martin 2005, *Der Monarch im Skandal. Die Logik der Massenmedien und die Transformation der wilhelminischen Monarchie*, Berlin: Akademie Verlag.

Koszyk, Kurt 1953, *Anfänge und frühe Entwicklung der sozialdemokratischen Presse im Ruhrgebiet (1875–1908)*, Dortmund.

Koszyk, Kurt 1966, *Die Presse der deutschen Sozialdemokratie. Eine Bibliographie*, Hannover: Verlag für Literatur und Zeitgeschehen.

Koszyk, Kurt 1979, 'Kultur und Presse der Arbeiterbewegung', in *Beiträge zur Kulturgeschichte der deutschen Arbeiterbewegung*, edited by Peter von Rüden and Kurt Koszyk, Frankfurt/M., Vienna, Zurich: Büchergilde Gutenberg, pp. 63–77.

Kroboth, Rudolf 1986, *Die Finanzpolitik des Deutschen Reiches während der Reichskanzlerschaft Bethmann Hollwegs und die Geld und Kapitalmarktverhältnisse (1909–1913/14)*, Frankfurt/M., Bern and New York: Peter Lang.

Kruedener, Jürgen von 1987, 'The Franckenstein Paradox in the Intergovernmental Fiscal Relations of Imperial Germany', in *Wealth and Taxation in Central Europe*, edited by Peter-Christian Witt, Leamington Spa: Berg, pp. 111–23.

Kruse, Wolfgang 1993, *Krieg und nationale Integration. Eine Neuinterpretation des sozialdemokratischen Burgfriedensschlusses 1914/15*, Essen: Klartext.

Kruse, Wolfgang 1989, '"Welche Wendung durch des Weltkrieges Schickung". Die SPD und der Beginn des Ersten Weltkrieges', in *August 1914. Ein Volk zieht in den Krieg*, edited by Berliner Geschichtswerkstatt, Berlin: Nishen.

Kučera, Rudolf 2016, *Rationed Life: Science, Everyday Life, and Working-Class Politics in the Bohemian Lands, 1914–1918*, Oxford: Berghahn.

Kutz-Bauer, Helga 1983, 'Arbeiterschaft und Sozialdemokratie in Hamburg vom Gründerkrach bis zum Ende des Sozialistengesetzes', in *Arbeiter in Hamburg*, edited by Arno Herzig et al., Hamburg: Verlag Erziehung und Wissenschaft, pp. 179–92.

Kutz-Bauer, Helga 1988, *Arbeiterschaft, Arbeiterbewegung und bürgerlicher Staat in der Zeit der Großen Depression*, Bonn: J.H.W. Dietz Nachf.

Lammel, Inge 1984, *Arbeitermusikkultur in Deutschland, 1844–1945*, Leipzig: Deutscher Verlag für Musik.

Lammel, Inge 2002, *Arbeiterlied-Arbeitergesang. Hundert Jahre Arbeitermusikkultur in Deutschland*, Teetz: Hentrich & Hentrich.

Lange, Annemarie 1967, *Das Wilhelminische Berlin*, Berlin: Dietz Verlag.

Langewiesche, Dieter and Schönhoven, Klaus 1976, 'Arbeiterbibliotheken und Arbeiterlektüre im wilhelminischen Deutschland', *Archiv für Sozialgeschichte*, 16: 135–204.

Laschitza, Annelies 1969, *Deutsche Linke im Kampf für eine demokratische Republik*, Berlin: Dietz Verlag.

Laschitza, Annelies 1996, *Im Lebensrausch, trotz alledem. Rosa Luxemburg*, Berlin: Aufbau Verlag.

Laschitza, Annelies 2007, *Die Liebknechts*, Berlin: Aufbau Verlag.

Lehnert, Detlef 2014, '"Bürger sind wir alle" – "Arbeiter sind wir alle": Demokratie und Wohlfahrtstaat bei Lassalle', in *Ferdinand Lassalle und das Staatsverständnis der Sozialdemokratie*, edited by Peter Brandt and Detlef Lehnert, Baden-Baden: Nomos.

Lepsius, M. Rainer 1993, 'Parteiensystem und Sozialstruktur. Zum Problem der Demokratisierung der deutschen Gesellschaft', in *Demokratie in Deutschland*, Göttingen: Vandenhoeck & Ruprecht, pp. 25–50.

Lewis, Ben 2015, 'Karl Kautsky's Democratic Republicanism', MA dissertation, University of Sheffield.

Lidtke, Vernon L. 1966, *The Outlawed Party: Social Democracy in Germany, 1878–1890*, Princeton, NJ: Princeton University Press.

Lidtke, Vernon L. 1979, 'Lieder der deutschen Arbeiterbewegung, 1864–1914', *Geschichte und Gesellschaft*, 5.

Lidtke, Vernon L. 1980, 'Social Class and Secularisation in Imperial Germany: The Working Classes', *Leo Baeck Institute Yearbook*, 25: 21–40.

Lidtke, Vernon L. 1985, *The Alternative Culture*, Oxford: Oxford University Press.

Lih, Lars T. 2006, *Lenin Rediscovered: What is to be Done? in Context*, Leiden: Brill.

Lindenberger, Thomas 1994, 'Die Fleischrevolte am Wedding. Lebensmittelversorgung und Politik in Berlin am Vorabend des Ersten Weltkriegs', in *Der Kampf um das tägliche Brot. Nahrungsmangel, Versorgungspolitik und Protest 1770–1990*, edited by Manfred Gailus and Heinrich Volkmann, Opladen: Westdeutscher Verlag, pp. 282–304.

Linton, Derek S. 1991, *'Who has the Youth, Has the Future!' The Campaign to Save Young Workers in Imperial Germany*, Cambridge: Cambridge University Press.

Lipgens, Walter 1964, 'Bismarck, die Öffentliche Meinung und die Annexion von Elsass und Lothringen 1870', *Historische Zeitschrift*, 199: 31–112.

Loreck, Jochen 1977, *Wie man früher Sozialdemokrat wurde*, Bonn-Bad Godesberg: Verlag Neue Gesellschaft.

Maehl, William Harvey 1980, *August Bebel: Shadow Emperor of the German Workers*, Philadelphia: American Philosophical Society.

Matthias, Erich 1957, 'Kautsky und der Kautskyanismus', *Marxismusstudien*, II: 151–97.

Mayer, Gustav 1928, *Bismarck und Lassalle: Ihr Briefwechsel und ihre Gespräche*, Berlin: J.H.W. Dietz Nachf.

Maynes, Mary Jo 1998, '"Genossen und Genossinnen": Depictions of Gender, Militancy, and Organizing in the German Socialist Press, 1890 to 1914', in *Between Reform and Revolution: German Socialism and Communism from 1840 to 1990*, edited by David E. Barclay and Eric D. Weitz, Oxford: Berghahn, pp. 141–66.

Messerschmidt, Manfred 1979, 'Die politische Geschichte der preußisch-deutschen Armee', in *Handbuch zur deutschen Militärgeschichte, 1648–1939*, Vol. IV, Munich: Bernard & Graefe.

Morgan, Roger 1965, *The German Social Democrats and the First International, 1864–1872*, Cambridge: Cambridge University Press.

Moses, John A. 1982, *Trade Unionism in Germany From Bismarck to Hitler, 1869–1933*, Vol. I, London: George Prior.

Mosse, George L. 1975, *The Nationalization of the Masses*, New York: Howard Fertig.

Mühlberg, Dietrich, with authors' collective 1985, *Arbeiterleben um 1900*, Berlin: Dietz Verlag.

Müller, Lothar 2014, *White Magic: The Age of Paper*, translated by Jessica Spengler, Cambridge: Polity.

Müller, Theodor 1972 [1925], *Die Geschichte der Breslauer Sozialdemokratie, Erster Teil*, Breslau [reprint: Glashütten i.T.: D. Auvermann].

Na'aman, Shlomo 1971, *Lassalle*, Hannover: Verlag für Literatur und Zeitgeschehen.

Na'aman, Shlomo 1974, '"Er soll an der Organisation festhalten": Zum Wortlaut von Lassalle's Testament', *IRSH*, 19: 396–400.

Neff, Bernhard 2004, *'Wir wollen keine Paradetruppe, wir wollen eine Kriegstruppe …'. Die reformorientierte Militärkritik der SPD unter Wilhelm II. 1890–1913*, Cologne: SH-Verlag.

Nichols, J. Alden 1958, *Germany after Bismarck: The Caprivi Era 1890–1894*, Cambridge, MA: Harvard University Press.

Nipperdey, Thomas 1968, 'Nationalidee und Nationaldenkmal in Deutschland im 19. Jahrhundert', *Historische Zeitschrift*, 206: 529–85.

Nishikawa, Masao 1990, 'Rosa Luxemburg in Bremen. Eine Dokumentation', *Internationale wissenschaftliche Korrespondenz zur Geschichte der deutschen Arbeiterbewegung*, 26.

Nolan, Mary 1981, *Social Democracy and Society: Working-class Radicalism in Düsseldorf, 1890–1920*, Cambridge: Cambridge University Press.

Nonn, Christoph 1994, 'Fleischteuerungsprotest und Parteipolitik im Rheinland und im Reich 1905–1914', in *Der Kampf um das tägliche Brot*, edited by Manfred Gailus and Heinrich Volkmann, pp. 305–15.

Nonn, Christoph 1996, *Verbraucherprotest und Parteiensystem im wilhelminischen Deutschland*, Düsseldorf: Droste.

Offermann, Toni 2002, *Die erste deutsche Arbeiterpartei. Organisation, Verbreitung und Sozialstruktur von ADAV und LADAV 1863–1871* (= *Archiv für Sozialgeschichte* Beiheft 22), Bonn: J.H.W. Dietz Nachf.

Opitz, Eckardt 1995, 'Allgemeine Wehrpflicht – ein Problemaufriß aus historischer Sicht', in *Allgemeine Wehrpflicht. Geschichte, Probleme, Perspektiven*, edited by Eckardt Opitz and Frank S. Rödiger, Bremen: Ed. Temmen.

Paul, Johann 1987, *Alfred Krupp und die Arbeiterbewegung*, Düsseldorf: Schwann.

Petzina, Dietmar (ed.) 1986, *Fahnen, Fäuste, Körper. Symbolik und Kultur der Arbeiterbewegung*, Essen: Klartext.

Pollmann, Klaus Erich 1989, 'Arbeiterwahlen im Norddeutschen Bund 1867–1870', *Geschichte und Gesellschaft*, 15: 164–95.

Pracht, Elfi 1990, *Parlamentarismus und deutsche Soziddemokratie 1867–1914*, Pfaffenweiler: Centaurus.

Prinz, Michael 1996, *Brot und Dividende. Konsumvereine in Deutschland und England vor 1914*, Göttingen: Vandenhoeck & Ruprecht.

Prüfer, Sebastian 2002, *Sozialismus statt Religion. Die deutsche Sozialdemokratie vor der religiösen Frage 1863–1890*, Göttingen: Vandenhoeck & Ruprecht.

Quataert, Jean H. 1979, *Reluctant Feminists in German Social Democracy, 1885–1917*, Princeton, NJ: Princeton University Press.

Rausch, Helke 2006, *Kultfigur und Nation. Öffentliche Denkmäler in Paris, Berlin und London, 1848–1914*, Munich: Oldenbourg.

Renzsch, Wolfgang 1980, *Handwerker und Lohnarbeiter in der frühen Arbeiterbewegung*, Göttingen: Vandenhoeck & Ruprecht.

Retallack, James 2017, *Red Saxony: Election Battles and the Spectre of Democracy in Germany, 1860–1918*, Oxford: Oxford University Press.

Reuter, Ursula 2006, *Paul Singer (1844–1911). Eine politische Biographie*, Düsseldorf: Droste.

Ribhegge, Wilhelm 1973, *August Winnig. Eine historische Persönlichkeitsanalyse*, Bonn-Bad Godesberg: Verlag Neue Gesellschaft.

Ritter, Gerhard A. 1959, *Die Arbeiterbewegung im Wilhelminischen Reich*, Berlin: Colloquium Verlag.

Ritter, Gerhard A. and Tenfelde, Klaus 1992, *Arbeiter im Deutschen Kaiserreich 1871 bis 1914*, Bonn: J.H.W. Dietz Nachf.

Roberts, James S. 1984, *Drink, Temperance and the Working Class in Nineteenth-Century Germany*, Boston: Allen & Unwin.

Rohe, Karl 1992, *Wahlen und Wählertraditionen in Deutschland*, Frankfurt/M.: Suhrkamp.

Röhl, John C.G. 2014, *Wilhelm II, Vol. 3. Into the Abyss of War and Exile, 1900–1941*, Cambridge: Cambridge University Press.

Roth, Guenther 1963, *The Social Democrats in Imperial Germany*, Totowa, NJ: The Bedminster Press.

Rüden, Peter von 1973, *Sozialdemokratisches Arbeitertheater 1848–1914*, Frankfurt/M.: Athenäum.

Rüden, Peter von (ed.) 1979, *Beiträge zur Kulturgeschichte der deutschen Arbeiterbewegung 1848–1918*, Frankfurt/M., Vienna, Zurich: Büchergilde Gutenberg.

Saldern, Adelheid von 1995, *Häuserleben. Zur Geschichte städtischen Arbeiterwohnens vom Kaisereich bis heute*, Bonn: J.H.W. Dietz Nachf.

Saul, Klaus 1972, 'Der Staat und die "Mächte des Umsturzes"', *Archiv für Sozialgeschichte*, 12.

Saul, Klaus 1974, *Staat, Industrie, Arbeiterbewegung im Kaiserreich*, Düsseldorf: Bertelsmann Universitätsverlag.

Saul, Klaus 1981, 'Zwischen Repression und Integration. Staat, Gewerkschaften und Arbeitskampf im kaiserlichen Deutschland 1884 bis 1914', in *Streik. Zur Geschichte des Arbeitskampfes in Deutschland während der Industrialisierung*, edited by Klaus Tenfelde and Heinrich Volkmann, Munich: C.H. Beck, pp. 209–36.

Schellack, Fritz 1988, 'Sedan- und Kaisergeburtstagsfeste', in *Öffentliche Festkultur*, edited by Dieter Düding et al., Reinbek bei Hamburg: Rowohlt, pp. 278–97.

Schildt, Gerhard 1986, *Tagelöhner, Gesellen, Arbeiter: Sozialgeschichte der vorindustriellen und industriellen Arbeiter in Braunschweig 1830–1880*, Stuttgart: Klett.

Schmidt, Jürgen 2011, 'The Secularisation of the Workforce in Germany in the 19th Century', in *Secularisation and the Working Class: The Czech Lands and Central Europe in the 19th Century*, edited by Lucas Fasora et al., Eugene, OR: Pickwick Publications, pp. 39–59.

Schmidt, Jürgen 2015, *Arbeiter in der Moderne. Arbeitsbedingungen, Lebesnwelten, Organisationen*, Frankfurt/M.: Campus.

Schmidt, Jürgen 2018, *Brüder, Bürger und Genossen. Die deutsche Arbeiterbewegung zwischen Klassenkampf und Bürgergesellschaft 1830–1870*, Bonn: J.H.W. Dietz Nachf.

Schönhoven, Klaus 1978, 'Arbeiterschaft, Gewerkschaften und Sozialdemokratie in Würzburg 1848–1918', in *Würzburgs Sozialdemokraten. Vom Arbeiterverein zur Sozialdemokratischen Volkspartei 1868–1978*, edited by Hans Werner Loew and Klaus Schönhoven, Würzburg, pp. 1–39.

Schönhoven, Klaus and Braun, Bernd (eds) 2005, *Generationen in der Arbeiterbewegung*, Munich: Oldenbourg.

Schorske, Carl E. 1955, *German Social Democracy, 1905–1917: The Development of the Great Schism*, Cambridge, MA: Harvard University Press.

Schraepler, Ernst 1972, *Handwerkerbünde und Arbeitervereine 1830–1853*, Berlin and New York: De Gruyter.

Schröder, Wolfgang 2013, *Wilhelm Liebknecht. Soldat der Revolution, Parteiführer, Parlamentarier. Ein Fragment*, edited by Renate Dressler-Schröder and Klaus Kinner, Berlin: Karl Dietz Verlag.

Schulze, Hagen 1985, *Der Weg zum Nationalstaat*, Munich: dtv.

Seidel, Jutta 1986, *Wilhelm Bracke. Vom Lassalleaner zum Marxisten*, Berlin: Dietz Verlag.

Selo, Heinz 1930, *Die 'Freie Volksbühne' in Berlin. Geschichte ihrer Entstehung und ihre Entwicklung bis zur Auflösung im Jahre 1896*, Berlin (= dissertation, University of Erlangen).

Seyferth, Alexander 2007, *Die Heimatfront 1870/71. Wirtschaft und Gesellschaft im deutsch-französischen Krieg*, Paderborn: Schöningh.

Sinjen, Beke 2015, *Prosa der Verhältnisse. Die Entdeckung der Erzählliteratur durch die Arbeiterbewegung*, Essen: Klartext.

Sperber, Jonathan 1997, *The Kaiser's Voters: Electors and Elections in Imperial Germany*, Cambridge: Cambridge University Press.

Spiekermann, Uwe 2010, 'Dangerous Meat? German-American Quarrels over Pork and Beef, 1870–1900', *Bulletin of the German Historical Institute*, 46 (Spring).

Spoerer, Mark 2004, *Steuerlast, Steuerinzidenz und Steuerwettbewerb. Verteilungswirkungen der Besteuerung in Preußen und Württemberg (1815–1913)*, Berlin: Akademie-Verlag (= *Jahrbuch für Wirtschaftsgeschichte*, Beiheft 6).

Spree, Reinhard 1988, *Health and Social Class in Imperial Germany*, translated by Stuart McKinnon-Evans with J. Halliday, New York: Berg.

Stargardt, Nicholas 1994, *The German Idea of Militarism: Radical and Socialist Critics, 1866–1914*, Cambridge: Cambridge University Press.

Steenson, Gary P. 1981, *'Not One Man! Not One Penny!' German Social Democracy, 1863–1914*, Pittsburgh, PA.

Steinberg, Hans-Josef 1979, *Sozialismus und deutsche Sozialdemokratie*, 5th edn., Berlin/Bonn: J.H.W. Dietz Nachf.

Stürmer, Michael 1971, 'Bismarck in Perspective', *Central European History*, 4: 291–331.

Stürmer, Michael 1984, *Die Reichsgründung*, Munich: dtv.

Tenfelde, Klaus 1981, *Sozialgeschichte der Bergarbeiterschaft an der Ruhr im 19. Jahrhundert*, Bonn: J.H.W. Dietz Nachf.

Tenfelde, Klaus 1982, 'Adventus. Zur historischen Ikonologie des Festzugs', *Historische Zeitschrift*, 235, no. 1: 45–84.

Tenfelde, Klaus 2010, 'Forced Labour in the Second World War: The German Case and Responsibility', in *Work in a Modern Society*, edited by Jürgen Kocka, Oxford: Berghahn.

Tenfelde, Klaus and Trischler, Helmuth (eds) 1986, *Bis vor die Stufen des Throns. Bittschriften und Beschwerden von Bergleuten im Zeitalter der Industrialisierung*, Munich: C.H. Beck.

Tenfelde, Klaus and Volkmann, Heinrich (eds) 1981, *Streik. Zur Geschichte des Arbeitskampfes in Deutschland während der Industrialisierung*, Munich: C.H. Beck.

Tennstedt, Florian 1981, *Sozialgeschichte der Sozialpolitik in Deutschland*, Göttingen: Vandenhoeck & Ruprecht.

Torp, Cornelius 2005, *Die Herausforderung der Globalisierung. Wirtschaft und Politik in Deutschland 1860–1914*, Göttingen: Vandenhoeck & Ruprecht.

Trautmann, Günter 1983, 'Das Scheitern liberaler Vereinspolitik und die Entstehung der sozialistischen Arbeiterbewegung in Hamburg zwischen 1862 und 1871', in *Arbeiter in Hamburg*, edited by Arno Herzig et al., Hamburg: Verlag Erziehung und Wissenschaft.

Trempenau, Dietmar 1979, *Frühe sozialdemokratische und sozialistische Arbeiterdramatik (1890–1914)*, Stuttgart: Metzler.

Trotnow, Helmut 1980, *Karl Liebknecht. Eine politische Biographie*, Cologne.

Turk, Eleanor L. 1982, 'The Great Berlin Beer Boycott of 1894', *Central European History*, 15, no. 4.

Uexküll, Gösta von 1974, *Ferdinand Lassalle in Sebstzeugnissen und Bilddokumenten*, Reinbek bei Hamburg: Rowohlt.

Ullmann, Hans-Peter 1995, *Das Deutsche Kaiserreich 1871–1918*, Frankfurt a. M.: Suhrkamp.

Ullmann, Hans-Peter 2005, *Der deutsche Steuerstaat. Geschichte der öffentlichen Finanzen vom 18. Jahrhundert bis heute*, Munich: C.H. Beck.

Ulrich, Bernd, Jakob Vogel, and Benjamin Ziemann (eds) 2001, *Untertan in Uniform. Militär und Militarismus im Kaiserreich 1871–1914*, Frankfurt/M.: Fischer.

Vollert, Michael P. 2014, *Für Ruhe und Ordnung. Einsätze des Militärs im Innern (1820–1918)*, Bonn: J.H.W. Dietz Nachf.

Walter, Franz 2013, 'Ferdinand Lassalle. Zwischen Kult und Kitsch', in *Mythen, Ikonen, Märtyrer. Sozialdemokratische Geschichten*, edited by Franz Walter and Felix Butzlaff, Berlin: vorwärts buch, pp. 15–25.

Weber Eugen 1976, *Peasants into Frenchmen*, Stanford, CA: Stanford University Press.

Wehler, Hans-Ulrich 1971 [1962], *Sozialdemokratie und Nationalstaat*, Göttingen: Vandenhoeck & Ruprecht.

Wehler, Hans-Ulrich 1985, *The German Empire, 1871–1918*, translated by Kim Traynor, Leamington Spa: Berg.

Wehler, Hans-Ulrich 1995, *Deutsche Gesellschaftsgeschichte, Bd. 3: 1849–1914*, Munich: C.H. Beck.

Welskopp, Thomas 2000, *Das Banner der Brüderlichkeit. Die deutsche Sozialdemokratie vom Vormärz bis zum Sozialistengesetz*, Bonn: J.H.W. Dietz Nachf.

Welskopp, Thomas 2010, 'The Vison(s) of Work in the Nineteenth-Century German Labour Movement', in *Work in a Modern Society*, edited by Jürgen Kocka, Oxford: Berghahn.

Wette, Wolfram 1987, *Gustav Noske. Eine politische Biographie*, Düsseldorf: Droste.

Wiedner, Hartmut 1982, 'Soldatenmißhandlungen im Wilhelminischen Kaiserreich (1890–1914)', *Archiv für Sozialgeschichte*, 22: 159–99.

Witt, Peter-Christian 1970, *Die Finanzpolitik des Deutschen Reiches von 1903 bis 1913*, Lübeck and Hamburg: Matthiesen Verlag.

Wyrwa, Ulrich 1990, *Branntewein und 'echtes' Bier. Die Trinkkultur der Hamburger Arbeiter im 19. Jahrhundert*, Hamburg: Junius.

Zwahr, Hartmut 1978, *Zur Konstituierung des Proletariats als Klasse: Strukturuntersuchung über das Leipziger Proletariat während der industriellen Revolution*, Berlin: Akademie-Verlag.

Index

Abendroth, Wolfgang 12, 28
Anderson, Benedict 142
Audorf, Jakob 18, 19, 23, 169n
Auer, Ignaz 4
August Wilhelm, Prince 167
Aveling, Edward 131

Baader, Ottilie 69, 145, 148–149, 156
Bachmann, Karl Otto 114
Bachofen, Johann Jakob 131
Badia, Gilbert 178
Ballod, Karl 192
Bebel, August 7, 12–13, 21, 23, 26, 28, 33, 35, 36, 37–38, 39, 40, 41, 43, 44, 46, 47, 48, 49, 58, 59, 69–70, 79, 105, 115n, 130, 131–132, 134, 137, 141, 143, 148, 157, 161, 176, 177, 183, 184–185, 190, 195
Becker, Bernhard 14
Becker, Johann Philipp 14, 38, 39
Belli, Joseph 104–105
Berger, Stefan 1
Bernstein, Eduard 15, 21, 98, 132, 140, 141, 143–144
Bethmann Hollweg, Theobald von 118
Bismarck, Otto von 6, 20, 33, 34, 35, 38, 39, 40, 41, 44, 48, 49, 76, 79, 80, 102, 108, 129, 148, 178, 187, 190, 198
Blessing, Werner 182–183, 186
Bloch, Joseph 139
Block 124, 144
Bogdanowitz, B. 166
Bolger, Fritz 20
Bonaparte, Louis-Napoleon (Napoleon III) 40, 43, 45, 46, 48
Bonhorst, Leonhard von 41, 45
Borchardt, Julian 143
Boyen, Hermann von 101
Bracke, Wilhelm 36, 41, 42, 43, 45, 132, 134
Brandt, Peter 26
Braun, Lily 85
Brecht, Bertolt 60, 150
Brentano, Lujo 138
Brod, J. 70–71
Bromme, Moritz 57–58, 59, 113, 140
Bronsart von Schellendorf, Paul 109

Buchwitz, Otto 149
Bülow, Bernhard von 76, 81, 85, 91, 93, 94, 159, 193, 194

Caligula 180
Calwer, Richard 140
Caprivi, Leo von 79, 80, 81
Cohn 193
Corvin, Otto von 130

David, Eduard 142–143, 157, 194
Deist, Wilhelm 125
Dietz, Heinrich 131
Dikreiter, Heinrich Georg 122, 147
Dittmann, Wilhelm 88
Domann, Peter 190
Dönniges, Helene von 13
Dowe, Dieter 29n
Dühring, Eugen 21n, 129
Dumas, Alexandre 130
Düwell, Bernhard 144

Eberhard, Konrad 185
Ebert, Friedrich 108, 195
Eisner, Kurt 180
Elm, Adolf von 145
Emig, Brigitte 126, 153
Erbe 171–172
Ewald, Heinrich 46
Eley, Geoff 5
Engels, Friedrich 12, 20, 21, 23, 25, 26n, 32, 39, 43, 56, 73, 129, 130–131, 132, 134, 137, 139, 141, 143, 146, 147, 161, 175, 189–190
Eulenburg, Philipp 167
Evans, Richard J. 51, 52, 60, 94, 124, 149, 187, 188

Fabrice, Alfred von 110
Fahrenwald, Agnes 95, 147
Falkenhayn, Erich von 118
Fehmlich, Eduard Woldemar 115
Fischer, Carl 58, 113
Fischer, Emil 81
Fischer, Ernst 85
Förster, Stig 101

INDEX

Fourier, Charles   191
Frank, Ludwig   183–184
Friederici, Hans Jürgen   28
Friedrich, Grand Duke of Baden   183–184
Friedrich Wilhelm IV   182
Fritzsche, Friedrich Wilhelm   44, 46
Frohme, Karl   119, 186
Fuchs, Eduard   140

Garibaldi, Giuseppe   103
Geary, Dick   5n, 61, 72, 130, 154
Geib, August   42
Geiser, Bruno   129
Georg, Duke of Saxony   118
Gerschenkron, Alexander   76, 77
Göhre, Paul   59, 113, 123–124
Gorky, Maxim   53
Gradnauer, Georg   113, 192
Gräf, Robert   112
Grebing, Helga   1, 12, 15, 186–187
Greulich, Hermann   176
Griessinger, Andreas   66–67
Groh, Dieter   3
Grote, Heiner   29, 30
Guttsman, William L.   1, 133

Haase, Hugo   180
Haberland, Karl   26–27
Hahn, Bertha   16
Hake, Sabine   49n, 60n, 154
Hall, Alex   186
Hasenclever, Wilhelm   16, 32, 44, 46–48, 64, 102–104, 105, 108, 123
Hasselmann, Wilhelm   32, 43, 62
Hatzfeldt, Countess Sophie von   13, 14, 15, 18, 29n, 36
Hauptmann, Gerhart   155
Heine, Heinrich   194, 195
Heine, Wolfgang   143
Heinrich, Prince   188
Heinzen, Karl   191
Hepner, Adolf   48, 176, 177
Hess, Moses   14
Hinz (*Schutzmann*)   84, 150
Hoffmann, Lieutenant   123
Hoppe, Martha   95, 193

Jaurès, Jean   190

Kautsky, Karl   3n, 4, 19, 20–21, 129, 130, 131, 133, 134, 135, 136, 137, 139, 140, 142–143, 146, 149, 174–175, 181, 183, 191, 192–193
Kegel, Max   169
Keil, Wilhelm   58, 183
Kennan, George   4
Kitchen, Martin   101n, 121
Klein, Peter   124
Kolb, Wilhelm   183–184
Koszig, Otto   120
Krajewski, Paul   167
Kramer (*Schutzmann*)   85
Krille, Otto   148
Krupp, Alfred   66
Krupp, Friedrich   66n
Kuhn, August   45
Kummer, Fritz   73–74

Lafargue, Paul   135, 189–190
Lassalle, Ferdinand   7, 11–33, 35, 36, 50, 64, 103, 132, 134, 138, 157, 158, 161, 162, 176n, 190–191
Laurence, Max   167
Le Bon, Gustave   4
Ledebour, Georg   127
Legien, Carl   81
Lehnert, Detlef   26, 176n
Lenin, V.I.   3, 4
Lepsius, M. Rainer   151
Levenstein, Adolf   59, 124
Levi, Paul   118–119
Lewandowsky, H.   167–168
Lidtke, Vernon L.   1, 12, 19, 149, 153, 156, 158, 170–171
Liebknecht, Karl   115n, 117, 126–127, 159n, 184
Liebknecht, Wilhelm   12, 21, 24, 35, 36, 37, 38, 39, 40, 41, 42, 43, 44, 46, 48, 49, 50, 70, 113–114, 132, 154, 161, 176–177
Lindenberger, Thomas   77
Litolff, Henry   169
Loreck, Jochen   57, 58n
Louis XVI   193
Ludwig, Prince of Bavaria   185
Lütgenau, Franz   81
Luxemburg, Rosa   118–119, 136, 137, 144, 173–174, 181–182, 190–191, 193

Marx, Karl   3n, 8, 12, 20, 21, 22, 25, 26n, 31n, 32–33, 38, 39, 43, 56, 61, 70, 71, 72, 73, 75, 128–129, 130, 131, 134, 135, 136, 137, 138, 139, 140, 141, 143, 148, 149, 150, 155, 158, 161, 175, 176, 191
Matthias, Erich   3n
May, Eugen   112–113
Mayer, Gustav   11, 33n
Mebus (police constable)   54
Mehring, Franz   1, 28, 30, 153, 157, 163, 178, 181, 190–191
Meibryck, Willy   168
Meissner, Otto   129
Mende, Fritz   46
Michels, Robert   3–4, 11–12, 27, 28, 34n, 108, 144, 163, 171, 173
Mimi (rabbit)   137
Molkenbuhr, Hermann   97
Moltke, Helmuth von ("the Elder")   101, 108
Morgan, Roger   1
Motteler, Julius   39

Napoleon III   see Bonaparte, Louis-Napoleon
Naumann, Friedrich   59
Neff, Bernhard   126
Nicholas II, Tsar   52, 53, 185
Niendorf, Gustav   120
Nolan, Mary   5n, 99
Nonn, Christoph   77, 81n, 83, 99
Noske, Gustav   126, 194

Offermann, Toni   29n
Osterroth, Nikolaus   122

Plekhanov, Georgi V.   135
Pohl, August   146
Pohl, Frau   146
Popp, Adelheid   69
Prüfer, Sebastian   29–30

Quarck, Max   32n
Quataert, Jean   69
Quessel, Ludwig   178, 195
Quidde, Ludwig   180

Rehbein, Franz   57, 59, 125, 126–127
Retallack, James   2, 69–70

Reuleaux, Franz   62, 65
Ribhegge, Wilhelm   108
Ritter, Gerhard A.   1
Rittinghausen, Moritz   63
Roberts, James S.   88
Rosenfeld, Kurt   118
Rospitzky   124
Roth, Guenther   1, 3
Rouget de Lisle, Claude-Joseph   18
Rousseau, Jean-Jacques   155, 156n

Saul, Klaus   179
"Scävola, C.M." (pseud.)   33n, 163
Scheidemann, Philip   58–59, 87
Schmidt, Jürgen   1, 30, 49, 70n
Schmoller, Gustav   93
Schneltzer, Max   168
Schoenlank, Bruno   133, 134, 135, 136, 142
Schorske, Carl E.   1, 3, 4
Schraps, Reinhold   46
Schulz, Heinrich   157, 159
Schumann, Lilly   166, 167
Schweitzer, Johann-Baptiste von   13, 14, 22, 35, 36, 37, 39, 43–44, 46, 47n, 48
Sergei Aleksandrovich, Grand Duke   53
Shakespeare, William   155
Sievers (printer)   45
Singer, Paul   80, 81, 97, 161
Spier, Samuel   45
Stadthagen, Arthur   97
Steenson, Gary   1, 174n
Steiger, Edgar   19
Steinberg, Hans-Josef   4, 23, 128–130, 131, 137, 140
Strauss, David Friedrich   122–123
Stripp (*Rezitator*)   169
Ströbel, Heinrich   120
Strzelewicz, Boleslaw   23, 164–165

Taube, sailor   125–126
Taylor, Frederick W.   73–75
Tenfelde, Klaus   59
Thalheimer, August   146
Tirpitz, Alfred von   79, 80, 112
Torp, Cornelius   81n, 99

Vahlteich, Julius   13, 15
Vollmar, Georg von   157

Wabersky, Gustav 180
Waldersee, Alfred von 120–121
Adalbert (Max?) Weber 128n
Weber, Alfred 5–6
Weber, Eugen 101
Weber, Max 27–28
Wehler, Hans-Ulrich 6, 45
Welskopp, Thomas 59, 61
Weyl, Klara 98
Wiedner, Hartmut 117
Wiesenthal, Karl 143
Wilhelm, Crown Prince 185
Wilhelm I, Kaiser 189
Wilhelm II, Kaiser 8, 30, 55, 107, 115, 117, 120, 121, 161, 167, 173, 178, 179, 180, 181, 182, 185, 186, 187, 188, 189, 192, 193, 194–195
Winnig, August 102, 105–108
Wissell, Rudolf 112, 120, 122–123
Woldt, Richard 73–74
Wurm, Mathilde 95

Zetkin, Clara 69, 138, 157
Zietz, Luise 81
Zimmermann, Wilhelm 130
Zinne, Karl 119
Zola, Emile 130
Zschaler, Gustav Hermann 119
Zubeil, Fritz 124, 194